Aristotle and moral realism

Aristotle and moral realism

EDITED BY
Robert Heinaman
University College London

WESTVIEW PRESS
Boulder • San Francisco

© Robert Heinaman and contributors 1995

First published the UK in 1995 by UCL Press.

UCL Press Limited
University College London
Gower Street
London WC1E 6BT

The name of University College London (UCL) is a registered
trade mark used by UCL Press with the consent of the owner.

First published in 1995 in the United States by

Westview Press
5500 Central Avenue
Boulder, Colorado 80301-2877

All rights reserved. No part of this publication may be
reproduced or transmitted in any form or by any means,
electronic or mechanical, including photocopying, recording,
or any information storage and retrieval system, without
permission in writing from the publisher.

ISBN: 0-8133-2646-X HC

Library of Congress Cataloging-in-Publication Data

Aristotle and moral realism / [edited] by Robert Heinaman.
   p. cm.
 Includes bibliographical references and indexes.
 ISBN 0-8133-2646-X (alk. paper)
 1. Aristotle--Ethics. 2. Ethics, Greek. 3. Realism.
I. Heinaman, Robert.
B491.E7A75   1995
171 ′ .3′092--dc20   95-17199
                                                                 CIP

Typeset in Palatino.
Printed and bound by
Biddles Ltd, King's Lynn and Guildford, England.

Contents

Preface   vii

Introduction   *Robert Heinaman*   1

Acting as the virtuous person acts   *Bernard Williams*   13
The virtuous agent's reasons: a reply to Bernard Williams
Rosalind Hursthouse   24

The twofold natural foundation of justice according to
 Aristotle   *Pierre Aubenque*   35
Justice at a distance – less foundational, more naturalistic: a reply to
Pierre Aubenque   *Troels Engberg-Pedersen*   48

Testing the limits: the place of tragedy in Aristotle's ethics
Jonathan Lear   61
Tragedy, reason and pity: a reply to Jonathan Lear   *Stephen Halliwell*   85
Outline of a response to Halliwell   *Jonathan Lear*   96

Aristotelian ethics and the "enlargement of thought"
Sabina Lovibond   99
Pitfalls in doing post-Hegelian ethics with Aristotle: a reply to
 Sabina Lovibond   *Troels Engberg-Pedersen*   121

Aristotle and modern realism   *David Charles*   135
Aristotle and the explanation of evaluation: a reply to David Charles
Stephen Everson   173

Eudaimonism and realism in Aristotle's ethics
John McDowell   201
Eudaimonism and realism in Aristotle's ethics: a reply to John McDowell
David Wiggins   219

Index of persons named   233
Index of passages cited   235

Preface

Since 1981, an annual S. V. Keeling Memorial Lecture has been given at University College London.[1] The same anonymous donor whose generosity founded that series has now further benefited University College London by establishing the S. V. Keeling colloquium in ancient philosophy, which is to be held regularly in coming years. To him, all students of ancient philosophy owe a great debt.

The present volume contains the proceedings of the first Keeling colloquium which took place at the Warburg Institute in London from February 16 to 18, 1994. The theme of the conference was Aristotle and moral realism, examining Aristotle's views on the objectivity of morality, and the connection of his views to contemporary discussions of moral realism. We were fortunate in being able to attract a distinguished group of speakers and commentators: Bernard Williams, Rosalind Hursthouse, Pierre Aubenque, Troels Engberg-Pedersen, Jonathan Lear, Stephen Halliwell, Sabina Lovibond, David Charles, Stephen Everson, John McDowell and David Wiggins. I would like to thank them all for making the colloquium a success, and especially Stephen Everson and Stephen Halliwell for stepping in as commentators at the last minute. I also thank Roger Jones from the UCL Press for his unfailing assistance.

Robert Heinaman
May 1994

---

1. Those given between 1981 and 1991 have now been published in *Modern thinkers and ancient thinkers*, R. Sharples (ed.) (London: UCL Press, 1993).

Introduction

ROBERT HEINAMAN

In this introduction I will very briefly discuss a few of the philosophical views associated with the topic of the colloquium, and summarize the main points contained in the principal papers.

Questions connected with the issue of moral realism fall into the branch of ethics known as meta-ethics, which deals with foundational issues in moral philosophy. One of these issues is the question of how, if at all, morality can be justified.

Although one might try to "justify" morality in other ways, moral realism attempts to do so by showing that it is objective. To explain what this involves, the moral realist must address several questions, including:

- What is the meaning of statements to the effect that something is morally right or wrong, or of (non-moral) value?
- Are judgements that positively assert that something is valuable, or morally good or evil, ever true?
- If so – as the moral realist will assert – what kind of fact is reported by such a true statement, and how can we acquire knowledge of it?
- What precisely does ethical objectivity consist in, and how can the belief in objectivity be maintained in face of the seemingly irresolvable disagreements about value between different societies and individuals?

However, the label "moral realism" can be taken to suggest not merely the idea that morality is objective, but the further claim that there are moral properties "out there" that may be correctly attributed to objects by true moral statements. Some philosophers regard morality as objective but reject this sort of metaphysical commitment. For example, some think that the objectivity of morality can be established on the basis of explaining what counts as a good reason for action. Here the objective truth of an ethical claim such as "I ought to

INTRODUCTION

X" issues from facts about practical reasoning rather than being based on the accurate depiction of the possession of moral properties by objects independently of our beliefs. Something like this view finds echoes in the papers of Williams, Lovibond and McDowell, which appeal to the role of the virtuous and practically wise man in Aristotle's ethics, the practical reasoner par excellence. At the same time, however, McDowell argues against one version of such a view which would seek to justify ethical reasons for action on the basis of a prior, non-ethical notion of rationality.

Another approach to the objectivity of value maintains that there are indeed moral properties depicted by true ethical statements and that they can be identified with, reduced to, or at least explained by, reference to *natural* properties. Such a view is plausibly attributed to Aristotle on the basis of his famous function argument, which appears to answer the question of what the highest good for man consists in by specifying the kind of activity that distinguishes humans from other animals, i.e by specifying the human function. So, for example, one of the activities comprising the human function is *contemplation*. Hence a *good* for a human being *is* contemplation, an activity that can be described in a value-neutral way. Aristotle makes it clear that a parallel function argument would determine what counts as good for any other kind of living thing. Warthogs, bats and daisies, like human beings, have their own peculiar natures that make certain things good and evil for them where these activities appear to be specifiable in a value-neutral manner. The function argument as it applies to humans is only one instance of a general pattern of argument that applies to all living things.

Naturalism may also be suggested by Aristotle's apparent reduction of different kinds of good in different categories in *Nicomachean ethics* I.6 and *Eudemian ethics* I.8. Thus, for the body to be in a good condition *is* for it to be healthy. Or it may be suggested by Aristotle's analysis of the virtues, for example when justice is explained in terms of geometrical and arithmetical proportion. Pierre Aubenque's paper presents such a view.

But it is far from clear how Aristotle's notion of the "natural" is to be explained, and some people doubt that he has any neutral, value-free conception of nature that would provide a non-normative foundation for his ethics. As an interpretation of Aristotle, naturalism in the sense explained finds little favour among the authors of the present volume.

An important question raised by Aristotle's function argument concerns the connection he makes between non-moral value and moral value. Aristotle would claim that what we regard as moral virtues and moral behaviour are necessary for a human being to attain the human function which is the highest human good, where the "good" refers to the valuable without, apparently, incorporating the idea of *moral* value. John McDowell's paper discusses this issue and, consistently with his previously noted view regarding rationality, argues that Aristotle would – correctly – reject the suggestion that there is a notion of the "best life" that can be explained prior to and independently of considerations of ethical value.

One contemporary position, which both believes that morality can be given an objective foundation and was directly inspired by Aristotle's discussion of the virtues, is known as "virtue theory." Rosalind Hursthouse, the commentator on Bernard Williams' paper, is a prominent exponent of this approach.[1] According to this neo-Aristotelian view, progress in our moral thinking requires a richer vocabulary than that which is typically limited to the notions of "right" and "wrong." This more fruitful vocabulary, ("courageous", "truthful", "honest", "just", etc.) is especially connected to *virtues of character*, and the analysis of these character traits should play a larger role in moral philosophy than it has in the recent past. Of course, such analysis plays a conspicuous part in Aristotle's moral philosophy, and his discussions of specific virtues in the ethical treatises is often seen as providing a paradigm of the sort of analysis the virtue theorists have in mind. The present volume's references to practical wisdom (*phronesis*) and the practically wise man (*phronimos*) recall this kind of approach.

The problem of the objectivity of ethics is a comparative question: can ethics be assimilated to science, or does it at least possess a kind of objectivity that is close enough to the objectivity of science to vindicate our speaking of ethical objectivity? For example, do ethical concepts play the same sort of explanatory role as scientific concepts? Or should we rather regard the objectivity of ethics as quite unlike scientific objectivity? To make their position clear, moral realists must explain the differences and similarities between moral truth, knowledge and fact, and scientific truth, knowledge and fact. David Charles' paper investigates some aspects of Aristotle's position in this regard, and argues that it is the close continuity between his concep-

---

1. See, for example, her book *Beginning lives* (Oxford: Basil Blackwell, 1987).

tions of practical knowledge and theoretical knowledge that grounds Aristotle's belief in ethical objectivity.

One might try to strengthen the claim of ethics to objectivity by maintaining that the belief in its subjective character is often based on an exaggeration of the differences between it and science. Nowadays, this sort of approach is sometimes based on coherence theories of justification.[2] Such a picture is related to the recurrent talk of "internal" validation in the papers by Lear, Lovibond and McDowell, and in the latter's reference to Neurath's well known image of the sailor who must repair his boat at sea plank by plank. Aristotle's dialectical method, which he applied to natural science as well as to ethics, could easily be taken to suggest this sort of epistemological position. For when it addresses a specific question, it begins with the reputable opinions that already exist, and most of these should be retained and explained at the end of the inquiry. In an important recent book, Terry Irwin[3] has examined at length the problem of whether Aristotle's undoubtedly realist conception of truth is consistent with his dialectical method.

As even these brief remarks should make clear, Aristotle's writings are suggestive of different approaches to the problem of the objectivity of ethics. These differences are reflected in the variety of approaches to the problem found in the contributors to this volume.

Professor Williams' paper, "Acting as the virtuous person acts", approaches the topic of Aristotle and moral realism obliquely by first proposing an interpretation of a statement in *Nicomachean ethics* II. 4, where Aristotle explains what has to be true in order for the agent of a virtuous action to be virtuous himself. Aristotle says that the agent must act with knowledge, must act from a firm disposition, and must choose the action for its own sake. Professor Williams concentrates on this last condition and explains it in terms of the idea of acting for certain kinds of reason. A person with a particular virtue of character will have "a specific repertoire of considerations that operate for or against courses of action." And it will be for such reasons that the virtuous person acts.

Moral realism enters the picture in the connection of this idea to

---

2. See, for example, D. Brink, *Moral realism and the foundations of ethics* (Cambridge: Cambridge University Press, 1989).
3. *Aristotle's first principles* (Oxford: Oxford University Press, 1988).

phronesis (practical wisdom). There are certain "thick" ethical concepts (e.g. "inconsiderate", "disloyal") where there is, in general, an essential link between seeing that it is *true* that (e.g.) actions of kind X are inconsiderate, disloyal, and so on, and seeing that the concepts are *relevant* to deliberation. When the man of practical wisdom exercises his perception and judges that such considerations apply, he may judge something **true**. *Perhaps* this is enough for realism, but it will not be enough if moral realism is understood to require such ethical concepts to "pick up on" aspects of the world.

Professor Aubenque's paper, "The twofold natural foundation of justice according to Aristotle", examines Aristotle's accounts of distributive and corrective justice as they are found in Book V of the *Nicomachean ethics*. As is well known, in Aristotle's view distributive justice turns on the idea of geometrical or proportional equality, and concerns public goods disposed of by the polis. If we take as an example the distribution of goods G1 and G2 to, respectively, recipients R1 and R2, justice exists if

$$\frac{\text{the value of G1}}{\text{the value of G2}} = \frac{\text{the value of R1}}{\text{the value of R2}}$$

Since Aristotle regards it as a natural fact that a person has the worth or value that he has, this provides one natural foundation for Aristotle's account of justice.

If we take political offices as paradigms of publicly distributable goods, people disagree on the criterion of value that should underlie their distribution: wealth, virtue or freedom. On the basis of a controversial interpretation of *Nicomachean ethics* 1135a2–5, Professor Aubenque makes the novel suggestion that Aristotle does not regard virtue as the sole best criterion. Rather, in each particular case natural justice is what coheres with its institutional environment, whether it be democracy, oligarchy or aristocracy. So, for example, in an oligarchic form of government, the naturally just and best distribution of political offices will be based on wealth.

Corrective justice, on the other hand, concerns not public goods but private matters such as contractual and penal rights. The equality relevant to corrective justice is arithmetic equality. If person A suffers harm equal to M at the hands of B as a result of theft, for example, equality is re-established (in the simplest case) by the restitution of M to A, so that the quantity possessed by the two individuals after restitution will be equal to the sums possessed on both sides prior to the theft.

The justification for this principle of equality is the equality between men with regard to their *right* to possess certain fundamental goods, such as life and health, on the basis of the fact that the same human nature is found in all men.

Hence, for Aristotle, justice has a twofold natural foundation. In relation to the political community, one receives a share of social goods proportional to one's natural worth, which will vary from person to person. But all human beings are equally human beings, and therefore everyone has the same right as every other to possess certain fundamental goods.

Jonathan Lear, in "Testing the limits: the place of tragedy in Aristotle's ethics", argues that Aristotle attempts to use his account of tragedy to construct an internal validation of his moral realism by vindicating his conception of practical reason. The appeal to tragedy at the same time tests the limits of practical reason.

Although Aristotle's ethical and political writings also present internal justifications of his ethical views, Lear looks for such a justification in Aristotle's discussion of tragedy. In its depictions of violence and death inflicted on one member of a family by another, tragedy presents attacks upon the primordial bonds of reason that hold the polis together. Aristotle sees such representations of irrationality as testing the adequacy of reason to explain human nature.

Tragedy was banished from Plato's ideal polis on the grounds that it encourages violence and destructiveness not controllable by reason. Plato believed that we all possess lawless desires that, although normally repressed, find expression in dreams and in the dramatic representation of violent behaviour in tragedy. The mimesis of such behaviour in tragedy stirs up in its audience the lawless desires present in us all, and hence encourages destructive behaviour of the sort which would lead to the death of the polis.

Aristotle rejects Plato's banishment of tragedy. Hence, the polis should tolerate representations of attacks on the bonds that hold the polis together. In fact, tragedy plays an important role in the self-validation of reason. "The point of tragedy, for Aristotle, is to reveal logos manifest even in attacks upon logos, and thus to establish the adequacy of logos to account for even the most destructive aspects of human nature."

Witnessing the tragic events arouses our pity only because rationality is present in tragedy. The events follow reasonably on one another and the protagonist makes a mistake, which explains why the downfall occurs; he or she must be good enough to arouse the audience's pity, but not so virtuous as to be incapable of error; the reversal and discovery must intelligibly follow from the preceding events. Catharsis takes place because there is a rationale for the terrible events that produce the audience's emotional response, and hence there is reassurance that the terrible events can be grasped by reason. If the sequence of events had not proceeded rationally, the audience would have felt not pity but terror at the sight of something so dreadful happening for no intelligible reason.

Whereas, for Aristotle, tragedy is supposed to test the limits of human destructiveness, tragedy also involves the emotion of pity, which requires rationality. Hence, in contrast to Plato, irrational destructiveness is deemed non-human. But then tragedy vindicates reason's ability to explain human destructiveness only because it rejects irrational destructiveness. As a result, Aristotle's conception of tragedy fails to provide an adequate test for his conception of human nature.

Sabina Lovibond's contribution, "Aristotelian ethics and the 'enlargement of thought'", investigates the question of whether moral realists of the present day might find some support for their position in Aristotle. A distinctive feature of Aristotle's ethics is its focus on practical wisdom or practical rationality: *phronesis*. It is his conception of *phronesis*, Lovibond believes, that commits Aristotle to moral realism. The habits of judgement characterizing the practically wise man "determine a quasi-perceptual *norm* analogous to the perceptual norms which dictate, for instance, what colour it is right to describe something as having."

For Hegel, the idea of modernity was grounded in the ability of the individuals of a society to evaluate critically the system in which they find themselves from an independent perspective. The postmodern world, with its awareness of cultural diversity and ethical perspectives other than our own, makes it difficult to accept that the man to whom *phronesis* is attributed makes *correct* moral judgements. The problem for the status of the idea of *phronesis* arises from our inability to accept uncritically any claim to practical rationality. Aristotle's moral epistemology appears precarious, then, since it is based on the questionable notion of *phronesis*.

INTRODUCTION

The rest of Lovibond's paper responds to this problem by arguing for the idea that the Aristotelian notion of proficiency in moral judgement can be successfully joined with the idea of *universal* criteria for assessing a proposed moral position.

Aristotle's ethical views take for granted the moral position of his own society. But his appeal to human nature supplies a basis for rational criticism of proposals about the human good and the content of *phronesis*. Hence, we can claim that, human nature being what it is, it is a truth that some social practice of an alien culture is morally unacceptable.

Another reason for believing that we can attain ethical truth is based on Aristotle's view of how the moral virtues are acquired. It involves the acquisition of *phronesis* at the same time that one's pleasures begin to move beyond the mere physical. One's behaviour, after at first arising from impulse, begins to be influenced by considerations of prudence and, finally, is devoted to realizing the fine (*to kalon*). The notion of the fine determines a standard by which the genuinely worthwhile can be judged. Such an idea can be associated with Bernard Williams' image of the "abstracted, improved neighbour lodged in one's inner life", whose reactions of approval and indignation can influence one's behaviour.

Kant's maxim of "enlarged thought" states that we should think from the standpoint of everyone else. It proposes that the critical examination of our own thoughts should involve examining them from other points of view, and that we should not be unduly impressed by what is immediately before us. This suggests a Kantian approach to enlarging the notion of practical wisdom: when we adopt an ethical position, we should ask ourselves whether there is an unobjectionable perspective from which our own view could be properly regarded with scorn. If so, then our ethical position needs revision.

By thus freeing *phronesis* from a local point of view, we can justifiably speak of moral judgements that are true and which therefore record an aspect of reality.

In his paper "Aristotle and modern realism", David Charles starts by elaborating and critically examining an interpretation of Aristotle which takes his assertion that

(1) a is good if and only if a seems good to the good

to mean that neither side of (1) has priority over the other, and hence that no account of the good can be given independently of our practices of moral approval and disapproval.

This approach opens up the possibility of a novel characterization of moral realism which does not involve the correspondence theory of truth, or the idea that real properties are those that causally interact with other properties according to the best scientific theory, or the view that real properties must be explicable independently of our moral practices. Charles sets out the various claims involved in this interpretation, and objects that, *inter alia*, it fails to provide an adequate account of objective truth and misrepresents Aristotle's moral psychology.

In his view Aristotle was committed to a reaction-independent theory of moral objectivity on the basis of the close analogy between ethical or practical knowledge and theoretical knowledge. The objectivity of ethics can be established by the similarity between the ways in which concepts are acquired in both cases, and by the similarity in the explanatory role of ethical concepts and concepts from theoretical disciplines.

In the case of theoretical knowledge, our grasp of the first principles proceeds through three stages. (1) We grasp the concept. (2) We realize that the concept picks out a natural kind that is involved in explanations. At this point, we know that the concept has objective validity. (3) We realize that the concept is a principle, playing a central explanatory role for the discipline in question.

Aristotle believes that mastery of a concept for a natural kind involves the thinker being causally affected in a certain way: the intellect is assimilated to the kind, where this involves mastery of an explanatory framework. The same thing happens in the ethical sphere. The concept of generosity, for example, connects us to a property enmeshed in an explanatory theory. Furthermore, the explanation of the ethical concept will not refer to what *we* find pleasant or painful, in the way in which the explanation of the concept of the humorous must refer to what we find amusing. So we can know that the concept of generosity puts us in touch with an objective feature of the world. As in the case of health, Aristotle sees our ethical concepts as forming "a reaction-independent structure whose legitimacy does not rest solely with our judgements of what is reasonable and worthwhile, but is grounded rather in a reaction-independent theory of a properly functioning human."

The conclusion of Aristotle's function argument – that eudaimonia or living well consists in rational activity – is based on a theory of human nature plus certain general requirements such as self-sufficiency. It is these theoretical considerations rather than a consideration of our reactions to particular cases that ground Aristotle's understanding of eudaimonia. Furthermore, the concept of wellbeing plays the role of a basic organizing principle in ethics as health does in medicine. "From its perspective, the particular subgoals can be seen to hang together in a non ad hoc way which constitutes a coherent world."

For Aristotle, these close analogies between the scientific and ethical spheres suffice to justify our belief in ethical objectivity.

John McDowell, in "Eudaimonism and realism in Aristotle's ethics", rejects the view that Aristotle provides an external, extra-ethical foundation for his belief that eudaimonia consists in living according to virtue. On this view, Aristotle proves that living according to virtue is the best life by showing that it best satisfies standards independent of ethical values. The best life is then interpreted in terms of an optimal combination of goods. Ethical reasons for action are validated by showing that, on a prior non-ethical notion of rationality, ethical reasons provide rational grounds for action.

One version of this view identifies eudaimonia with the optimal combination of goods. But this identification is not consistent with Aristotle's central claim that eudaimonia consists in *action* and *activity* in accordance with virtue, for many important goods are not activities. Another reading retains that central claim, but still appeals to the notion of an extra-ethical, optimal combination of goods to justify Aristotle's account of eudaimonia: virtuous action is most likely to secure the optimal combination of goods. The difficulty here is that, in making the value of virtuous action derivative on the combination of goods, the *intrinsic* value of virtuous action is not adequately recognized.

It might be thought that Aristotle's function argument appeals to the idea that humans, having a certain position in a teleologically organized natural world, possess a natural inner nisus towards living according to virtue. But the function argument merely applies to the case of human beings a quite general conceptual connection between the ideas of *an X's being such as to act as it befits an X to act* and *an X's having the excellence proper to Xes*. This general link "leaves entirely open what sort of evaluative or normative background fixes a substance for applications of the notions of *ergon* or excellence, in any particular exemplification of the general connection."

The value of the ethical virtues is encapsulated in the idea of "the noble." "Because it is noble" gives a reason for action that is not based on any prior extra-ethical notion of rationality. Although other values exist besides the noble, only the noble is in question when Aristotle speaks of acting for the sake of *eudaimonia*. Hence, the notion of eudaimonia does not provide a general theory of reasons for action. Nevertheless, it is primary and, if the noble needs to be brought to bear on a particular situation, it alone should determine one's action, whatever its effects on other values important for one's life.

Aristotle is not entirely dogmatic since he believes that reasons can be given for accepting his scheme of values, not by validating it from outside the scheme of values but by seeing how one's previously piecemeal perceptions of value – instances of possession of the *that* – hang together into a coherent scheme for life, resulting in possession of the *because*. Although Aristotle is dogmatic in not envisaging the possibility that revision may require rejection of the initial perceptions themselves, we can allow this without doing violence to Aristotle's realism. On the other hand, if a set of initial perceptions survives critical examination, we have reason to accept them as true – even if that validation can never be regarded as better than provisional.

Modern readers of Aristotle have frequently sought more than a Neurathian internal validation of his ethical position, because they thought that objective truth could not be achieved by internal reflection on a set of moral beliefs and a way of thinking inherited by chance. But this is a distinctly modern problem that did not trouble Aristotle. And in any case, it is far from clear that it *ought* to have troubled him. "On the contrary, we might say: organizing our metaphysics around the idea of transcending historicity is profoundly suspect . . . we have only our own lights to go on, and they are formed by our particular position in the history of enquiry."

Acting as the virtuous person acts

BERNARD WILLIAMS

This paper is not mainly directed to questions about moral realism in Aristotle, but it does end with a suggestion about that subject. It starts from a question that Aristotle raises about virtuous action, and gives what I think should have been Aristotle's answer to it, an answer which I think was also, broadly speaking, Aristotle's own answer. At the end I ask where (if anywhere) this leaves questions of moral realism in relation to such a theory.

In *Nicomachean Ethics* II.4 Aristotle raises the question of how it can be true, as he claims it to be, that someone becomes (e.g.) just by doing just things: for how can someone do virtuous things without already having the appropriate virtue? His answer is that the things done by the learner, although they are in a sense virtuous things, do not yet fully display the virtue. We may say that they are minimally virtuous things: they are not done *as* the virtuous person does them. He holds, in effect,

(A) A (fully) V act is what a V person would do, but only if it is done as the V person does such a thing.

The conditions on an act's being done as the virtuous agent would do it are these:

(i) the agent knows (*eidos*)
(ii) he does it *proairoumenos kai proairoumenos di' auto*: choosing, and choosing it for its own sake
(iii) he is in a steady, unchangeable state.

There is a question about how much (i) imports. There are conditions of intention here that are uncontroversially relevant. In many cases, however, their relevance is to an earlier question: not whether the V act was done as a V person would do it, but whether an even minimally V act was done at all. This is what is at issue if someone tackles the armed robber believing him not to be armed, or, differently, attempts a malicious act which misfires, doing the intended victim a good turn. These matters of intention are importantly different from questions of motive. Someone who sends a cheque to the hospital to advance his reputation is not like someone who puts the cheque into the wrong envelope: he intends, with regard to the outcome, what the generous person intends – he is, after all, seeking a reputation for generosity. He certainly does not act as the generous person would act, but his failure to do so falls under condition (ii), to which we shall come later, and not under condition (i).

It may seem puzzling that Aristotle says (*NE* 1105b1f.) that knowledge counts for everything in relation to *technai* (arts) and for little or nothing in the case of the virtues. Surely both virtue and *techne* require one to know what one is doing? I take the point to be this. There is a sense of "knowing what one is doing" that applies both to virtue and to *techne*; if there were not, Aristotle could not make the comparison in these terms. The proper possession of a *techne* can be picked out by saying that the person in general, habitually, knows what he is doing when he chooses to exercise the *techne*[1]; a person who gets it right occasionally does know, on those occasions, what he is doing, but on other occasions does not. In the case of the virtues, it *is* necessary to being a V person (and, indeed, we have already seen, even to doing a minimally V action) that one knows what one is doing, in that same sense, but the state of being a V person is not picked out by saying that he is standardly or regularly in that state of knowledge.

This is fairly straightforward, and it makes sense of Aristotle's contrast. However, it has a significant consequence. Just given condition (i), one might take it to refer to some kind of moral knowledge, the presence of which distinguishes the truly V person from those who do occasional V acts, or, again, acts that are less than fully V. If you are looking at that contrast, and are disposed to express virtue in terms of knowledge, this interpretation will be attractive. But in terms of Aristotle's contrast with the craftsman, it is not inviting at all. If moral knowledge is the virtuous person's special possession, then

---

1. "When he chooses to exercise" already picks out a difference from the virtues, of course: one that is picked up by condition (iii), as noted below.

that knowledge will make *all* the difference, and not, as Aristotle says, little or none. The knowledge mentioned in condition (i) is everyday knowledge relevant to effective intentions, as it is with *technai*.

I shall not say much about condition (iii). It is important that it can be taken to include, as well as generality over time, a requirement, in the style of Hume, of (appropriate) generality over people. The generous act must not be merely a whim; in addition, the agent's generosity will not count as the virtue if he is only generous to Lulubelle. The demand that the V person should be in the appropriate state *ametakinetos* (unchangeably) also covers, as Sarah Broadie has well pointed out,[2] two considerations that distinguish a virtue from a *techne*: that one cannot choose to exercise it or not, and (a less familiar thought, perhaps) that it counts against one's having virtues that one can be distracted by passion from exercising them, whereas this is not so with the *technai*: a carpenter who makes a bad job of it because of rage or sexual distraction is not shown by this to be a bad carpenter.

There are several complexities in this area that are connected with the unity of the virtues. My clumsy formulation "it counts against having virtues" was designed to contain, without developing, the point that, if one does not accept Aristotle's view about unity, it may make a difference what distraction is in question: if a man is distracted from brave deeds by lust rather than fear, he is not shown to lack courage. Further, there will be some skills (notably, some political ones) that require some virtues, above all the executive virtues of courage and self-control: I shall briefly come back to these later.

The question I want principally to discuss arises from condition (ii), specifically from the requirement that the V person chooses V things "for their own sake." My concern is with this phrase, and I shall not discuss the condition more generally (e.g. the question of how the two conjuncts are related). As Broadie says in her very helpful discussion of Aristotle's definition of virtue,[3] a virtuous disposition is expressed in choice (but not only so expressed), and this is not simply a matter of deliberation. The virtue is expressed in "reason-structured responses", such as the emotions, which link rational and

---

2. *Ethics with Aristotle* (Oxford: Oxford University Press, 1991), 89.
3. Particularly on the force of *proairetike*, ibid., p. 78. On the relation of the conjuncts, see p. 87. It is worth saying that the question whether *kai* is "epexegetic" is quite complexly related to questions about the role of *proairesis* in the good life. It should be remembered that *proairesis* is not peculiar to the virtuous. See below, p. 20 and *n*. 8.

non-rational aspects of the agent.

The first question is whether (iii) entails

(B) A V person chooses V acts qua V acts.

(A) and (B) together seem to make the ideas of a V act and a V person depend on each other. There is no problem just in this, but there will be a problem if it leads to vacuity. This will be so, if we cannot distinguish one virtue from another, and/or the V agent is left with no determinate content to his thoughts. Both of these threaten if (B) and no more is adopted.

But (B) is in general false, in a *de dicto* sense: courageous people rarely choose acts as courageous, and modest people never choose modest behaviour as modest. Justice is about the only case in which it clearly holds. So what might be put in place of (B)? Various alternatives might be suggested.

(a) Might the acts be chosen qua *kala* (qua fine or noble)? Aristotle repeatedly says that virtuous people act for the sake of *to kalon* (the fine or the noble), and stresses that this is something common to all the virtues.[4] Moreover, the presence of this idea to the mind of a virtuous agent would be less objectionable to Aristotle than it is to post-Christian thinkers. But this proposal does not tell us what it is to do a particular sort of V thing for its own sake. It leaves us with the problem of distinguishing the virtues, even to the extent that Aristotle needs to distinguish them. (Both Socrates and Aristotle, despite their views on the unity of the virtues, need to secure the minimal result that the names of the virtues have different senses, which they must have even if they have the same reference (as Socrates held), or (as Aristotle held) they pick out different dispositions, but those dispositions all imply and are implied by one and the same virtue, *phronesis* (practical wisdom)).

On the present proposal, the distinctness of the virtues will be under-represented in the agent's thought, as in (B), interpreted *de dicto*, it is too directly represented.

(b) I lay aside the suggestion that the V person's fully V act can be picked out as having been done as a result of what Broadie calls "Grand End" *proairesis*. This again would not help with the distinction of the virtues; and I accept Broadie's view that, so far as we can, we should disembarrass Aristotle of the Grand End view. In any case,

---

4. *NE* 1115b12, 1120a23, 1122b6.

even the greatest enthusiast for the Grand End View will surely not say that each fully V act is the product of a Grand End deliberation.

(c) The fully V act of the V person is an expression of *phronesis*: it is done *ek tou orthou logou* (for the right reason). I take it that this (as opposed to the Grand End interpretation of it) is true, but there is a difficulty in supposing that it could answer this problem. First, *phronesis* will add something to the account only if it takes us beyond the mere expression of a V disposition in a V act. Let us assume that it does so by adding the idea that the V act is the result of deliberation, actual or (let us say) appropriately understood as in the offing. Then that deliberation will offer the answer that this is the thing to do; this thing will be the V thing, and the conclusion being that of a V person, this conclusion will be appropriately related to the deliberation and to the person. But how? This is just a version of the question we are already trying to answer. Adding the fact that the V person has deliberated well (or can be seen as having deliberated well, or that there is a good deliberation in the offing) does not seem to help in answering it: it merely provides a new focus for it. What we need seems to be something, at least in central cases, about the *content* of the V person's deliberation (but not the content offered by (B)).

(d) The right answer starts from the idea that *di' auto* should be read negatively: the agent does the V thing not for the wrong reasons. This is correct, but it needs positive reinforcement, in the form of an account of the kinds of reasons that appropriately go with various Vs. When developed in this direction, this can indeed lead us back to the original formulation (B). (B) is very roughly right, but only if "qua V" is read *de re*. We say that the agent did the generous (e.g.) thing because it was the generous thing to do, and we understand what this means because we understand what it is about the situation and the action that makes this action in this situation something that would seem to a generous person the appropriate thing to do. It will follow from this that the philosophical understanding of the various virtues will require some, at least, of the understanding that comes from having the virtues: which is of course what Aristotle holds.

This does imply that there is a way in which the action seems to the agent the appropriate thing to do: a way in which such an action commends itself in such a situation to a generous person. What this means is that typically there is a kind of reason or consideration present to the agent's thought that goes with the act's being of this particular V kind. One important sort of consideration involved is that which serves to dismiss alternative courses of action as variously unworthy: thus, a modest person might dismiss a course of action as vainglorious. A person with a particular V disposition will have a specific repertoire of considerations that operate for or against courses of action. We may include both kinds, positive and negative, under the label "acting for X reasons."

The V agent, then, does the V act because he thinks it is the thing to do for X reasons, where "for X reasons" is part his thought, and the type X is tied (both positively and negatively) to the V in question. (As we have already seen in considering (B), X is only rarely the same notion as V, as it occurs in "V act": justice is the leading case in which it is). The role of the distinctive types of reason helps to answer the question about the separation of the virtues.

We can now have non-vacuous mutual dependence:

– A V act is an act done for X reasons
– A V person is disposed to do V acts.

This does not simply make acts primary, because "an act done for X reasons" is not a type of act independent of its agent's state; it is an act done by an agent with a certain disposition. The account locates an important role of desire focused on *to kalon*, in explaining the "because" of "he did it because it was the V thing." The business of concentrating on the X reasons, allowing them to have force, can be assisted by thoughts of how it would be shameful not to. There is no reason for Aristotle to deny this, even though he seems to think that the word *"aidos"* ("shame") relates only to a motivation of the immature (*NE* 1128b15f.).

There is a vital role, too, for *phronesis*: without it, one could not reliably see what acts X reasons could lead to, or what more specific considerations might fall into the class of X reasons. We shall have to ask how much, if anything, that might imply in the direction of moral realism. Before turning to this, however, we have to register that there are some of Aristotle's virtues for which this account does not work. These are the so-called "executive" virtues of courage and *sophrosune* (temperance). I shall discuss the latter in terms of "self-control", which is not Aristotelianly correct: "self-control" is *enkrateia*, a virtue that, for Aristotle, a really virtuous person does not need, and hence is not strictly speaking a virtue. This, like some other views associated with the mean, seems just to represent a substantive and tedious Aristotelian ideal, which we can ignore.

The problem with courage and self-control is not just that courageous and self-controlled people do not choose acts as courageous or self-controlled; as we have seen, that is standard. The self-controlled person may reject actions as shameful, unsuitable, exploitative, etc., but his self-control is manifested not so much in that recognition – although it is partly manifested in the fact that he can achieve that recognition – as in the fact that he can carry that recognition through into action. The courageous person may (although he does not have to) reject acts as cowardly, and he may possibly do acts as *kalon* – as Aristotle was happier to accept this than we are, having a more self-conscious idea of nobility.[5]

The real problem is that there is no X such that courageous or self-controlled people choose their acts for X reasons. Rather, for various other V-related X reasons, they choose acts for those reasons in the face of fear or desire: the structure of the situation is that they do those things for those reasons, although . . . We shall say that those other reasons are V-related, of course, to the extent that we sympathize with Aristotle's unity of the virtues. We could, and I believe reasonably should, say that people can display courage or self-control in doing things for reasons *not* related to some other virtue; but that does not matter much for the present question. The point is that even if we put in the V-related restriction on what counts as a reason for doing some courageous or self-controlled thing, courage and self-control still do not fit the account. This is because they will not fit Aristotle's tripartite structure, which the account is explicating: no version of (ii) applies to them.[6] Courageous or self-controlled things are not done "for their own sake", and doing them for their own sake would be something quite special: something like doing a certain thing in a certain situation to display or develop one's courage or self-control.

If the account of virtuous action looks like this, where, if anywhere, does that leave questions of moral realism? The answer must lie in the relations of all this to *phronesis*, a topic that has been briefly touched on before. Aristotle uses that language of knowledge and of a kind of

---

5. One of the passages mentioned in note 4 above relates the general role of to *kalon* to the case of courage: "the brave man holds his position for the sake of to *kalon*: for this is the *telos* of virtue", 1115b12.
6. It is worth saying that this result is not a product of my taking "self-control" as the executive virtue in question. On Aristotle's account of *sophrosune*, the point is still more obvious.

perception in relation to *phronesis*. Is there an element in the *phronesis*/deliberation structure that could invite a kind of picture that might be labelled "moral realism" (MR)?

Might it come in, first, in explaining what the *phronimos* comes to know when he comes to see *what to do*? Surely not, since Aristotle gives us no reason to say that the conclusion of practical reasoning is *in itself* different when the virtues are being expressed from what it is when it is a matter of the crafts. On the contrary, the idea of a distinctive content that is introduced at this point, just when the virtues are involved in practical reasoning, is alien to Aristotle's approach, which is essentially to incorporate the account of ethics into the theory of rational action in general.

There is, of course, a tradition according to which there is in Aristotle no distinctive conclusion of practical reasoning at all: there is only the actual doing of the action. I do not want to discuss this unappealing account here: in any case, if this were correct, the suggestion I am presently considering for where we might find a place for MR would fall away altogether.

We might add, further, that conclusions about what to do can also be reached by non-moral or anti-moral agents who are presumably not in touch with any such supposed subject matter. Aristotle does not say much about the deliberative activities of such people. A description of the *akolastos* (self-indulgent), that he thinks it always appropriate to pursue the present pleasure, does not eliminate such activities: on the contrary, Aristotle says of this character, as opposed to the *akrates* (incontinent), that he *agetai proairoumenos* (is led on in accordance with his own choice), and this must imply that he arrives at deliberative conclusions.[7]

All this shows is that MR is not going to show up by considering the outcome of the *phronimos'* deliberations. Now Aristotle says that *phronesis* is related to cleverness (*deinotes*), but he holds that *phronesis* is not identical to this, although it cannot exist without it (NE 1144a29). *Phronesis* is essentially connected to virtue of character: and it is important that this is not a verbal point ("treason never prospers"). The thought of the *phronimos* is structurally and materially peculiar; and this is because he thinks of "ends" – we might say, more generally, considerations – that do not occur to other people. As Broadie points out, this capacity is part of his intelligence. He sees that certain

---

7. NE 1146b23-24; cf. 1151a7 for an association between *kakia* (vice) and *proairesis*.

considerations apply, are relevant, carry more weight than others. These include examples of the reasons X that are tied to the various virtues.

To some extent, one can distinguish between seeing that a statement is correct, and seeing that it is relevant to the practical situation at hand. Some of the reasons X will be simply "factual" statements ("it will embarrass her") which might be seen to be true by someone not disposed to count them as reasons in a V-linked way. But it is easy to move out of this area (consider "she needs help"), and many of the most significant reasons X – notably among the negative considerations mentioned before – will be "thick" ethical concepts ("inconsiderate", "disloyal", "shabby"), where the questions of truth and of relevance can be separated only in relation to particular cases. At a general level, those questions cannot be separated, since you cannot make the judgements without having the concept, and you have the concept only if you do count such considerations as relevant in deliberation.[8]

MR will come in, it seems to me, only if it comes in with such concepts. The *phronimos* will exercise his perception, presumably, in seeing that certain considerations of this sort apply. In so judging, he can judge something true. Equally, someone who misses the point, is obtuse, fails in *phronesis*, may be said to have missed a truth, overlooked something, and so forth. Is this enough to speak of realism?

One might say so. However, much of what is said about realism suggests a stronger condition than this. The requirement will be not only that true judgements can be made under the concept, and that one user of the concept can point out to another that he has missed an application. It will, further, have to be true that people who do not use that concept at all are missing something – that the concept "picks up on" an aspect of the world that an attentive and interested observer should acknowledge. But this further condition does not follow from what is indisputably true about thick concepts. With regard to many of them, it is hard to accept; and it is impossible to accept it of all of them taken together (because the thick concepts of different societies

---

8. It is important that "having the concept" here means "possessing it as one's own", where this implies being disposed to use it in judgements with which one is identified. One can understand such a concept, as an anthropologist does, without satisfying this condition.

are often not combinable, and we have no idea of how they might all be mapped onto one grid).

Aristotle did hold a quite strong position about such concepts: that a definitive set of them represented the best achievable human understanding of the ethical. Is Aristotle's position a version of the view which, I have just suggested, might be identified with MR? Only, I suggest, if one accepts more of Aristotle's philosophy than his ethics. For Aristotle, a certain set of thick ethical concepts, including those that define the virtues themselves, provide the best achievable human understanding of the ethical in this sense, that their intelligent use in a life that they serve to define as virtuous is the most satisfying life accessible to a human being. The set of concepts is, one might say, ethically categorical. This is not, for us, obviously the same idea as that expressed by MR (as we are presently interpreting it), which is rather that of certain concepts being cognitively categorical: one who does not use some or all of them has left an important element out of his understanding of the world. So for us, the basic Aristotelian idea, and the suggested interpretation of MR, are distinct. Aristotle himself, however, had further conceptions in the light of which those two ideas are not distinct, but come to much the same thing.

We can, in our own way, seek to remove the gap between the two ideas, by saying that the sense of "understanding the world" that is appropriate to these concepts must be that of ethically understanding the world: these concepts are, after all, hardly going to help us make a contribution to the physical or biological sciences. But our difference from Aristotle's situation is measured precisely by the fact that we need to make this point. Aristotle could see ethics as connected to biology in a way that made human flourishing, understood in terms of a rational ethical life, as straightforwardly an application to us of explanatory categories that apply to all species; you would mention this kind of flourishing in saying what kind of living thing a human being was. We do not share this picture, and it is a denial of history and of scientific change to pretend that we do.

Of course it is we, and not Aristotle, who deploy such formulae as "moral realism", and we must decide what we mean by them. We also must decide how to make the best use, in our circumstances, of Aristotle's ethics. But if we mean the kind of thing by "moral realism" that I have suggested, then even the fullest use we might reasonably make of Aristotle's ethics will not in itself lead us to MR. It would do that only if we accepted Aristotle's own account of the relation of human ethical life to everything else, and that, certainly, we cannot reasonably do.

The virtuous agent's reasons: a reply to Bernard Williams

ROSALIND HURSTHOUSE

According to Williams, Aristotle's claim, in *Nicomachean ethics* II.4, that "The virtuous agent chooses virtuous actions 'for their own sake'" should be taken as meaning different things, according to which virtues are in question.

If it is any virtue but justice, temperance[1] or courage, choosing the act for its own sake means choosing it for at least one of a certain type or range of reasons, X, "where the type X is tied (both positively and negatively) to the virtue in question", but is not "the same notion" (p. 18).

If the virtue in question is justice, choosing the act for its own sake means, roughly, choosing it because it *is* just.

And if the virtue in question is temperance or courage, it can mean only something "quite special: something like doing a certain thing in a certain situation to display or develop one's courage or self-control" (p. 19). In fact, courage and temperance just don't fit Aristotle's II.4. account of acting virtuously at all.

That justice should emerge as a bit of an odd man out might not surprise us; Hume, after all, is right that there is something distinctive about it. But I do find something perverse in an interpretation of II.4 that not only makes justice a slightly special case but also makes courage and temperance not fit, the two virtues (along with justice) that Aristotle mentions time and again to illustrate his general claims about the virtues in Book II, and thereby (one might plausibly say) the two he is least likely to have forgotten about when claiming that the virtuous agent chooses virtuous actions "for their own sake."

For several reasons, some the same as Williams', some rather different (in particular connected with inculcating the virtues in children), I too have long believed that "The V agent chooses what is V for X reasons" is a good way of understanding "The V agent chooses what is V 'for its own sake'." But I have always taken this in such a

---

1. I do not agree with Williams that temperance is a "tedious Aristotelian ideal", so I talk in terms of it, not self-control. But nothing I say in disagreement with him hangs on this.

way that it is as true of the courageous and the temperate as it is of the liberal, the sincere, the agent with the virtue of *philia*, and so on. So it is over the nature of X reasons that I particularly disagree with Williams, and that is what I shall explore.

Like Williams, I think of X reasons as those that enable us to understand "what it is about the situation and the action that makes this action in this situation something that would seem to [an agent with a particular virtue] the appropriate thing to do." (p. 17). But, perhaps unlike him, I thereby think of them as encompassing a large range. Thinking of the range of reasons a courageous agent might have for a courageous act, I come up with such things as, "I could probably save him if I climbed up there", "Someone had to volunteer", "One can't give in to tyrants", "They'll suffer if I don't get to them". Thinking of the range of reasons a temperate agent might have for a temperate act, I come up with "I'm driving", "I'd like you to have some", "You need it more than I do", "The cheaper one's fine by me", "She said 'no'", "I'm waiting to see if I'm HIV positive". With respect to the liberal, I think of "He needed help", "He asked me for it", "It was his 21st birthday", "She'll be so pleased". With respect to the agent with the virtue of *philia*, "He's my friend", "He's expecting me to", "I can't let him down". And for justice we get "It's his", "I owe it to her", "She has the right to decide", "That would mean breaking my promise". And so on and so forth, with many examples of Williams' "negative" reasons as well.

These ranges of reasons seem to me to be a fairly uniform lot. Post-Hume, we might see the reasons given for just acts as being slightly special, insofar as the concepts of *ownership* or *owing* or *rights* or *promising* get a foothold only given the institution of justice. But, aside from that point, they all seem much of a muchness. When we imagine them as sincerely given, in the situation in question, in appropriate tones of voice, with appropriate further answers to further questions about why alternative courses of action were ruled out, and so on – as of course we must – they are all such as to enable us to understand why the agent, in virtue *of* the virtue in question, saw her action as an appropriate thing to do. Moreover, viewed abstractly, they all secure this understanding in the same way – by showing or indicating what good the agent took herself to be pursuing, or what evil she took herself to be avoiding.

And this harmonizes with Williams' point that we should "start from the idea that *di' auta* should be read negatively: the agent does

THE VIRTUOUS AGENT'S REASONS

the V thing not for the wrong reasons" (p. 17) and then fill this out. *In showing or indicating which* good the virtuous agent took herself to be pursuing (or which evil she is avoiding) the reasons given distinguish the way *she* is acting from the way the licentious, or cowardly, or merely self-seeking, or merely docile, agent happens to do the same sort of action; the latter will be pursuing or avoiding quite different goods and evils, doing what is temperate or liberal "for the wrong reasons" (in the particular case).

So far, so good. Why, then, does Williams think that courage and temperance are odd men out? Well, I think he *has* spotted a contrast between them and the other virtues, but I do not think he has characterized it in the right way. Moreover, the contrast does not, I hope to show, undermine my claim that the ranges of X reasons I have given for courage and temperance capture the sense in which the agents with those virtues who choose their V acts for such reasons act *"di' auta."*

What is this contrast? Suppose we said this: Aristotle's virtues, apart from courage and temperance, are distinguishable or separable by reference to the end or good for the sake of which the V agent characteristically acts when she does what is V; an end that, unlike the common end of *to kalon* or *eupraxia*, really does distinguish them, but which, unlike "doing a liberal action" or "doing the action-of-a-friend", somehow does not make them over-distinct.

We get at this end by asking ourselves: suppose the V agent to have succeeded in doing what she intended – what will she, typically, have *done*? And the answers come fairly readily. What will the liberal agent have done – benefited another materially; the munificent – benefited the public materially; the amiable – contributed to the pleasure of others/avoided causing them pain; the sincere – spoken or otherwise revealed the truth about themselves; the "patient" – revenged an unwarranted injury; the agent with the virtue of *philia* – secured his "friend's" good (where "friend" covers friend, lover, associate, wife, child); the modestly ambitious and the *megalapsychos*; these are inevitably tricky, but let's try "secured an honour (small or large) befitting him."

With respect to all of these actions, except those last tricky two (and I think one could even make out a case there), it is clear that they could be done intentionally, i.e. knowingly, but for an ulterior reason – to put the recipient in one's debt, to show off one's wealth, to gain money, under compulsion, and so on. And we know that that's not "the way" the V do them; they do them "because of themselves"; what they were aiming at, the very good or end they were pursuing in acting just was – benefiting someone else materially; benefiting the public, giving others pleasure/or saving them from pain, speaking or revealing the truth about oneself, exacting justified revenge, and so on.[2]

But when we turn to courage and temperance we find that we cannot, in the way we can with the other virtues, say what the courageous or temperate agent *does di' auta*, picking out *the* end he characteristically pursues.

Of course, what the courageous agent characteristically does, in a way, is face danger, but here we do not want to add *"di' auta"* – "because of itself." For although adding *"di' auta"*, would, as before, nicely distinguish the courageous agent from the agent who faces danger for some other reason, under compulsion say, it does so at the price of making him irrational, singling out danger as the good he took himself to be pursuing. But danger is an evil. Face danger *because* it's danger? You would have to be a maniac or insensate.

Similarly, what the temperate agent characteristically does, in a way, is reject some proffered physical pleasure; here again we do not want to add *"di' auta"* for once again, although adding it would nicely distinguish the temperate agent from the agent who does the same for some other reason – to heighten another pleasure say – it does so at the price of making him irrational, singling out physical pleasure as the evil he took himself to be avoiding. But physical pleasure is a good. Reject pleasure *because* it is pleasure? You would have to be perverse or unhealthy.

So courage and temperance really do contrast with the other virtues in this respect. With respect to them we cannot say – what the V agent characteristically does is pursue *this* good or end; instead we say, what the courageous or temperate agent characteristically does is: pursue *some* good or end despite the danger or despite the occasion of temptation.

This is indeed very like Williams' account. But it is not quite, which is why I said above that I thought he had not characterized correctly what was distinctive about courage and temperance. For on Williams' account, the courageous and temperate pursue goods or ends

---

2. Justice, once again, emerges as a slightly special case, since what the just agent will characteristically have aimed to do is – what is just.

related to the other virtues despite etc.; or rather, we must add that qualification insofar as "we sympathize with Aristotle's unity of the virtues" (p. 19).

I certainly have some sympathy with some interpretations of that notoriously difficult doctrine, but in order to get as much of it as I want, I do not, I think, need to claim that the goods or ends pursued by the courageous and temperate are all related to the other virtues. All I need is the assumption that the goods in question are *real*, not merely apparent, goods – *just as*, please note, we assume that the benefit aimed at by the liberal and munificent is real, not apparent, benefit, and the pleasure and pain aimed at and avoided by the amiable is real not apparent pleasure and pain, and the good of one's friend aimed at is a real good, and so on. (This is an important feature of this method of distinguishing the virtues, whereby it avoids making them too distinct; the same judgements about goods and evils, benefits and harms, pleasures and pains, crop up all over the place. I particularly envisage them (I am not sure whether Williams does or not) as coming up in the negative X reasons – "but that would have harmed him (even though it would have given him pleasure)"; "that's not the sort of 'help' he needs even though he thinks it is").

In being "real rather than apparent goods", the goods the courageous agent pursues (and the evils he avoids) despite the danger will thus be not *un*related to the other virtues; but this much, as I just noted, is true of all the others, and I take it Williams means something stronger: that in giving us something of the unity of the virtues, at least enough to rule out courage being displayed by the licentious and unjust, they must all be *proper* to the other virtues – the good aimed at is, say, just action (if one is fighting for the state in which this is possible, against the threat of an unjust regime), or the good of a friend; the evil being avoided is unjust action (if one is resisting a tyrant's demand that one do something unjust), and so on.

I can see that one might say this is sometimes so, but why should one say it is always so, either in Aristotle or more generally? Does Aristotle suppose that every good that is worth pursuing, despite the danger, is the proper object of some particular virtue? Where? And why should he? It is true that his account of courage is lamentably obsessed with warfare; it is thereby, I suppose, conceivable that he would not count, as examples of courageous actions, a lot that we would, such as saving the lives of strangers, or saving the crops and buildings, or Plato's library, from fire, despite the danger. But one rather supposes he would; and these goods or ends are not proper to any of his other virtues.

Moreover, when, like him, we do concentrate on courageous acts in warfare, isn't it a mistake to think of the goods or ends the courageous agent pursues, despite the danger, as having to be goods or ends in themselves? Can't they be instrumental goods or subordinate ends such as "getting the needed message through" or "saving the supplies", or even "obeying orders"?

Similarly, I see no reason for saying that the (real) goods and evils the temperate agents pursue and avoid, despite the occasion of temptation, must be proper to the other virtues, either in Aristotle or more generally. Indeed, for temperance, unlike courage, there do seem to be *some* goods and evils proper to it. Her own health is not, of course, the only good the temperate agent pursues despite etc.; but it is not an end characteristically pursued by agents with any of the other virtues; nor is the evil of eating until one is full to bursting, despite etc. characteristically avoided by any but the temperate.

Now let us take all this back to the question of how we are to understand Aristotle's claim that the courageous and temperate choose to do what *is* courageous or temperate *"di' auta"*, and my claim that this is captured by my X reasons.

I claimed that the ranges of reasons I gave for courageous, temperate, liberal, "friendly", etc. acts done *"di' auta"* were "a fairly uniform lot", notwithstanding a post-Humean qualification on those for just acts. Once we have noted the way in which courage and temperance are unlike the other virtues, we might look at the ranges again and say, "Not so uniform after all; here's an interesting difference. The range of X reasons, or at least the range of *positive* X reasons associated with any particular one of the *other* virtues all work by singling out, in a way, the *same* particular end. Whatever the variations, we can see all the positive reasons, perhaps even some of the negative ones, associated with, say, liberality, as indicating (given the context) that the agent's end is benefiting another materially; the ones associated with *philia* as indicating seeking one's friend's good, and so on. But the ranges associated with courage and temperance are not like that."

True enough. But that does *not* prevent the two ranges I gave from doing the very same job that the others do, namely making it clear (in context), in a non-vacuous way, that the agent is not acting "for the wrong reasons." What do the courageous and temperate do? They pursue a (real) good (or avoid a real evil) despite the danger or temptation. And, *unlike* the cowardly or licentious, they do so because they think the good (or evil) in question *is* a good (or evil), a good (or evil) in comparison with which the danger isn't worth avoiding, or the pleasure pursuing, in the circumstances, whereas the cowardly and licentious will be pursuing or avoiding quite different goods and evils. So the reasons that enable us to understand what made the action in question seem appropriate to the courageous or temperate agent will be those that show us what appears as a good worth pursuing (or an evil worth avoiding) in the situation to such an agent, despite. . . . That's all that is needed. And my X reasons do it.

And it will indeed follow, as Williams says, that the understanding will require some, at least, of the understanding that comes from *having* the virtues; to the real coward, the knowledge that to *that* agent, saving someone else's life, or gaining knowledge, appeared as a good worth pursuing despite the risk to her own life, will seem a clear indication that the agent is reckless to the point of insanity; only the courageous, or those who have been properly brought up, will find that it makes the action comprehensible and typical of the courageous. Similarly, when the licentious discover that the temperate agent saw someone *else's* physical pleasure as a good to be pursued, instead of her own, they think the agent must be an idiot, or incapable of real physical enjoyment, and so on. Which is just what we want.

And now to moral realism, or better, following Wiggins and Foot, moral cognitivism. What can we say the *phronimos* knows? It seems that Williams is reiterating, from *Ethics and the limits of philosophy*, that the *phronimos* cannot know that his thick concepts are "the right ones", and on some of the same grounds. We will not say that Aristotle's *phronimos* knows that *his* thick concepts are the right ones, because we find it "hard to accept" (p. 21) that some of them *are* right; (cf. some of them "belong to another world"[3]; we would produce a different catalogue now[4]). Even if we do accept them (which I must say I do) and add some further ones such as charity, we cannot, even assuming we are *phronimoi* ourselves, say that we know we have the right ones, because we know that other societies have at least some different ones not combinable with ours. And we cannot say, giving any *justification*, that we have got it right and they have

---

3. *Ethics and the limits of philosophy* (London: Fontana/Collins, 1985), p. 35.
4. Ibid., p. 135.

got it wrong. The only justification for such a claim would have to be an "objective" account of human nature which revealed that a certain kind of life was best for human beings and enabled us to recognize that that sort of life involved using *these* thick concepts and not *those*. And, unlike Aristotle, we do not think this is available.

Actually, going by *Ethics and the limits of philosophy*, it rather looks as though the knowledge that we do not accept some of Aristotle's virtue concepts (if we don't), or that other societies have different virtue concepts and they can't all be combined with ours or each other's, is strictly irrelevant to the impossibility of justifiably claiming to know "We have got it right." It merely provides a context that would give that claim a further bite, namely that we could *add* "and they have got it wrong." But knowledge claims, or claims about their impossibility, do not need that context; they just need room for genuine doubt and the reflective discovery that one has, or has not, *nothing* to say to counter it. Williams' claim, in *Ethics and the limits of philosophy*, seems to be that, *when* I reflect on my thick concepts, never mind about whether the reflection is prompted by other societies or not, I will find myself floating, wanting to say that my thick concepts are the *right* ones, pick out *good* ends or ways of going on, but unable to find any way (short of the "objective", "biological" account of human nature that delivers the architectonic end that governs all that Aristotle thought he had) to ground these "thin" concepts – "right" and "good."

Rather than attempting to summarize the objections that others have made to Williams' position here, I shall leave them for discussion and produce a modest one of my own that involves applying plain basic Foot to a most interesting suggestion of Nussbaum about the virtues. I have (following, I supposed, Williams) distinguished many of the virtues by reference to a particular end for the sake of which the V agent characteristically acts when she does a V act. (A strategy that might indeed be seen as leading straight to the idea that the *phronimos* cannot know that his thick virtue concepts are the right ones without having an objective account of human nature, precisely because one can't assess particular ends (such as those set by one's virtue concepts) as good or bad, right, all right or not right, except in terms of the last architectonic end that governs all.) But in "non-relative virtues",[5] Nussbaum distinguishes the virtues a different

---

5. In M. Nussbaum & A. Sen (eds), *The quality of life* (Oxford: Oxford University Press, 1993).

way, by associating each with "a (particular) sphere of human experience that figures in more or less any human life."[6] "The point is", she says, "that everyone makes some choices and acts somehow or other in these spheres" – n.b. actually, that's too strong – "if not properly, then improperly",[7] and the associated virtue specifies what is involved in acting and choosing properly. So, for example, she associates liberality with the sphere of "management of one's personal property where others are concerned", temperance, obviously, with the sphere of "bodily appetites and their pleasures", justice, more tendentiously, with "distribution of limited resources"; but the particular details need not concern us.

What this suggests to me is that we might look at virtue (and vice) concepts as specifying good and bad ways for human beings, in society, to operate in particular spheres of life that all, or some, will inevitably find themselves in. And now basic Foot: *way for human beings (in society) to operate with respect to the physical pleasures*, or *in the management of their personal property where others are concerned*, although laborious noun phrases, are still *noun* phrases; "good" is properly attributive when attached to them, and the noun phrase determines what can count for or against such a way being good, as the noun "roots" determines "good roots." We might note straight away that just the beginning of the noun phrase with "good" attached (good way for *human beings* to operate) makes room for such a counter-claim as, "That might be a good way for *men* to operate (because, say, it secures them pleasure), but it can't be a good way for *human beings* to operate because, far from securing women anything, it harms them." (I should not have to say, but know I need to, that, for example "good way for human beings in society to operate with respect to their possession of great wealth in relation to others" does *not*, in the same way, make room for "That can't be a good way for *human beings* to operate because not everyone has great wealth." But *it* allows, as some of the others manifestly do not, "That doesn't *have* to be sphere of human life; here is a good way for human beings to operate without it" and then the reasoning has to go on from there).

As with what makes for a cactus being good, "*We*, or *they*, like it, or go for it" said by, or of, some group, does not even get into the running as counting in favour of a way of human beings operating as

---

6. Ibid., p. 245.
7. Ibid., p. 247.

being good. "*We* (or *they*) find it works pretty well" gets off the ground, but only as an opening to "because it combines well with what's done *here*, enables *this* to be done, avoids *that* problem, secures *this* advantage" any of which is at least of the right shape to be subject to further assessment – "but this *other* way does all that and also combines well with . . ."; or "but it means losing out on so and so." "Good", combined with such a noun phrase, *is* "thick"; indeed, unless Foot has written for forty or more years in vain, why did it not strike us all immediately that, according to Williams' characterization of "thick" concepts as simultaneously "world-guided and action-guiding", "good" is obviously sometimes thick and sometimes not (in different ways), depending on what it is attached to.

What "counts" for or against a particular way's being a good way for human beings to operate in society, with respect to so and so, will be *reasons* all right, and indeed, reasons for the belief that so and so is a good way (or a bad way, or a fair way that could be improved on) for human beings to operate with respect to whatever. But they are not such reasons in virtue of being grounded in some "objective" account of human nature.

Of course, this is not about reasons a *phronimos* could present to the Samurai warrior, nor indeed to the Ayatollah Khomeni or Baroness Thatcher, in the expectation that they will be led to change their ways or their views; it is not supposed to be. And it is certainly not about how a reflective human being might arrive at the belief "Here is the definitive, i.e. complete list of virtue (and vice) concepts, covering every sphere of life that could ever be important to us, however our lives develop"; I have no idea how reason could ever lead one to such a belief. It *is* about how a reflective human being might arrive at the belief "This thick virtue (or vice) concept, and this, and this, really does pick something out, a good (or bad) way for human beings to go on with respect to certain aspects of life" (and indeed, the further belief, if we want to add the extra bite "and those chaps, who haven't got it, or anything that does anything like the same job, have missed out on something"). And it says that a reflective human being could believe such a thing on the basis of reasons – other beliefs – that are not grounded in anything as fancy as an "objective" account of human nature; which is what Williams declares to be impossible.

The twofold natural foundation of justice according to Aristotle[1]

PIERRE AUBENQUE

I wish to examine Aristotle's theory of justice in the strict sense, with the aim of uncovering its foundations. Book V of the *Nicomachean ethics*, where this theory is developed at length, possesses a certain autonomy, and my analysis will not refer to other, more general moral theories of Aristotle, such as his views on happiness and virtue. Rather, on the basis of the interpretation of the theory of particular justice I will endeavour to draw more general consequences for the interpretation of Aristotle's ethics and its special characteristics.

The general sense of justice, which I will not be examining in detail here, is the sense according to which "the just man is he who is in conformity with the law" (1129a33).[2] On the Aristotelian view that asserts that the law (i.e. the civil law) orders what is good, justice taken in this broad sense is coextensive with "the sphere of action of the virtuous man" (1130b5), i.e. with the entire domain of morality. Justice in this sense is distinguished from particular virtues at most by the juridically constraining character that it confers on acts born of the particular virtues: thus, one can stay unshaken at one's post in war either from courage or – if courage fails – from justice, i.e. by somewhat mechanically observing the law that forbids desertion.

Justice in the guise of legality might appear to be no more than the complement of a morality too weak to be effective on its own. But it also possesses two positive characteristics that make it into a com-

---

1. Translated by Robert Heinaman from the French original.
2. Unless otherwise indicated, all references are to the *Nicomachean ethics*.

plete (*teleia*) virtue: it is not merely a disposition but the use (*chresis*) of other virtuous dispositions (1129b31; cf. 1130b20), and this use manifests itself "in relation to others and not only in itself" (1129b32; cf. 1130b2). Justice is a good that realizes itself in relation to other people (*allotrion agathon*, 1130a2). Certainly this last trait is what secures a kind of unity for the multiple senses of justice,[3] and we will meet it later, in more specific form, when analyzing particular justice.

Particular justice is that "part of virtue" (1130a14) which aims at equality. At 1130a13 it is put simply: "the just man is equal." But one can also take the passage to say – and the context, assimilating equality to justice, fits this sense – that "the just man is *the* equal man." This positive characterization emerges most clearly from the examination of the opposed, vicious disposition, which is *pleonexia* (1129a32). In conformity with etymology, *pleonexia* is the desire to have more (*to pleon haireisthai*, 1129b7).[4] But the question immediately arises: more of what, and more than what or more than who? Aristotle is clear enough on the first point. The goods of which the greedy man wants "more" are not all goods, but only those that refer to good and bad fortune (1129b2–3), i.e. the goods that do not depend on us, which Aristotle elsewhere calls external goods, *ta ektos agatha* (1099a31). A bit later Aristotle explains that it is a matter of "honour" (*time*) and "wealth" (*chremata*) and "all the other things which may be divided between members of the political community" (1130b31–32). This enumeration holds for *pleonexia*, and therefore it also applies to its contrary – justice.

A preliminary remark must be made here about the function of justice and its range of action. Since the goods in question relate to fortune or chance (*tuche*), they are apparently not subject to deliberation and choice. What share of them a person possesses appears to be a matter of chance (*apo tuches*). But the virtue of justice is not satisfied with a situation in which by luck we are born furnished with goods or noble titles; or in which we benefit, thanks to the wealth or culture of our family, from an education which renders us capable of exercis-

---

3. This is what is explicitly asserted in 1130a33: the relation to others belongs to the generic definition of justice; justice is therefore a univocal term, *synonymos*. This conclusively removes the suspicion of hidden homonymy, which had been introduced in 1129a27.
4. It is a matter of secondary importance to point out, as Aristotle does, that the man with *pleonexia* is also the man who wants to have less (of disadvantage) because "less evil is a good."

ing "honours", i.e. political functions; or in which, on the contrary, we are deprived of these advantages. By proposing to distribute these goods in an "equal" fashion, the virtue of justice works in opposition to the chance inequalities that randomly result from our birth and social situation. The virtue of justice, as is said of Greek ethics in general,[5] is a means for rationalizing chance and, thus, for suppressing it up to a certain point.

Therefore, the man characterized by *pleonexia* is the one who desires to have more of these goods or – what comes to the same – the one who desires to endure fewer of the inconveniences that would result from their just distribution (for example, the man who would like to pay fewer taxes). The just man, by contrast, is he who agrees to take an *equal* share of these goods or of the corresponding burdens. But equal to what? Aristotle gives in succession two answers to this question. The first arises, in a way by preterition, from the absence of any explicit relation: the just man is called purely and simply "equal" (1129a34), the greedy man purely and simply "unequal" (a33). It is the same for the qualities of what is just and what is unjust, which reside respectively in equality and inequality (a34, b1). It follows that this equality (or its contrary) is in some sense intrinsic: it is a matter of equality in relation to oneself, of the correct appropriation, on the part of each individual, of his own essence; of the acceptance of one's own value, with the rights and obligations that this implies. The man with *pleonexia* is he who claims more than his due or who does less than he should because he believes himself to be more than he actually is. There is no doubt that this recalls the Platonic definition of justice: according to the *Republic*, for each individual (or each class in society, or each part of the soul), justice consists in "doing one's own" (*ta heautou prattein*), i.e. in accepting one's condition, fulfilling one's function or, negatively, in not overstepping one's limits. Plotinus will further simplify the formula and define justice in itself as *to heautou*,[6] which we could translate as self-appropriation, identity to oneself.

In the Platonic conception this equality to oneself does not exclude, but on the contrary implies, a distinction between the different subjects governed by justice. Fulfilling one's own function means not infringing on that of others; thus, in a just city, the warrior must not

---

5. Cf. M. Nussbaum, *The fragility of goodness* (Cambridge: Cambridge University Press, 1986).
6. Plotinus, *Enneads* I, 2. For Plato, cf. also the *Charmides* on *sophrosune*.

usurp the power of the magistrate, nor the producer usurp the power of the warrior.

Since difference involves a hierarchy, one can say that the equality of each in relation to himself implies an inequality – of inferiority or of superiority – in relation to others. Aristotle does not draw such an inegalitarian conclusion from the concept of equality. He at least leaves open the possibility that the equality of each in relation to himself implies equality in relation to others. If the "self" by which equality is measured is the essence or the form of a man, and this is common to all individuals of the species "man", then there is indeed equality between men precisely in so far as they are men. If one defines man as a rational animal, one can say that all men are of equal value and dignity in so far as they participate in the *logos* inscribed in their essence. Aristotle does not explicitly draw such a conclusion in the *Ethics*[7]; but it seems to me that this conclusion serves as an implicit premiss for the theory of commutative justice, which is one of the two species – and not the least important – of particular justice.

However, the second way of determining the equality constitutive of justice will initially engage the analysis from another direction. The man with *pleonexia* is not only the man who wants to have more absolutely, but the man who wants to have more than others. Here the term of the relation is clearly specified: it is a question of inequality or equality of "one in relation to another" (*heteron heterou*, 1130b33). We should understand that it is a question of inequality or equality of the citizens of the same political community (*politeia*, b32) with regard to the manner in which honours, wealth and other such goods are distributed (*dianomai*) among them. Here we should point out that this element of comparison only enters the picture in relation to distributive justice, which is merely one of the two species of particular justice, the other species being commutative or corrective justice (*diorthotikon*, 1131a1).[8] As nothing new is said on the sort of equality that corrective justice represents, what had been said about equality *tout court* still stands, i.e. what was said about absolute equality, an equality with no other relation besides the one in respect to oneself.

---

7. In the *Politics*, Aristotle connects the fact that "man is by nature a political animal" (1253a2), which implies that he "possesses language (*logos*)" (a10), with the capacity to detect the just and unjust, a capacity tied to *logos* (a14–15, 17) and, among animals, possessed by man alone. Hence all men, in virtue of their nature, appear equal with respect to this capacity.

8. On this, see further below, p. 45f.

Since the theory of distributive justice is the best known part of the Aristotelian theory of justice, I will largely confine myself to points that appear to create difficulties. The principle of distributive justice is not absolute equality but relative equality, and even doubly relative equality: *pros ti kai tisin* (1131a16); relative on the one hand to the value of the distributed good, and on the other hand to the quality of the person who receives it. This twofold relation allows the reintroduction of equality under the form of the equality of two relations: the relation between the things must be equal to the relation between the persons. Each beneficiary must receive a quantity of goods proportional to his value (*axia*, 1131a24). This evidently implies (that without which the principle of proportionality would be of little interest) an inequality of value between persons, which requires a corresponding inequality in the goods respectively distributed to each person. This equality, which introduces between unequals not an absolute equality (as an arithmetical equality would be) but an equality of relations, is what Greek mathematicians called geometrical equality or equality by analogy. The application of the mathematical structure of analogy to the virtue of justice, clearly articulated by Aristotle[9] and largely taken up by the subsequent tradition, is what we will call the Aristotelian model of justice, even though, as we will see, it is not the only one that Aristotle proposed.

The proportional principle justifies unequal persons receiving unequal shares. Rather than using theoretical arguments directly to

---

9. Relating the analogy or geometrical equality to justice goes back at least to Plato. Cf. *Gorgias* 508a:
> Wise men, Callicles, affirm that Heaven and Earth, gods and men, are bound together by friendship, respect for order, moderation and justice, and for this reason they call the universe *kosmos*, i.e. "order", and not disorder or irregularity. You do not pay attention to this, I believe, despite all your science, and you forget that geometrical equality is all powerful among the gods as among men. You are of the opinion that it is necessary to labour to gain an advantage over others (*pleonektein*): this is because you neglect geometry.

Note that in Plato it is a question of the cosmological–theological foundation of virtue in general. This aspect is entirely absent from Aristotle and, moreover, for him it is only a question of founding a species (*eidos*) of particular justice, which is itself a part of justice (1130b30–31). Further, in Plato, if geometrical equality governs the order of things in general, it does not extend as far as the particular; thus, contrary to Aristotle's opinion, it does not hold for individuals of the same class, as is shown by the sanctioning of the guardians' common possession of goods in the *Republic* (423e, 457a–466d).

justify the principle of proportionality, Aristotle points out the difficulties that arise when it is disregarded. Proportional justice is productive of social peace because "quarrels and complaints arise when, being equal, people possess or are awarded unequal shares, or when, people being unequal, they possess or are awarded equal shares" (1131a22–23). It is important to distinguish these two cases of non-application of the principle, which have very different consequences. What is meant by the situation in which "equal persons receive unequal advantages"? Two types of case might be involved. It may be a question of fortuitous circumstantial equality, which is not recognized by the unequal distribution; such is the situation when two labourers accomplish the same work and do not receive the same salary.

But one can also think of a natural equality that would be violated in action or by the toleration of circumstantial inequalities; e.g. if the equality of citizens before the law – the principle of *isonomia* which Solon had introduced to Athens – is violated by corrupt practices or favouritism, with the result that citizens are treated unequally when they should start with the same chances. (For example, applicants for a job). It is clear that this second sort of injustice is more fundamental than the first. Inequality of treatment for those who are equal can only be attributable to an error and it will be easily corrected if it is recognized; but one can also dispute its reality by arguing that the supposition of equality disregards the difference in the situations and contexts, which are never completely identical for two different individuals (differences of sex, age, concrete conditions of production, if it concerns remunerated work). Thus, today, in the name of proportionality, one could easily justify the fact that, for the same work, the salary differs from one country to another, from one business to another, and even for two workers in the same business, depending on their relative seniority. A total equality of situation between two individuals is probably never to be found.

It is not the same for equality of rights such as *isonomia*: here, equality is absolute, clearly definable and recognizable, and its non-recognition constitutes what men agree to be an injustice. But here injustice is due to a fault other than failure to respect the principle of proportionality, since the equality of relations amounts to an equality of terms when the members of the proportion are equal. Equality between citizens entails equality in their rights.

The second case of injustice envisaged by Aristotle merits attention for the contrary reason. It is difficult to see at first what moral principle is violated by the equal treatment of unequal persons. Where is the evil when persons of unequal merit receive the same share, if no one is harmed? Precisely this sort of case is envisaged in another tradition of thought by the Gospel's parable of the twelve labourers at the eleventh hour (*Matthew*, 20, 1–16), and I will recall those elements of it that are relevant for our comparison. The Lord has agreed to a "just salary" with each of the labourers successively hired during the course of the day (20, 4) – let it be one farthing. When at the end of the day he starts to pay the same salary of one farthing to all the hired labourers beginning with the last – those who only started their work at the "eleventh hour" – he runs into recriminations from the first, from those who have worked all day and who "thought that they would receive more" (20, 10). The Lord replies to one of them: "My friend, I do not harm you in any way: did we not agree to one farthing? Take what comes to you and go ... Must you be jealous in order that I be good?" (20, 13–15). In the Gospel's parable, clearly, a principle other than the Aristotelian principle of justice is at work. But which one? Is it enough to invoke the giver's freedom of choice ("don't I have the right to dispose of my goods as I please?", 20, 6)? Undoubtedly, Aristotle wants to avoid a distribution of goods according to the arbitrary will of the distributing power: this must be guided by an objective criterion of equality. Now, to treat unequals like equals is to infringe the rule of (geometrical) equality.[10] Nevertheless, one can, *from an Aristotelian point of view*, attempt to justify the situation described, and this in two ways. The first consists in saying that the labourers are remunerated equally because, despite the difference in their performances, they are equal in a way: they all have the same needs or they all possess the same dignity. Here we would find ourselves in the same situation mentioned above, that of the limiting case where, the value of the persons being equal, geometrical equality amounts to an arithmetical equality. We will be obliged to ask ourselves whether this situation is not more frequent, even for Aristotle, than the introduction of the principle of proportionality (having become superfluous in this case) would have allowed him to believe.

---

10. In a text of the *Politics* (1263a11f.), Aristotle explicitly characterizes as unequal, and therefore unjust, the situation described in the Gospel's parable:
    If pleasure and labour are not distributed according to the rule of equality, but in an unequal manner, recriminations will inevitably arise against those who enjoy or receive much in exchange for little labour from those who receive less and work more.

But the Gospel's parable is open to another "Aristotelian" interpretation that would grant proportionality all of its claims. One could argue thus: the labourers at the eleventh hour are certainly overpaid, since, receiving the same salary for one hour of work as those who have laboured twelve hours, they are, in reality, paid twelve times as much as these others; but this advantage that they receive can be defended as a "just" compensation for their initial weakness. If the labourers at the eleventh hour have not laboured earlier, this is not because of laziness but because "nobody had hired them" (*Math.* 20, 7): they are those left behind, the unlucky, the timid – in a word the weak, those on the bottom rung of society. So is it not legitimate to afford them an initial advantage, a kind of indemnity, which would not be arbitrary since it would be proportional to the difficulties they have encountered more than others, to the sufferings they have endured, etc.? To make those who are last first, as the parable concludes, is, in a way, to re-establish equality by a supplementary advantage accorded to the most disadvantaged.

Today this interpretation, which is doubtlessly not that of the Gospel nor, to be sure, that which Aristotle would have given, has a certain topical interest. Only the negative application of the principle of proportionality (inverse proportionality of the advantage accorded in relation to the social advantages of the beneficiary, or, what comes to the same thing, direct proportionality of advantage to disadvantages previously suffered) allows one to justify, from what would today be called a "socialist" or "social-democratic" perspective, the disadvantaged receiving as much as (i.e. proportionally more than) those who are already advantaged. It is in this way that the opportunity for the sons of workers to attend a university without needing to prove the same abilities as other candidates was justified in the former Communist countries of eastern Europe; or again, it is in this way that the system of quotas is justified in the USA (even with inferior funds, the protected candidate receives the right of equal opportunity, indeed superior access); that special rights for minorities are justified; or again, that a system practised everywhere in civilized countries is justified: tax reductions for the least advantaged, and progressive taxation for the wealthiest. (Thus, the same share of income is taxed more for the rich than for the poor; or again, persons with different incomes pay the same tax depending on their family situations).

It is likely that Aristotle would have refused such an application of the system of proportionality, probably because the advantage freely accorded to certain people – from goodness, as the Gospel indicates (*Math.*, 20, 14), more than from strict justice – cannot fail to harm those who do not benefit from this favour, given that the quantity of goods to be distributed is limited. Now this is just the condition posed by the Gospel's parable itself: the labourer frustrated by his proportional wage is told "I do not harm you in any way." The difficulty, indeed impossibility, of fulfilling this condition can be used to object to Rawls' view of justice. According to him, the principle of equal distribution of primary goods may favour an unequal distribution provided that nobody is harmed and everyone is better off with an unequal distribution.[11] But in a closed economic setting one cannot prove that overpaying the weak does not obstruct paying more to others as would be demanded by proportionality of wages.

Rawls would doubtlessly reply that everything depends on what is meant by an *advantage*. This may naturally be the advantage of the least favoured in accepting differences in wages that benefit the most competent, provided that the latter's competence directly or indirectly benefits all. Of course, this may rather be the advantage of the most favoured in renouncing a part of their advantages (for example, in paying proportionally more tax) if this renunciation contributes to social peace, from which they too will benefit. However, since the advantages of inequality are more subjective than objective (and in a certain way secondary), acceptable inequalities must be based on an agreement between the members of society. Hence, the lack of any recourse, in Rawls, to an objective principle of proportionality and the concomitant necessity of supplying a *contractual* foundation for inequalities.

Nothing of the sort is to be found in Aristotle. Justice is not the product of a decision, a kind of secondary quality projected onto persons or situations by the judgement that declares them just, but a real property of persons and situations recognized as just. All men agree (*homologousi pantes*, 1131a25–26) on the point that distributions must be based on value. As one sees in other assertions with the same universal structure,[12] universal or quasi-universal agreement is not the result of a convention, but a sign of the natural character of the subject

---

11. J. Rawls, *A theory of justice* (Oxford: Oxford University Press, 1972), para. 11.
12. Cf. 1095a17–20: "The majority of men agree in giving the highest good the name of happiness . . . Both the many and the cultivated say that [the highest good] is happiness, and identify living well and doing well with being happy."

of the agreement. Hence, in this sense the principle of proportionality is natural. But if men agree to recognize this natural principle in its generality, nothing prevents their divergence on the interpretation of its content – as is the case with happiness. What is the "value" by which the justice of distribution is measured? It varies, Aristotle tells us, according to the political regime: for democracy, it is freedom (by which one must understand the condition of the free man); for oligarchy, wealth or noble birth; for aristocracy, virtue (1135a27–29).

We find it surprising that Aristotle presents this disagreement without attempting to settle it. Doesn't this refer justice back to the arbitrary conditions of its application, and so deprive it of its natural character? There are two possible replies to this objection. The first would admit that there is a natural hierarchy of political regimes, the most perfect being aristocracy, which makes virtue the criterion of distribution. Natural justice would then distribute goods in proportion to the virtue of each, the question of what defines virtue remaining open (but not insoluble). But Aristotle appears uninterested in this theoretical possibility. The most likely interpretation is that Aristotle considers justice sufficiently defined when it is related to the constitution in which it is exercised (cf. 1130b33): natural justice is what in each particular case coheres with its institutional environment. Later, Aristotle says that the rules of natural justice "are not the same everywhere, since the form of government itself is not" (1135a2–5). Unlike fire, which burns in the same way in Greece and in Persia, the rules of justice are not non-natural as a result of the fact that they vary from one country to another. Human nature manifests itself differently in different places, and the fact that justice realizes itself in different ways conforms with nature, if this realization is always appropriate to the constitution that is best for people in the given circumstances.[13] In human affairs, naturalness does not exclude variability.

But the variability of the criterion does not exclude the presence of constant features as well. And the principle of proportionality, which implies inequality, need not always be applied – as in the absence of

---

13. We are clearly giving a partitive rather than a collective sense to *pantachou* in line 1135a5: "everywhere on each occasion there is one constitution which is best according to nature", and not: there is only one constitution which is everywhere by nature the best. Cf. H. G. Gadamer, *Wahrheit und methode* (Tübingen, 1962), p. 303; and P. Aubenque, "La loi selon Aristote", *Archives de Philosophie du Droit* **25**, 1980, pp. 147–57, especially p. 154.

inequalities which it would have to equalize. We learn this from the Aristotelian analysis of the second species of particular justice: corrective or commutative justice (*diorthotike*).[14] Although Aristotle develops this at greater length than the first kind of justice, it has often been less studied by the tradition, which has retained above all the first species' model of proportionality. Commutative justice assures the rectitude of interpersonal relations (*synallagmata*, 1131a1). The difficulty here arises from the fact that Aristotle applies this name to two very different types of situation: on the one hand, "voluntary" transactions, regulated by contract (sale, purchase, loan, letting, etc.); on the other hand, relations governed by the passions – called "involuntary" by Aristotle – which are not controlled by rational desire. (Here Aristotle gives a long list of such cases which constitute what we would call misdemeanours: theft, adultery, prostitution, perjury, murder, sequestration, outrage, etc.). Hence, this new form of justice covers the fields of contractual rights and penal rights. One might wonder whether it also covers the area of economic exchange.[15] What differentiates this immense area from that governed by distributive justice is its concern with private relations, whereas distributive justice distributes public goods (*chremata koina*, 1131b28–29), i.e. goods disposed of by the polis, whose distribution must therefore be proportional to the contribution each makes to the community (1131b31).

In the sphere of private relations, all men are equal, and so here the principle is one of respecting "arithmetical proportionality" (1132a2). If an individual A has suffered a share of harm equal to M at the hands of an individual B who has unduly appropriated this share for himself, equality will be re-established by the restitution of M, so that the quantities possessed by the two individuals after restitution will be equal, according to the arithmetical mean, to the sums possessed on both sides prior to the theft. According to the commentary of J. Tricot (*ad loc.*), the aim of this needlessly complicated bookkeeping is to show that "corrective justice restores people to their natural state of equality." Since it cannot be a matter of equality of situation (for example, the person robbed may be richer than the thief and

---

14. "Commutative" is the traditional translation that derives from St Thomas. One can retain it to the extent that this form of justice concerns exchange (*commutationes*) in general, including economic exchange.
15. This is what seems to arise from 1131b25, where commutative justice is presented as the sole remaining species, which therefore includes economic exchange, distinguished by the supplementary character of reciprocity.

he will recover his wealth after restitution), it can only be a matter of equality of persons independent of their respective social positions.

It is this absolute rather than relative principle of equality that must be applied, so that both strict respect for contracts will be assured and the equilibrium destroyed by an offence will be re-established. In this last case, it will be the role of the judge to "equalize" (1132a24): in the simplest case previously referred to, by restitution; and, when restitution is no longer possible (e.g. in a case of wounding), by compensation; to which is added a penalty whose function is to equalize as much as possible, through the suffering inflicted on the condemned, the suffering experienced by the victim. The judge (*dikastes*) is a mediator; that is, according to an imaginary etymology, he who divides in two (*dicha*).

From this principle without proportionality Aristotle draws an important consequence, which is probably new and indeed revolutionary for his time: that justice must judge without favour. That is, it must judge without regard to the rank or station of the victim or of the guilty party (1132a1–6): a nobleman who murders a slave must not be punished any the less than a slave who murders a nobleman. Such at least is the principle – an absolute principle – of commutative justice.[16] But what is the justification for the principle itself? It can only be the equality between men in their right to possess certain goods. The list of offences enumerated by Aristotle enables us to see which goods are not to be allowed to be subjected to criminal attack with impunity: life, health, personal integrity, property as such (not in so far as it is quantified), good reputation and self-respect (both shaken by defamation), and so on. Since the enjoyment of some of these goods, such as property, health or life itself, partly depends on chance, the equality that Aristotle claims for all men can only concern

---

16. The absoluteness of the principle is not weakened by Aristotle's refusal – to be explained shortly – to interpret the principle of equality in terms of simple reciprocity, which would be the equivalent of the law of retaliation. For equality is not identity (which would justify the formula "an eye for an eye, a tooth for a tooth"). Equality presupposes an evaluation, which is evidently necessary in the case of murder, for example. In the evaluation of the crime, and thus of the penalty, the circumstances play an important role. This is the reason why an injury inflicted on a magistrate will be punished more severely than an injury inflicted on a private individual (1132b28–30); not because the magistrate would have greater worth, but because what is attacked through him is not only the man, but the office.

a *right* of possession, the exercise of which assumes equal opportunity of access to the goods. Hence, for Aristotle, men have an equality of rights founded on a human nature equally shared among men, which is itself the foundation of commutative justice.

Thus, in Aristotle's view, every aspect of justice has a natural foundation. But this foundation is itself twofold: in his relation to the political community, each man occupies a position, fulfils a function, and must see himself recognized as having a value in proportion to which he receives a determinate share of social goods. But seen in his private relations with other men (those that do not pass through the political community), each man possesses the same right as every other to enjoy a certain number of elementary and inalienable goods.[17] If the exercise of the rights of the citizen demands respect for proportionality, the rights of man are indivisible, unquantifiable, universal, and therefore can only belong to all men as such. Human nature is twofold: variable and inwardly diversified in its political manifestations, at the same time it is everywhere the same in the right it confers on each man to realize, even if in different ways, the capacities inherent in his human essence.

---

17. This duality of models – regulated distribution of a finite mass of goods, or an equal attribution to all men of a universal capacity – is the basis of the myth of Protagoras, according to the *Protagoras* of Plato. Protagoras was clearly inclined to favour the second model. Plato prefers the first with its hierarchical conception of the polis. Aristotle accepts the duality of models.

Justice at a distance – less foundational, more naturalistic: a reply to Pierre Aubenque

TROELS ENGBERG-PEDERSEN

In his chapter on "Relativism and reflection" in *Ethics and the limits of philosophy*,[1] Bernard Williams had some difficulty with fitting justice smoothly into his idea of an ethical "relativism of distance." On the one hand, Williams stated, "there is some pressure, if one thinks historically at all, to see modern conceptions of social justice, in terms of equal rights, for instance, as simply not applying to hierarchical societies of the past."[2] Yet, as he continues,

> there are strong pressures for the justice or injustice of past societies [and hence also, we may add, for their theories of justice] not merely to evaporate in the relativism of distance. Even if we refuse to apply to them determinately modern ideas, some conceptions of justice were used in those societies themselves, and it is not a pun or a linguistic error to call them that. One can see some modern conceptions of social justice as more radical . . . applications of ideas that have existed elsewhere and informed other societies; equally, historical continuities may be put to ethical use in the opposite direction . . . if radicals can identify more egalitarian modern conceptions as descendants of past conceptions of justice, so can conservatives try to find some less egalitarian analogue of the old conceptions to serve them now.[3]

Williams concludes, however: "There is much more that should be said on these issues. It may be that considerations of justice are a central element of ethical thought that transcends the relativism of distance."[4]

This sets the scene well for Pierre Aubenque's paper. In a discussion of Aristotle and moral realism, his treatment of justice must have a very high priority, as even Williams' generally relativistic approach

---

1. London, Fontana/Collins, 1985.
2. Ibid., p. 165.
3. Ibid., p. 166.
4. Ibid.

indicates. In my response, however, I shall not focus directly on this broader issue. Since the general burden of Aubenque's paper is not only that we can (in Williams' words) "identify more egalitarian modern conceptions as descendants of past [in this case, Aristotelian] conceptions of justice", but that we can even find them in Aristotle, I shall rather discuss the issue of whether that is in fact so. My basically historical approach may seem slightly disappointing but, clearly, in discussing Aristotle and moral realism we also want to get Aristotle right.

Two premisses

Let me make two general remarks before I begin. The first concerns the overall character, as I see it, of Aristotle's philosophizing on ethical and political issues. Very briefly, I take Aristotle to be not so much a naïve as a robust realist. Although he was well aware of relativistic alternatives in matters ethical and political, he was not very strongly *impressed* by them. Instead he thought that by careful analysis of the *endoxa* – beliefs held in good repute and shared by either few or many – it is possible to arrive at genuine truths on the given subject.[5]

There is no need to rehearse the various statements that support this interpretation. One example from the *Rhetoric* will suffice: "Human beings are by nature sufficiently oriented towards the true and most often they hit upon the truth" (1355a15–17).

The important point in the present context is that with such a robust confidence both in the very existence of truths (in general and in ethical and political matters) and in the human capacity to reach them, Aristotle felt no need to develop a substantive understanding of human nature to serve as the foundation for whatever conception of justice he might present. As Aubenque himself notes, in several places in *Nicomachean ethics* (Book V) Aristotle refers to what "all

---

5. For Aristotle the relativistic alternative on ethical and political issues took the form of the view that ethical and political beliefs are conventional (*nomoi*) as opposed to natural (*physei*). See, for instance, NE 1094b14–19. Aristotle rejects this and draws the consequence – from the "variety and fluctuation of opinion" in this area, which he acknowledges (1094b15–16) – that the conclusions he will present will only "show the truth roughly and in outline" (1094b19–22). Still, what is shown remains "the truth" (*talethes*). Thus, Aristotle acknowledges the difficulty and takes steps to handle it, but it does not unsettle the basic direction in which he is going.

mean by justice" (1129a7), what "all men suppose it [the just] to be, even apart from argument" (namely, Aristotle's kind of argument, 1131a13–14), what "all men agree" on (1131a25–26), and the like. On my reading of Aristotle, that sufficed. In particular, he felt no need to seek a justification for the truth of what men agree to in a special understanding of human nature, man's essence or what not. Aubenque, by contrast, seems to be looking for indications of just that. At least, he seems to take it that, behind Aristotle's statements about what is or is not just, there lies such an understanding. But if I am right, that goes clearly and importantly beyond Aristotle.

My second remark is related to this. I take it that Aubenque intends to give a *reading* of (parts of) what Aristotle has to say about justice. *His* claim is not merely that there is a more or less tenuous line between Aristotle on justice and certain more modern conceptions that Aubenque himself obviously cherishes. As already indicated, that is where my problems begin. But it matters a great deal for the appositeness of my comments that I should be right in my diagnosis on this point: Aubenque intends his paper as a reading of Aristotle. And it is as a *reading* of Aristotle that I respond to it.

Two difficulties in Aubenque's account of particular justice as a whole

Aristotle defines the second of his two main types of justice – particular justice – in terms of equality (*to ison*, cf. 1129a32-b1, b10–11). The corresponding form of injustice is characterized by an attitude of "grasping", of *pleonexia*. Aubenque reasonably asks, concerning the notion of equality: equal to what? He claims, however, that there are two answers to this question. First, there is a sense of equality that is "in some sense intrinsic: it is a matter of equality in relation to oneself, of the correct appropriation, on the part of each individual, of his own essence; of the acceptance of one's own value, with the rights and obligations that this implies" (p. 37). Aubenque also speaks of "self-appropriation" and "identity to oneself" and suggests that Aristotle leaves open the possibility that "the equality of each in relation to himself *implies* an inequality – of inferiority or of superiority – in relation to others" (p. 38, my emphasis). For that, of course – that is, equality with the others – is the second form of equality that Aristotle must have had in mind.

I have difficulty in following Aubenque here. He goes on to speak in the following way: "If the 'self' by which equality is measured is the essence or the form of a man, and this is common to all individuals of the species 'man', then there is indeed equality between men precisely in so far as they are men" (p. 38). To my mind this not Aristotle but, for instance, Stoicism. I can find no indications in the treatise on justice that we should bring in such an idea.

Aubenque, however, thinks it is involved when Aristotle says (NE 1129a31–33) that "both the lawless man and the grasping and unfair (or unequal) man are thought to be unjust, so that evidently both the law-abiding and the fair (or equal) man will be just." But first, if Aristotle was thinking of a person as being either unequal or equal in relationship to himself, namely to himself as a human being, then he should have explained the point since it is a far from obvious idea. And secondly, one reason why Aristotle explicitly begins his account of justice from a consideration of injustice (1129a17ff.) is presumably that in the notion of *pleonektein* or grasping one can see most clearly that particular justice is about equality – and in exactly the sense of not getting the better of others.[6] The idea that those involved will have an intrinsic value just as human beings or persons seems to me completely foreign to Aristotle's thought here. Nor can I see any need for it. I shall come back to this point later.

My second difficulty concerns Aubenque's claim that equality in relation to others is only relevant with regard to one of the two subspecies of particular justice, namely so-called distributive justice. The other subspecies, "commutative" or corrective justice, is only concerned with what Aubenque calls "absolute equality, an equality with no other relation besides the one in respect to oneself" (p. 38). But even if – as I just denied – this last idea were to be found in Aristotle, it seems clear that corrective justice is called for precisely to correct or adjust an imbalance brought about by *pleonexia*: when person A has acquired (in whatever way) more than his due (or his own) *in compar-*

---

6. In fact, as I have argued elsewhere (*Aristotle's theory of moral insight* (Oxford: Oxford University Press, 1983), pp. 57–60), Aristotle intends to define particular injustice in NE 1130a16–32, by showing that the man of particular injustice has a special motive, that of making a "gain" in terms of natural goods, of getting "more" for himself of such goods than the others. That idea may seem unduly restrictive to us, but it fits well into what appears to be a characteristic of Greco-Roman ("zero-sum") society, the constant comparison with others about access to the social goods.

ison with person B who has suffered from a given transaction. It is the "equality" or balance between the two people defined by the situation before the transaction that a judge will attempt to re-establish.

Thus, Aubenque's attempt to find the notion of the intrinsic value of the individual person behind Aristotle's talk of equality has not convinced me. I do not find the notion in Aristotle's text, nor do I think Aristotle needs it.

I now turn to three points in Aubenque's more detailed discussion of one of the two subspecies of particular justice, namely, distributive justice.

Three difficulties in Aubenque's account of distributive justice

Aubenque rightly highlights (pp. 39–40) an interesting remark of Aristotle:

> Rather than using theoretical arguments directly to justify the principle of proportionality [which serves to define distributive justice], Aristotle points out the difficulties that arise when it is disregarded. Proportional justice is productive of social peace because [as Aristotle says] "quarrels and complaints arise when, being equal, people possess or are awarded unequal shares, or when, people being unequal, they possess or are awarded equal shares". (1131a22–23)

(a)   I have some difficulty with Aubenque's comments on the first case (where equals have unequal shares). If I understand him correctly, he is saying that what lies behind the quarrels and complaints that arise from *this* case, in other words what *explains* them, is a perception of a *natural* equality. This is the equality of citizens vis-à-vis the law, the principle of *isonomia* introduced by Solon in Athens – that equality of the citizens which gives rise to the equality of their rights (p. 40).

Again I think this goes much further than Aristotle wished to go. I cannot see that talk of a *natural* equality of citizens' *rights* has any basis in Aristotle himself. As I see it, Aubenque is himself *precisely* right in saying that Aristotle does not attempt to justify the principle of proportion by theoretical arguments, but instead shows the difficulties that follow from not respecting it: proportional justice generates social peace. Indeed, I think that there is a lesson to be learned here: namely, that the kind of justification for a principle of justice (in this case that of proportion) that Aristotle would be looking for is a pragmatic one.

(b) I also have some difficulty with Aubenque's discussion of the second case (where unequals have equal shares). He brings in, interestingly, as I hope to show, the Matthean parable of the labourers in the vineyard. He notes that it goes squarely against the Aristotelian principle that unequals should not have equal shares. He also quotes a passage from the *Politics* (1263a11–15) in which Aristotle expressly notes the injustice of a situation like the one described in Matthew. Here I would emphasize Aristotle's specific point that, if the work done and the benefit received are not equal but unequal, there will inevitably (*anankaion*) be ill feeling (*enklemata*, recriminations) towards those who get a good income without doing much work from those who work harder but get no corresponding extra benefit. Again, what concerns Aristotle is the fact of social dissatisfaction.

What worries me, however, is the way in which Aubenque attempts to make sense of the *Matthean* principle of justice (if such it is) *from an Aristotelian perspective*. He offers two possibilities. First, one might say that the labourers were in some way equal to one another: they have the same needs or the same dignity, their value as persons is the same (p. 41). Aubenque himself comments as follows on this possibility: "We will be obliged to ask ourselves whether this situation is not more frequent, even for Aristotle, than the introduction of the principle of proportionality (having become superfluous in this case) would have allowed him to believe" (p. 41). I take this to be a more or less veiled *objection* to Aristotle and thus an acknowledgement that this possibility of making sense of the Matthean principle of justice is not *Aristotle's* and hence does *not* constitute a justification of it "from an Aristotelian perspective." Rather, it brings in ideas which are precisely *not* Aristotelian ones.

Aubenque's second attempt to make sense of the Matthean principle of justice from an Aristotelian perspective develops the Aristotelian principle of proportionality in a direction almost exactly opposite to the sense in which Aristotle himself understood it. The idea is that the present advantage of those who have *few* merits to qualify them (the 11th-hour labourers who get full pay) is proportional to their earlier *dis*advantages. And so Aubenque speaks of a *"negative* application" of the principle of proportionality (p. 42, my emphasis).

But again, this is definitely not Aristotle. Aubenque obviously knows this since he says that Aristotle would probably have refused these applications (*aménagements*) of the system of proportionality (p. 42). But then what remains of the supposed justification of the Matthean principle of justice "from an Aristotelian perspective"?

Let us stop here for a moment and note two things. First, Aubenque is right that something like his principle of inverse proportionality lies behind many practices of distributive justice in modern states, from Eastern Europe to the United States. Where does it come from? Not, as we have seen, from Aristotle. Is it, then, part of our specifically Christian heritage? That, it seems to me, is an interesting historical question. What should be clear, however (and this is my second point), is that it is not lifted directly out of the *Matthean* story either. For that story is precisely not about justice. Aubenque rightly notes that the owner of the vineyard acts out of goodness (the term is *agathos*) "more than from strict justice" (pp. 43–4). I would go much further. The parable *presupposes* that *justice* would have required exactly what Aristotle says. But the owner of the vineyard chooses *not* (merely) to be just. In other words, the parable in Matthew is evidence that the *same* understanding of *justice* is to be found both in Aristotle and in this Hellenistic–Jewish author. What we have in Matthew is therefore not the modern principle of justice based on the idea of inverse proportionality. It may, however, be its ancestor.

So far, I see what Aubenque has been doing as an attempt to find some cherished modern ideas in Aristotle. The attempt is not, I think, successful. But it helps greatly to bring the differences between Aristotle and "us" into sharper focus. We shall see the same picture in connection with the third idea in Aubenque's discussion of distributive justice that I shall highlight.

(c)   Here I am referring to Aubenque's claim that Aristotle, against Rawls, would have nothing of the suggestion that views on justice have only a contractual foundation instead of being in some way based in nature. Initially, Aubenque is quite right here (p. 43): To Aristotle,

> Justice is not the product of a decision, a kind of secondary quality projected onto persons or situations by the judgement that declares them just, but a real property of persons and situations recognized as just. All men agree . . . on the point that distributions must be based on value . . . universal or quasi-universal

agreement is not the result of a convention, but a sign of the natural character of the subject of the agreement.

Aubenque further notes (p. 44), and again rightly, that the "value" (*axia*) in accordance with which goods are to be distributed varies with the political constitution: democrats say that it is the status of freeman (*eleutheria*), supporters of oligarchy that it is wealth (or noble birth), and supporters of aristocracy say that it is *arete* (1131a27–29). But how, Aubenque asks, can we then maintain the natural character of justice? Answer: "natural justice is what *in each particular case* coheres with its institutional environment" (p. 44, my emphasis). And we are not to ask which of these political constitutions is by nature the best one.

Initially, one might think that this is meant to make justice a completely formal matter that depends for its substantive content on the constitutional framework within which it is operating. That is probably part of the idea, but Aubenque also wishes to say that human nature itself may, *non*-hierarchically, manifest itself in different ways in different places. And so it is in accordance with nature (human nature, that is) that justice is realized in different ways in different places if "this realization is always appropriate to the constitution that is best for people in the given circumstances" (p. 44). Actually, Aristotle himself speaks of a single constitution as being "everywhere by nature the best one" (1135a5), but Aubenque reads the *pantachou* (everywhere) *distributively* (*n.* 13).

This interpretation of Aristotle's references to human nature is very congenial to modern tastes. But I disagree with Aubenque's reading of the particular text on which he builds his suggestion (1134b35–1135a5). The whole passage (1134b18ff.) is of course highly germane to the overall topic of Aristotle and moral realism. A short paraphrase will bring it before us. In the area of political justice, says Aristotle, something is natural(ly just, *physikon*) and something (just) by convention (*nomikon*). What is naturally just is, first, that which everywhere (*pantachou*) has the same force and, secondly, not because people take it in this or the other way. (This, incidentally, is one of the clearest statements in Aristotle of his moral realist position). What is just by convention is that which is originally indifferent, but makes a difference once it has been posited. Now some people think, Aristotle continues, that all justice is of this sort, because that which is by nature is unchangeable and has everywhere the same force (as fire

JUSTICE AT A DISTANCE

burns both here and in Persia), while they see change in the things recognized as just. But, as Aristotle replies, this is only half true. Natural and moral phenomena are all in one sense changeable, but still something is in accordance with nature and something not. For instance, the right hand is by nature stronger, yet it is possible that all men should come to be left-handed.

The idea is presumably (cf. *Magna moralia* 1194b30ff.) that all people might train their left hands to be stronger than their right hands, but still the human right hand is "by nature" stronger than the left hand, where "by nature" presumably means by birth and in accordance with human (genetic) nature. There may be difficulties in such a view, but it is certainly a recognizably Aristotelian position. The facts about which hand is the stronger are changeable in a way in which the burning of fire is not. Still something, the greater strength of the right hand, is in accordance with man's nature, and something else, the *possibly* greater strength of the left hand of all human beings, is not. Similarly, Aristotle held the corresponding moral or political view that, as human beings are, one political constitution is "by nature everywhere" the best – and will continue to be so even if at some time all societies decide on another form of political constitution. What is naturally just, then, is what corresponds, in the area of distributive justice, to the single constitution which is by nature everywhere the best.

Thus what Aristotle is saying in 1134b35–1135a5 is the following. He is speaking of "the things that are just not by nature but by human enactment (*ta me physika all' anthropina dikaia*)" (a3–4). Shortly before, he identified these things as what is just "by virtue of convention (*nomikon*) and contract (*syntheke* – agreement)" (1134b32), and he now reintroduces them as being "just by virtue of contract (*kata suntheken*) and (a mutual agreement on shared) expediency (*to sympheron*)" (b35–a1). They are like measures (a1–3) and thus (cf. the paraphrase of 1134b21–24 given above) they are posited. Of these things, then, it holds that they are "not the same everywhere (*pantachou*), since political constitutions too are not the same – *but still* (*alla*: nevertheless), a single one (*mia monon*, namely constitution) is *everywhere* (*pantachou*) *by nature* the best one" (a4–5).

It is difficult not to conclude that a distributive reading of the last *pantachou* goes directly against the clear sense of Aristotle's words.[7]

Summarizing so far, I have identified three points in Aubenque's discussion of distributive justice where he seems to me to find more modern ideas in Aristotle than can in fact be found there. This holds for his notion of a "natural equality of rights" as underlying Aristotle's principle of proportionality. It also holds for his notion of a "value of persons as persons" and of his attempted development of a negative application of Aristotle's principle of proportionality, both of which Aubenque finds to be in some way within the purview of Aristotle's principle. Finally, it holds for his construal of the notion of what is just by nature.

A difficulty in Aubenque's account of corrective justice

In the last pages of his paper Aubenque discusses corrective justice. There are some persuasive points: that this type of justice is concerned with the private relations between individuals, as opposed to the public distribution of goods, which falls under distributive justice (p. 45); that what Aristotle says in the interesting chapter V.8 of the book about economic exchange and the role of money belongs under corrective justice (p. 45). I have difficulties, however, when Aubenque develops what he calls the principle of equality that finds expression in this subspecies of justice. It is an equality not of situations but of persons, independently of their respective social situations, a non-relative, absolute equality (p. 46), a mutual equality of human beings "in their right to possess certain goods" (p. 46), with its foundation in "a human nature equally shared among men" (p. 47).

---

7. After the symposium Dr Bob Sharples kindly drew my attention to the ancient and Byzantine commentators, who concur on this; see the anonymous commentator in *CAG* 20 233.23ff. and Michael in *CAG* 22.3 48.21ff. – Aubenque refers for his reading to Hans-Georg Gadamer in *Wahrheit und Methode* (Tübingen: J. C. B. Mohr [Paul Siebeck], 3rd edn 1972), pp. 302–4. Gadamer's interpretation, however, is wilful. Aristotle's example of the conventionality of measures (1135a2–3) is translated as follows by Ross (rightly): "wine and corn measures are not everywhere equal, but larger in wholesale and smaller in retail markets". Here, however, is Gadamer (p. 303): "*Ein und dieselben Masse* [?] *nimmt man immer, wenn man mit ihnen Wein einkauft, reichlicher, als wenn man mit ihnen verkauft.*" (It is noteworthy that Gadamer virtually bases his whole claim about the general character of ethical knowledge, as modelled on Aristotle's notion of *phronesis*, on this mistranslation. It is found in a section of the book in which Gadamer is concerned to show *die hermeneutische Aktualität des Aristoteles*)!

JUSTICE AT A DISTANCE

As before, I cannot find the emphasis on personhood in Aristotle, or indeed find that notion at all. Aristotle does, of course, speak of equality (or the equal, *to ison*), but not (here: in connection with corrective justice) an equality of *people*. In fact, he emphasizes, as Aubenque notes (p. 46), that the kind of difference between people that might seem most pertinent, namely a difference in moral character, is considered wholly irrelevant when this kind of justice is in operation (1132a2–6).[8] Instead, I take it (cf. Aristotle's analysis in 1132a24–29, 1132b14 and 19–20) that what is compared and what must be equal are the two *situations* before and after a given transaction. *They* must be equal in the sense that each partner to the transaction must have the same amount of goods before and after it. The *status quo* must be maintained – is maintained by this kind of justice – no matter what the social or moral position of the partners may be.

But why? What, as Aubenque asks, is the justification for this principle of equality without proportionality? Aubenque's reply is: the mutual equality of human beings in their right to possess certain goods (p. 46). My own reply will go as follows. It is certainly worth asking what justifies the value of equality in the situations envisaged by Aristotle. If the question is taken to mean what Aristotle himself took to justify that value, it seems fairly clear, as we have already noted, that the answer should be: that is what all people think! Also, Aristotle would probably refer to the supposed fact that maintaining the value of equality in this area tends to promote social cohesion and to prevent recriminations and discord. If, however, the question is

---

8. Three points about this passage:
   – Aubenque reads Aristotle's talk of the *epieikes* and *phaulos* as referring to social location. In itself that is certainly possible, but passages such as NE 1128b21–29, and in particular 1113b11–14, make it more likely that Aristotle had in mind the moral sense of the two terms.
   – The sense of the phrase *pros tou blabous ten diaphoran monon blepei ho nomos* (1132a4–5) is contested. But what Aristotle needs for his argument is a reference to the "difference" made by the act to be corrected in terms of the "damage" incurred by the person who has suffered from the transaction. So, "the law looks only to the difference made (by the act) in terms of damage".
   – It is worth considering whether the word *isois* in *chretai hos isois ei . . .* should not be understood as grammatically neuter: the law considers equal the two *situations* that (*ei*) (i) A has done a wrong and B has been wronged and (ii) A has damaged and B has been damaged. (Here, however, as Dr Sharples has reminded me, the ancient and Byzantine commentators support taking the *isois* as masculine, see CAG 20 219.4ff. and CAG 22.3 25.19ff.).

taken to mean why *the Greeks* took the just to be the equal (as Aristotle, the philosopher, reflects it in his illumination of the reputable opinions), then we may come up with whatever answer appears congenial to us. A first step might lie in bringing in Richard Hare's notion of universalizability. But more would need to be said. The important point, however, as I have emphasized all through, is that we should not expect to find an Aristotelian attempt to justify the principles of justice in terms of a philosophical anthropology. There is no *more* justification to be found in Aristotle than in the reputable opinions that he canvasses and systematizes.

So, much as I would like to, I cannot find any sufficiently clear basis in Aristotle for Aubenque's notion of human rights to basic and inalienable goods. What we find in Aristotle, as I see it, is a different construal of justice from one we might wish to accept. It obviously has important and interesting affinities with what we would say. But it also has important differences and they are no less interesting. One difference has been highlighted by Aubenque in a thought-provoking way, namely that we, as I think, in contrast with both Aristotle and Matthew, tend to describe as just a political system that goes against the principle of proportional distribution so clearly developed by Aristotle. I find it interesting to speculate about how that change may have come about.

Concluding remarks

I have presented Aristotle as a robust moral realist; that is, as one who without compunction canvasses *endoxic* and pragmatic arguments for statements purporting to state *the truth* in the given area. It is noteworthy, however, that Aristotle is quite circumspect when it comes to stating those truths. He rarely leaves completely out of his final theory a point of view that appears sufficiently *endoxic* to have been given an initial hearing and he is often satisfied with fairly general accounts of the various notions he introduces, even the most basic ones. It is this feature that makes it possible to develop many central ideas in Aristotle's ethics beyond the way they were understood by Aristotle himself, but in a direction that does make it possible to claim that these ideas are valid for human beings as such, in all times and places. Most often that direction will be a Kantian one. Sometimes one need go no further than to Stoicism – but then the

Stoics and Kant had important affinities in their basic anthropology.

An example of this is Aristotle's formal principle of distributive justice: proportional equality relative to some value or other. For one may ask: why *equality*? Is there some underlying notion of an "intrinsic value of each individual person as an individual" that will account for why anybody should begin to think in terms of equality in the first place? The same question may be asked in connection with Aristotle's notion of corrective justice.

If these questions are about what Aristotle himself says, my answer has consistently been "No." But one might suggest that Aristotle's account of the two parts of particular justice, and the general understanding that it reflects, implies such a notion, which it was then left to later philosophers to develop in a process that began already with the Stoics. However, whether that suggestion will lead us to a notion that transcends Bernard Williams' relativism of distance remains to be seen.

Testing the limits: the place of tragedy in Aristotle's ethics

JONATHAN LEAR

I Introduction

Can mind comprehend its limits? Since Kant this has become a familiar question for theoretical reason, but for Aristotle it was crucial for practical reason. It is, after all, a primary task of practical reason to create, shape or sustain the polis; and, for him, the boundaries of the polis ought to capture the domain of robust human logos. That is, citizenship ought to be granted to all and only those capable of the practical reason involved in ruling and being ruled.[1] Legislators are to use their practical reason to determine who else is capable of the practical reason necessary for citizenship. So, in determining the shape and extent of the polis, practical reason should set its own boundaries. The polis becomes the field of human logos; at least in the sense that it is the arena in which practical reason achieves its full and proper expression.[2] Moreover, when legislators exercise their practical reason well, they craft a polis which both encourages and makes room for the exercise of theoretical reason on the part of those who are capable of it. The polis, then, is the place where both practical and theoretical reason reach fruition.

But there is also a deeper sense in which, for Aristotle, the polis is the field of logos. The polis is neither a brute element of the universe, nor is it the outcome of rigidly instinctual behaviour, as is, say, a bee-

---

1. *Politics* 1275a22–23, 1277b11–16, 1329a2–17, 1332b3–7, b25–29, b41–1333a3, a11–16.
2. Ibid., 1253a1–18.

hive.³ The structure of the polis ought to be the outcome of a certain kind of debate *inside the polis* as to what the polis ought to be like. Obviously, this is nothing like a modern liberal debate in which radically different conceptions of the good can fight it out or make room for each other, as the case may be. That, for Aristotle, would not be an exercise of practical reason. Only virtuous people are capable of practical reason – indeed, the virtues constitute practical reason – so the debate will be carried out by people who have already been educated into a broadly shared outlook. This Aristotle took to be the outlook of a truly excellent human being. These fine human beings are already living good lives, and it is their task, as legislators, philosophers and citizens, to discuss among themselves what this good life consists in and how it can best be facilitated within political space. Legislators will enact this practical wisdom into law. In short, the shape of the polis is to be decided by a few good men.

Let us for a moment set aside concerns we might have about the restricted social world that Aristotle thought capable of the full exercise of reason. Then I think we can see Aristotle as committed to the autonomy of human reason in this sense: through debate in the polis, human reason is setting its own standards of what constitutes a good life. This point is easy to miss if one is reading Aristotle in the shadow of Kant. For in Kant's anatomy of the psyche, reason has a "pure" form distinct from, and often set over against, human desires and passions. Aristotle does think that the debate on the good life must take into account basic biological facts of human existence, the nature of human desire, the emotions, etc. These conditions of human existence are ones to which any adequate debate must be responsive. The debate within the polis, then, is obviously not one Kant would recognize as an exercise of pure practical reason.

However, rather than viewing these conditions as exercising a heteronomous constraint, it is, I think, more illuminating to see Aristotle as trying to work out an embodied conception of human reason. First, the "non-rational" part of the psyche is by nature responsive to the dictates of reason. And when a person is well brought up, that is, brought up to virtue, the "non-rational" and rational parts of the psyche together constitute practical reason: "they" function together as a harmonious and seamless whole.⁴ So when the debate about the good life takes certain conditions of human existence into account, this, for

---

3. Ibid., 1253a7–8.

Aristotle, is part of the process by which human logos determines its own shape. The debate is constrained, to be sure, but not by something that is ultimately to be understood as external.

Secondly, the citizens of the polis, those who exercise practical reason, are themselves the final arbiters of what constitutes adequate responsiveness to these conditions of human existence. Being adequately responsive to the "facts of human nature" is equivalent to being taken to be adequately responsive by those who have practical reason. In that sense, there is no tribunal outside of reason to determine whether a given exercise of reason is or is not the exercise of correct reason (*orthos logos*).

Thirdly, Aristotle's claim that humans are by nature political animals implies that human nature is not an external constraint on the debate. For it is logos which, in Aristotle's opinion, distinguishes human nature. Humans differ from even other social animals in that they alone (*idion tois anthropois*) have logos or reason; and it is clear that this reason is normative and ethical.[5] The deepest reason that humans are by nature political is not, then, that a given nature forces them to huddle together, like sheep in a storm, but that human nature is realized in the political debate and enactment of what constitutes a good life. The debate is itself one of the higher expressions of human nature.

The human task, then, is to create an environment in which humans can become most fully themselves. The polis, for Aristotle, emerged naturally out of earlier forms of association – the household and village – which were themselves the outcome of natural instinct, notably for sexual union and protection.[6] Nature, working so to speak from below, facilitates forms of social organization that are ever less direct expressions of instinct. The polis culminates the development of human forms of life: it is the minimal (and maximal) self-sufficient unit that can successfully achieve its aim of securing the good life for humans.[7] And self-sufficiency here implies not merely that it is capable of catering to the material needs of the inhabitants, but that it is

---

4. Indeed, the distinction only makes sense from the perspective of explaining psychic pathology or of explaining how a person is educated so as to have practical reason in the full sense of becoming a virtuous person. See Sarah Broadie, *Ethics with Aristotle* (Oxford: Oxford University Press, 1991), pp. 61–72.
5. *Politics* 1253a15–18.
6. Ibid., 1252a26–34, 1253a29–30.
7. Ibid., 1252b27–1253a5.

self-sufficient for determining through debate what the good life for humans is. A polis in good shape will be able to establish its own standards of the good life, enact them into law, and transmit them to future generations through ethical education. And the claim that the polis is the minimal unit of human self-sufficiency implies that human autonomy is paradigmatically political. By actively participating in a healthy polis, virtuous people will themselves endorse and enact the lives that the polis, through its own internal debate, has determined to be good lives.

A moment ago, I asked to hold in abeyance momentarily any reservations we might have about the social exclusivity that accompanies Aristotle's conception of practical reason. Time's up. For Aristotle, the polis existed by nature, but he notoriously kept this realm of nature a restricted preserve. In the best polis women are excluded, as are metics, slaves, and anyone without education or virtue such as manual labourers and merchants – although they are all needed to support polis life. Only "the best" men, Aristotle thinks, should be granted citizenship; for only they are capable of ruling and being ruled. So, in shaping the ideal polis, Aristotle went well beyond the restrictive practices of his day. Were this merely an argument about citizenship, one might be tempted simply to dismiss it. But the political argument is grounded in a claim about the scope of human reason: all those creatures capable of exercising reason should be allowed inside. Of course, Aristotle interprets this constraint stringently. Although he admits that women, slaves, and so on, have various inferior capacities to respond to reason, he restricts citizenship to those who are able to have reason in the strong sense of having practical wisdom. A high standard perhaps; but for Aristotle it is only at this level that humans reach their *telos*, and thus fully realize their nature. If relatively few members of the biological species are granted citizenship, that is because only they are capable of becoming fully human.

This is an astonishing conclusion, but Aristotle seems willing to accept it. Humans are, for him, the only creatures who almost never realize their nature. Of course, there are various palliatives he attempts: that it is the nature of a slave to be such as he his, the nature of a woman to be such as she is, and so on. But this is tantamount to saying that, for a vast range of biological human beings, it is their "nature" never fully to realize human nature. That is, most of humanity in the biological sense is not fully human in Aristotle's sense.

Throughout the rest of nature the members of a species tend to become what it is their distinctive nature to be. Indeed, for Aristotle, this is virtually a methodological principle; albeit one confirmed by experience. For the rest of nature Aristotle observes what he takes to be typical members in the characteristic activities and environment of maturity, and concludes that these activities manifest the nature of the species. When it comes to humans, though, Aristotle shifts his ground: he resorts to philosophical reflection on the good life for humans. The effect of this shift is dramatic, although perhaps not obvious, because nature everywhere is normative. For any creature to fulfil its nature is what it is for that creature to live a good life. This is as true for humans as it is for chickens. But the shift in method has the following consequence: while almost all other animals are living good lives – for their lives conform to the pattern of a typical member of the species – almost no humans live good human lives – for they fail to achieve the standards set by philosophical reflection. The upshot is that, although the polis should contain everyone capable of realizing their human nature, virtually no one gets to belong.

There are two types of criticism of Aristotle's strategy. The first is a social criticism that points out the anti-egalitarian, anti-democratic base on which Aristotle's ethics rests. Although it is true that much modern discussion of Aristotelian approaches to ethics has ignored the elitist strain in Aristotle's thought, I find the social critique unsatisfying. For it remains unclear how crucial Aristotle's elitism is to his ethical–political outlook. Is it possible for a modern democrat to treat the elitism as a contingent bias of Aristotle's historical time and class, which can be eliminated from an acceptable, modern Aristotelianism? This question has not been adequately answered. Moreover, the social critique results in a standoff. It assumes a democratic inclusive standpoint, and invites us to condemn Aristotle's elitism. That may be fine if the social critique deliberately assumes an audience broadly committed to a democratic outlook; but that is certainly not an outlook Aristotle and his audience would share. From a democratic perspective Aristotle's politics will of course appear objectionably elitist; whereas from Aristotle's perspective the democratic outlook will appear incapable of grasping the truth about ethical life. This truth, as Aristotle eloquently argues, can only be grasped from within the perspective Aristotle himself holds. Of course, a modern democrat might not feel obliged to muster an argument that would persuade Aristotle. But from a philosophical perspective, one wonders whether there might not be something going wrong *within* Aristotle's philosophy. Might there not be strains inherent in Aristotle's outlook? If so, one could formulate an objection that was more than a bare dismissal of the outlook. Indeed, it would be one which even Aristotle would have to take seriously.

In this paper, therefore, I should like to explore a second possible objection, one that is internal to Aristotle's strategy. Has Aristotle begged the question of what constitutes human nature by simply excluding any possible counter-example? On this objection, Aristotle's conception of logos or reason trivially emerges as the distinguishing characteristic of human nature, because only those who can robustly exercise it are counted as fully human. From this perspective, Aristotle's ideal polis looks like an attempt to avoid disquieting thoughts about human nature. For his method begins to look as though it were designed to yield a noble conception of human nature: all those whose existence might challenge this alleged nobility are dismissed from consideration.

For Aristotle, the ultimate vindication of his ethical outlook was the judgement of the practically wise. Of course, practical wisdom is characterized by Aristotle as the exercise of correct reason; and for reason to be correct it must adequately capture the truth about the situation it is judging. *Orthos logos* is by definition accurately in touch with reality. One would expect the practically wise to study human nature, history and other forms of social organization, just as Aristotle did; but all of this study is seen from the distinctive perspective of the practically wise. Ultimately, it is the practically wise who are themselves determining what being adequately in touch with the truth consists in. There is thus the danger that those who take themselves to be "practically wise" are setting standards that confer an illusory vindication.

The significance of this issue transcends any qualms one might have with the specific limitations of Aristotle's social vision. Indeed, it confronts any ethical system that values autonomy. For there is, I think, an incipient tension between valuing autonomy and valuing that to which autonomy might lead. How much does any ethical theory that values autonomy have to restrict what it counts as "us", so that what "we" end up legislating turns out to be recognizably ethical? Kant restricts "us" to purely rational wills as he purports to offer a proof that such beings will autonomously will the categorical imperative. Aristotle, for his part, restricts "us" to virtuous people. In an ideal polis such citizens are, for Aristotle, in an "ideal speech situation": the outcome of their debate is *a fortiori* legislation of the good. But has the speech situation been made so "ideal" that genuine debate is short-circuited? Aristotle's virtuous man may be uniquely able to grasp the value of virtuous activity; but might he also be peculiarly unable to grasp the logos in women and slaves? It is therefore important that any attempt to draw the bounds of logos also supply certain tests that its delimitation is legitimate. This, I think, is the most general philosophical question raised by Aristotle's social exclusivity: how can any ethical system that offers an "internal" validation provide sufficiently strong internal tests that its claims to validity are more than self-serving ideology?

Aristotle himself tested the limits he had drawn in three ways. First, in the *Ethics* he offered an internal vindication of the virtuous person's outlook as manifesting logos. Secondly, in the *Politics* he surveyed existing poleis and tried to show that they are attempts to instantiate a field for logos which fail for comprehensible reasons. So, for example, an oligarchical polis fails because its judgement is distorted by too much appetite. The *Ethics* and *Politics* together thus comprise an attempted empirical vindication of Aristotle's boundaries.

But Aristotle also turned to the imagination. He wanted, I think, to test the boundaries with something stronger than any actual example could provide; and he thus turned to tragedy. The classic tragedies, for him, represent attacks upon the primordial bonds that hold the polis together.[8] And he encourages plots of family destruction: "Whenever the tragic deed is done among friends – when murder or the like is done or meditated by brother on brother, by son on father, by mother on son, or son on mother – *these* are the situations the poet should seek after." These are "unnatural acts", to be sure, but, within the context of Aristotle's political philosophy, tragedy is also a mimesis of a destructive attack on the elementary structures of reason. The polis is meant to provide protection from the ravages of uncivilized nature; yet there seems to be a need for the representation of the unnatural inside nature, the *alogon* inside logos. Why should the polis, the field of human logos, seek to contain within itself representations of attacks upon logos? Aristotle's answer, I believe, is that these representations help to test the adequacy of logos or reason to account for human nature. That is why he insists that these destruc-

---

8. *Poetics* 1453b10–22.

tive acts be perpetrated (or intended) by basically good people.[9] Tragedy, for Aristotle, represents the extremes of destructiveness to which a basically good person can fall. Such a person is good enough to be a citizen and thus good enough to be a representation of human nature, as Aristotle understands it. The philosophical significance of tragedy, for Aristotle, is that it shows that reason can give an account of even the most apparently "unnatural", *alogon*, irrational acts that truly *human* beings commit. The *Poetics*, then, is an attempted vindication of his ethical and political realism: it aims to show that the polis is adequate to capture all of *human* nature.

In this chapter, I would like to investigate Aristotle's use of tragedy as a constituent in the internal validation of his ethics. First, I shall discuss the Platonic legacy. Plato is important not merely because he sets the context for Aristotle's discussion, but because he has a darker view of the limitations of human reason. For Plato, the ultimate opacity of human destructiveness plays a crucial role in his decision to banish tragedy from the polis. From Plato, I should like to turn briefly to Freud. Plato's darker view of the human condition sheds light on Freud's postulation of a death drive. But, more importantly, Freud's argument provides a model of how logos might recognize that something beyond it is part of human nature. Finally, I shall turn to Aristotle's account of tragedy. My aim is to examine critically Aristotle's use of tragedy as a test of his conception of human nature, and thus as a legitimation of his ethics.

II The Platonic legacy

What lies beyond logos for Plato are certain forms of violence and undoing. Plato banished tragedy from the polis because he thought it encouraged a strain of destructiveness that logos could not contain. It does this by perverting the process of psychosocial development. The human psyche, for Plato, stands in a dynamic relation to the social world it inhabits. Primarily in youth, but throughout life, a person internalizes cultural influences; and these influences, once internalized, become motives. They are organized with other motives into an "inner polis", the psyche. In maturity a person externalizes these metabolized influences in activities that help to shape,

---

9. Ibid., ch. 15; see also ch. 13.

sustain or undo the social world. Tragic poetry, Plato thinks, turns this dynamic process into a vicious downward spiral.[10]

This deleterious trajectory is due in part to a type of desire in the human psyche that Plato calls *paranomos*. "*Paranomos*" is usually translated as "lawless", which suggests that these desires resist being informed, or even controlled, by law (*nomos*) and thus by logos. "*They are probably present in everyone*", Plato says, "but they are held in check by the laws and by the better desires with the help of logos. In a few men they have been eliminated *or a small number are left in a weakened state*, while in others they are stronger and more numerous."[11] They are incapable of lawful citizenship within the psyche, and the best case, in Plato's view, seems to be benign repression.[12] Even "the very best of us", Plato thinks, may have *paranomoi* desires, albeit in a weakened condition.[13] His reason for thinking this seems to be the dreams that even the best of us may have. These dreams, for Plato, represent *paranomoi* desires existing in the psyche, although repressed in daily life:

> They are aroused during sleep, whenever the rest of the soul, the reasonable, gentle and ruling part, is slumbering; whereas the wild and animal part, full of food and drink, skips about, casts off sleep and seeks to find a way to its gratification. You know that there is nothing it will not dare to do at that time, free of any control by shame or prudence. It does not hesitate, as it thinks, to attempt intercourse with a mother or anyone else – man, god or beast; it will commit any foul murder and does not refrain from any kind of food. In a word, it will not fall short of any folly or shameless deed.[14]

But, should the focus of attention shift from the activities, these desires motivate inside the psyche to the activities they motivate in the polis, they come to appear *paranomoi* in a stronger sense. They are now "against the law" in the sense of being destructive of law. It is these

---

10. I discuss the claims of this paragraph at length in my paper, "Inside and outside the *Republic*", *Phronesis* **37**, 1992, pp. 184–215.
11. *Republic* 571b–c.
12. In psychoanalytic terms, these desires resist any form of sublimation. Cf. Hans Loewald, *Sublimation: inquiries into theoretical psychoanalysis* (New Haven, Connecticut: Yale University Press, 1988).
13. Cf. *Republic* 605c–d. Thus Plato seems to admit that even in health there will be some, perhaps minimal, degree of intrapsychic conflict.
14. Ibid., 571c–d.

desires, expressed dramatically in dreams and in tragedy, that motivate attacks upon the elementary structures of human social relations.

Herein lies a basic tension in Plato's conception of human nature. Humans are by nature polis animals; but they seem to achieve fullest expression only by repressing an ineliminable part of themselves. Human nature, in Plato's vision, contains within itself motivation for attacks on the very structures in which it can be realized.[15] This dark thread running through Plato's account of human nature is occasionally masked by Socrates' enthusiastic hymns to the possibility of harmony in the psyche and in the polis.[16] But even in these hopeful trills there are intimations of darkness: this harmony is, after all, virtually impossible to achieve in actual life; and should it ever be achieved, it would eventually decay.[17]

Plato makes an equivocal attempt to offer a logos of this destructive tendency. The *paranomos* in human nature is conceived by him as a type of desire. It is as though there are omnivorous appetites that, in themselves, know no limit. Unless there is some constraint – whether political or intrapsychic (like shame) – these desires will motivate unbounded consumption. Human destructiveness, on this picture, is a byproduct of *pleonexia*: desire lurching out of control. But as desire starts gobbling up everything, we begin to lose grip on the idea that this force is a form of desire.[18] What can a truly unlimited and unchecked desire be a desire for? The answer cannot even be "everything": for should the *paranomos* ever have complete sway, it would not succeed in acquiring "everything", but in destroying everything. We see this in Plato's portrait of the tyrant. He does not acquire the polis but destroys it – as he is himself undone in the process.[19] The tyrannical psyche falls apart into a teeming mass of *paranomoi* "desires": there is no longer any organizational principle holding the psyche together. In full bloom, the *paranomos* cannot motivate the human subject to acquire anything, let alone everything; for the subject has already decomposed. The attempt to explain

---

15. Obviously, I am not here concerned with Plato's extreme dualist account in the *Phaedo*, where it not clear that human nature is embodied at all. I am here concerned with his attempt in the *Republic* to work out the nature of embodied human existence.
16. Ibid., e.g. 430e–432b, 441d–444a.
17. Ibid., 540d–541b, 546a–547a.
18. Cf. ibid., 577d–e: "The tyrannized psyche will do least of all what it wishes."
19. Ibid., 573c–579e.

human destructiveness in terms of unlimited desire seems itself to fall apart under the weight of what it is trying to explain.

It seems, then, that in Plato's conception of human nature there is a force for decomposition, the *paranomos*, which itself resists further explanation or understanding. The *paranomos* is *paralogos*. The polis can, then, be a field of logos only by forcibly suppressing an ultimately ineliminable part of human nature.

Tragedy, for Plato, is the return of the repressed. It not only loosens the important bonds of repression, it helps the *paranomos* to flow out of the psyche into polis life. Mimesis sets up homeopathic resonances inside the psyches of the audience: even "the best of us" are susceptible.[20] It stirs up the emotional and appetitive parts – the *alogistikon* – and thus encourages the audience to act out on the political stage the destructive impulses acted out in the theatre. Because mimesis sets us at no significant distance from the attacks on logos it represents, tragedy provides the bridge by which the worst products of the human imagination are made real. Tragic mimesis is thus a repetition that encourages repetition. It also plays a crucial role in legitimating tyranny.[21] The tyrant comes to feel justified in acting out the destructive attacks on his parents' estate, on his friends, family and fellow citizens.[22] And in establishing his tyranny, he must expel from the polis the brave and the wise, and surround himself with the cowardly and base.[23] "A fine catharsis!", Plato says.[24] Tyranny thus emerges, for Plato, as the true meaning of tragedy. By encouraging the *paranomoi*, always just below the surface of human nature, it facilitates attacks upon the elementary structures of human logos. The only way to deal with tragedy is to do away with it. By banishing tragedy Plato is trying to get rid of the *paranomoi* in psychic and political life. Of course, he realizes that there is no final solution: even in the best case there will be *paranomoi* desires in the psyche that are either weakened or repressed.

More importantly, Plato recognizes another source that is "against the law" in a deeper, if less violent, sense than the paranomoi desires. Even the best organized polis, Plato thinks, must eventually fall apart because of an inner tendency towards decomposition.[25] The finest

---

20. Ibid., 604e–605d.
21. Ibid., 568b.
22. Ibid., 547a–c, 569b.
23. Ibid., 567b–c.
24. *kalon ge . . . katharmon*, 567c.

guardians will eventually make a mistake about the proper time for mating; for their judgement must combine logos with perception. An inferior generation is born and the polis is on a path of dissolution. What undoes human logos is matter: the stuff that is perceived but not ultimately understood; the stuff that may be informed for a while but which eventually loosens itself from form. Matter is a principle in opposition to logos. In the human realm this is manifest both in the fact that it is ultimately responsible for the undoing of humanity's finest instantiation of logos and in the fact that it resists being understood. The ideal polis is undone for no reason at all. Matter, for Plato, is the basic *paranomos*.

III Freud on the death drive

Plato, then, thinks there is a strain in human nature that lies beyond the bounds of logos. In its most violent manifestation this strain becomes an attack on logos. But how can one conclude that this destruction is genuinely alogon, as opposed to having a logos that has thus far remained hidden? Aristotle holds, in opposition to Plato, that tragic destruction does have a logos, although one that may remain opaque to the participants. It may at first appear that Aristotle thereby accepts the reality of human destructiveness, and gives it a proper place in polis life. But, on further reflection, there is a question whether, precisely by giving it a place, Aristotle evades the reality of human destruction by assigning to it an ersatz logos. Here a comparison with a modern example may be of help.

At the beginning of his career, Freud thought that logos was adequate to give an account of human nature. That is, even the most bizarre neurotic symptoms could, he thought, be made intelligible through psychoanalysis. He treated the psyche almost like an inner polis and, like Aristotle, the only things he recognized as "citizens" had logos, at least in the minimal sense of being intelligibly directed towards a goal. Neurotic symptoms were the surface manifestation of civil strife. They were the outcome of conflicting lines of motivation, each line of which was intelligible. Freud's early work with neurotics convinced him that the human mind was basically pleasure-seeking. A person could be inhibited by societal prohibitions and conflicted by

---

25. Ibid., 546a–547c.

internalization of those norms, but the mind's basic task was to find pleasure under the constraints of reality. What on the surface appeared to be irruptions of irrationality were revealed to be intelligible, if non-optimal, attempts to perform this basic function. The early Freud thought he was justified in treating logos as adequate to capture human nature: after all, he could take purportedly extreme counter-examples and show that even there logos was at work.

However, Freud gradually shifted from this Aristotelian position to a more Platonic outlook in which some part of human nature must be recognized as beyond logos – indeed, as set over against logos. What changed his mind was a certain type of mimesis. In a classic discussion of repetition, Freud describes how he became the audience of a tragic mimesis acted out on a small stage within the micropolis of a family.[26] A little boy would throw away a wooden spool attached to a string, and cry out an infantile version of *"fort"* [gone], and then pull the spool back with a joyful *"da!"* [there]. Freud interpreted this as an enactment of the disappearance and return of the boy's mother. Significantly, the question of whether the drama is a tragedy or a comedy, at least in the modern senses of those terms, is up to the child. If the drama ends in *"fort"*, it is a tragedy; if it ends at *"da"*, the mother has returned and there has been a comic restoration. The child exerts imaginative control not merely over the ending of the drama but over its form.

Freud was puzzled that the *fort–da* game should regularly end at *fort*. There is no doubt some truth in the thought that the child is trying to gain imaginative mastery over a painful situation which, in real life, he passively suffered. But this thought does not explain why, if the game is really up to him, it should so regularly end as a tragedy rather than as a comedy. We seem to need a deeper understanding of what it is for the ending to be "up to him." Freud linked this drama with the repetitive enactments of people suffering from the so-called war neuroses and traumatic neuroses. It was not the destructiveness of the First World War that changed Freud's mind about the place of logos in human nature, but one psychological consequence of that destruction. Freud saw people repeat, in nightmares, daymares and compulsive rituals, the horrifying experiences they had suffered. The

---

26. Sigmund Freud, "Beyond the pleasure principle", in *The standard edition of the complete psychological works of Sigmund Freud (SE)*, J. Strachey (trans. and ed.) (London: Hogarth Press, 1981), XVIII, 14–15.

brute passivity of these enacted scenes, their compulsive durability, and the fierce anxiety they provoked, convinced him that they could not be understood as restorative or pleasurable in any way. Although he was a master in finding pleasures disguised in painful symptoms, when Freud finally looked hard at the horrific dramas of war neurosis, he abandoned the hypothesis that archaic mind always seeks pleasure. There must be a force that lies, as he put it, beyond the pleasure principle.[27]

In trying to account for these dramas, Freud imported a new force into the domain of psychoanalytic theory. The theory of the instincts is re-fashioned so that, following Plato, one is eros, a force that holds psyche and polis together. Sexuality is a manifestation of eros, as is logos. But there is another entropic force, tending towards decomposition. Freud called it the death drive; and it has long been puzzling how he could have thought of it as providing an explanation. For, unlike eros, the death drive is conceptualized as a purely biological force, having no psychological representation.[28] Freud thus abandons his regulative principle of providing psychological explanations for psychological phenomena.[29] So, while the death drive is imported into psychoanalytic theory, it remains, as it were, a resident alien. And because it is a biological force, from a psychological perspective one can only infer it from its results: as Freud put it, the death drive "works in silence."[30]

It is tempting to dismiss this conceptualization of the death drive as a manifestation of Freud's scientistic commitment to biological reduction.[31] But perhaps there is a deeper motivation for his choice. We are motivated to discover an explanation of eruptions of human destruction. In Aristotle's terms, we want a logos of attacks on the elementary structures of logos. In postulating a purely biological force, Freud is in effect admitting that there is a limit on any such attempt.

---

27. See ibid., *SE* XVIII, 12–23.
28. Ibid., *SE* XVIII, 37–61; "The ego and the id", *SE* XIX, 40; "Two encyclopedia articles", *SE* XVIII, 258.
29. "On narcissism: an introduction", *SE* XIV, 78–9; "The unconscious", *SE* XIV, 174–5; "Three essays on the theory of sexuality", *SE* VII, 243.
30. "Two encyclopedia articles", *SE* XVIII, 258; "An autobiographical study", *SE* XX, 57; "An outline of psychoanalysis", *SE* XXIII, 150; "Beyond the pleasure principle", *SE* XVIII, 52, 59–60.
31. This is the route I took in *Love and its place in nature* (New York: Farrar, Straus and Giroux, 1990), pp. 13–16.

In fact, Freud's thinking seems to vacillate among shades of darkness, almost as a shopper in front of a rack of dark suits hesitating as to which goes best. When he stresses the biological basis of the death drive, there is a disguised Aristotelian optimism underlying his surface Platonic pessimism. For as a brute biological force, the death drive will lack a logos from the perspective of psychoanalysis – that is, it will be unalterable by any talking cure – but presumably it will have a biological account. There would still be the hope of understanding it from a biological point of view; and perhaps of altering it via biological intervention.

However, in his mature theory, eros and the death drive take on the aspect of basic metaphysical principles. The death drive becomes a brute entropic force, running through the universe: a fundamental and inexplicable tendency towards decomposition. Certain forms of human violence are manifestations of this tendency, and thus they are utterly inexplicable. This is the deepest reason why the death drive must "work in silence": we will forever be taken by surprise, because such destruction has no logos. We can never see it coming; that is why it will always appear to us as an eruption. From this perspective, there could be no such book as, say, *Strife and its place in nature*. The point of postulating a biological death drive rather than a minded Strife is that, from the point of view of psychological motivation, there is nothing to be said about it. To understand it would be to bring it within the domain of logos, and it is of the essence of the death drive to attack any attempted assimilation. On this picture it remains a permanent possibility for human destructiveness to catch us by surprise; for there must be an element in human violence that remains inevitably surd. These are the moments when we suspect that all this carnage has happened for no reason at all.

These thoughts represent a challenge to psychoanalysis. For it is a regulative principle of psychoanalytic practice that it is possible, although perhaps only in the long run, to give a logos to the apparently disparate flotsam and jetsam that emerge from attempts to free associate. Interpretation is, by its nature, an organizing and unifying activity. On Freud's mature theory of the drives, it makes sense that psychoanalysis should be especially successful in interpreting sexual motivation. For sexuality, on the mature theory, is a manifestation of eros, a unifying and organizing force which has, as other important manifestations, interpretation, understanding, logos. Sexuality may be repressed, it may be confusing, and it may fuel the intrapsychic civil wars we call "neurosis", but it is comprehensible. As psychoanalysis has moved ever more towards the analysis of aggression, violence and destructiveness, however, it becomes less clear that what it is analyzing is analyzable. There are certainly intimations in Freud's later writings that, in attempting to analyze human destructiveness, analysis is bumping up against its own limits.

IV Aristotle's test

As Plato is packing tragedy's bags, he allows Socrates to issue his famous caveat: "if poetry that aims at pleasure and mimesis has any logos to bring forward to prove that it must have a place in a well governed polis, we should be glad to welcome it."[32] In this context, the *Poetics* takes the shape of a political argument: a plea to the Home Office to revoke a deportation order. Aristotle accepts Plato's constraint on how a justification is to be given. It must be via logos: an argument that tragedy earns its place in a well ordered polis.[33] But why should the polis permit representations of attacks on its elementary bonds? Aristotle's answer, I believe, is that tragedy plays a significant role in the self-validation of logos. The point of tragedy, for Aristotle, is to reveal logos manifest even in attacks upon logos, and thus to establish the adequacy of logos to account for even the most destructive aspects of human nature.

In myriad ways, Aristotle insists on the inherent rationality of tragic mythos. First, the events must occur plausibly or necessarily,[34] they must occur on account of one another rather than in mere succession,[35] and the protagonist makes a certain mistake (*hamartia*) which rationalizes his downfall.[36] Second, tragedy must exemplify the ethical structure of logos; it cannot portray a virtuous person falling to bad fortune, nor the rise of a bad person to good fortune.[37] The pro-

---

32. *Republic* 607c–d. Cf. *Apology* 22b–c. The idea that the *Poetics* is a response to this Platonic challenge is well canvassed. For one excellent account, see Stephen Halliwell, *Aristotle's Poetics* (Chapel Hill: University of North Carolina Press, 1986).
33. *Nicomachean ethics* 1094a26–27.
34. *Poetics* 1451a37–38, 1452a17–21, 1454a33–36, 1455a16–19, 1461b11–12.
35. Ibid., 1451a3–4, 1452a20–21.
36. Ibid., 1453a8–30.
37. Ibid., 1452b30–1453a8.

tagonist must have just the right amount of goodness: good enough to inspire our pity and fear, but not so virtuous that he cannot plausibly make a mistake which will intelligibly lead to his downfall.[38] Third, the reversal and discovery, although a surprise to the protagonist, must follow intelligibly from preceding events and thus make sense to the audience. In this way too, the audience can distance itself from, and thus domesticate, the eruption of horrifying surprise. The upshot of these constraints is that the unnatural acts of tragedy take on a peculiar logos of their own – a logos concealed within the drama, but available to the audience. In the light of the overall argument it would seem that, for Aristotle, tragedy achieves its catharsis by offering a logos for the terrible events (the objective *pathe*) which provoke the tragic emotions (the subjective *pathemata*). There is relief and reassurance in the thought that the portrayed destruction does not, in the end, represent a surd attack upon logos, but an attack that can be understood within the domain of logos. Aristotle thus reiterates "a fine catharsis!", but without Plato's irony.

Anyone who loves Greek tragedy will, I suspect, come away from the *Poetics* with a sense that, at some level, Aristotle "just didn't get it." But it is difficult to give a precise diagnosis of what is going wrong. It is tempting to think that Aristotle smothered tragedy with logos: that by insisting on logos inherent in tragedy, Aristotle abets the elimination of what he was purportedly trying to save. And yet, Aristotle's constraints are there in *Oedipus Tyrannos*. Indeed, Sophocles has Oedipus work through an argument of Euclidean rigor. Thus, even if, as I believe, Aristotle's account of tragedy is ultimately a failure, we must ask whether our sense of disappointment in his account flows from that failure; or whether, ironically, it flows from his success in describing certain aspects of tragedy. Vernant has brilliantly described how tragedy exists in a "border zone": "where human actions are hinged together with divine powers where, unknown to the agent, they derive their true meaning by becoming an integral part of an order that is beyond man and eludes him."[39] Strictly speaking, it is not a border zone, but an illusion of such a zone. Through a brilliant use of language and dramatic structure, Sophocles invites his audience into an imaginary world: a world in which

---

38. Ibid., 1454a17–20, b8–13.
39. J-P. Vernant & P. Vidal-Naquet, *Myth and tragedy in ancient Greece* (New York: Zone Books, 1990), p. 47.

they can share Oedipus's ignorance, pretend to be confronting the unfathomable, play with horrific surprise. Aristotle, in effect, is pointing out that this is just play. There is, of course, no room inside the play for such recognition.[40] And the question, then, is whether our sense of disappointment in Aristotle's account is actually a symptom of its accuracy, whether by pointing out the dramatic structure of an illusion, he disillusions us.

Aristotle does seem more interested than Sophocles in rationalizing Oedipus's downfall: thus the focus on Oedipus's mistake. Such a mistake pulls the downfall into (or at least toward) the realm of the humanly explicable; whereas for Sophocles, the origin of that downfall transcends the human realm as well as the human ability to understand. Yet Aristotle insists that the mistake is necessary for the play to be truly tragic. What entitles him to assume that only the plays meeting his constraints are tragic? Aristotle gives a psychological justification: only plays meeting these constraints can elicit pity and fear from the audience and thus effect the requisite catharsis. His guide to judging tragedy is thus not its accuracy in portraying human nature, but its success in eliciting a certain psychological response in the audience.[41] The plot must be persuasive to the audience; and this persuasiveness, Aristotle thinks, rests on the plot manifesting logos. It is not he, Aristotle can say, but the audience who is insisting on logos; only then can tragedy evoke the tragic emotions.[42]

Again, it is tempting to object that Aristotle should be concerned with the truth of human destructiveness, not a mere psychological reaction in the audience. After all, tragedy is meant to be a mimesis of a serious action, and there should be a question whether the mimesis is an accurate representation. What is to prevent tragedy from being a "noble" falsehood: an illusion that sustains a misleading image of human nature and political order? Aristotle's conception of human nature is meant to block this sceptical possibility. By insisting that humans are by nature polis animals, Aristotle is claiming that there are no deeper facts about human nature than those that could be revealed in polis life. Of course, polis life does give room for reflection

---

40. Cf. D. W. Winnicott, "Transitional objects and transitional phenomena", in *Through paediatrics to psychoanalysis* (London: Hogarth Press, 1975).
41. In the *Poetics* see, e.g., 1452b30–1453a8, b10–22.
42. Whatever catharsis happens precisely to be. See my paper, "Katharsis", *Phronesis* **30**, pp. 297–326; reprinted in *Essays on Aristotle's Poetics*, A. Rorty (ed.) (Princeton: Princeton University Press, 1992), pp. 315–40.

on destructiveness; and tragedy, in Aristotle's opinion, is a particularly significant example. If tragedy is found persuasive inside the polis, there is no tribunal outside – human nature as such – with which one could compare tragedy's account and find it wanting. For Aristotle there can be no further truth about the nature of human destructiveness: the emotional truth of mature citizens is all the truth tragedy could possibly have. So the fact that tragedy is experienced as psychologically convincing, far from opening the door to scepticism, is treated by Aristotle as evidence for its truth.

At this point it is difficult to avoid the sinking feeling that this is all too easy. Aristotle is using tragedy to test the boundaries of logos manifest in the polis; but he is using the polis to legitimate tragedy. Of course, for Aristotle any legitimation of logos must be internal. But here the circle seems too tight for comfort – or, rather, too comfortable to be uncomfortable. Our feeling of dissatisfaction has its source, I believe, in Aristotle's decision to cite pity as a tragic emotion. The point of pity, for Aristotle, is to secure a particular emotional relationship between the audience and the dramatized events. We feel pity *for others* – thus we must be at a certain distance from the dreadful events – but for others who are *like us* – and this allows a certain imaginative proximity to those same events.

> We pity those who are like us in age, character, disposition, social standing or birth; for in all these cases it appears more likely that the same misfortune may befall us also.[43]

In the imaginative setting of the theatre, pity makes fear possible. Because the characters are enough "like us" for us to pity them, we can also imaginatively identify with them and feel fear. And even if we do not identify with them, in pitying them we experience ourselves as sufficiently close to their condition to be threatened by it. For fear is elicited by the thought that a terrible event threatens one: "we shall not fear things that we believe cannot happen to us."[44] And yet, pity also ensures that there is not too much fear. If events become too terrible, dread drives out pity.[45] Aristotle cites the tale of Amasis, who did not weep when his son was taken away to his death but did weep when he saw a friend begging. Pity, as Aristotle's own example shows, sets us at a luxurious distance from the portrayed events: it is

---

43. *Rhetoric* 1386a24–27.
44. Ibid., 1382b31; cf. 1382a22–30, b28–1383a12.
45. Ibid., 1386a24–25.

safe enough to indulge one's fears while generously extending pity to the other.

In that sense, pity serves as a defence against terror: the very condition that makes fear possible insures us against terror. Pity thus domesticates fear, ensuring that it will not get out of hand. And once pity is installed as a necessary constraint, the tragic plot must also manifest logos. The reversal and recognition – the surprise! – must follow intelligibly from the preceding actions: if not, pity would be driven out by terror.[46] If terrible deeds can befall us out of the blue and for no reason, then, for Aristotle, there is no room for pity. Moreover, pity's requirement that the characters be "like us" is in fact a requirement that they be *taken by us to be like us*. That is, we, the audience, will feel no emotional tug towards pity if we do not feel the characters are like us, whether or not they are such. Pity thus provides ample room for idealized self-images to go unchallenged and for darker strains of our own nature to be disavowed. In particular, we can take ourselves to be fundamentally creatures having logos, and thus fail to feel pity for creatures we do not take to be such. This ensures, as Aristotle clearly saw, that the protagonists of tragedy be "good enough."

The inclusion of pity as a tragic emotion also enables the audience to play its own *fort–da* game with terror. As the child enacts a tragedy by throwing a spool, so the ancient audience can imaginatively throw itself into the drama, but always with the tacit knowledge that it could at any moment pull itself back. This tacit knowledge is guaranteed by pity. The audience needs to feel not only like the characters on stage but also assured that in their imaginative identifications they will not be overwhelmed by dread. The device of the chorus plays an important role in making pity a possible response. On the one hand, the chorus is meant to express the audience's fears but, on the other, the chorus also makes the audience an audience twice removed from the portrayed disaster.[47] The chorus of *Oedipus Tyrannos* is, after all, bound up in the miasma, as the audience is not. As the audience watches a dramatically involved audience, it can both identify with it and also step back from it. In its forward position, the audience experiences terror; in its return, there is pity alongside relief that the audience lives centuries later in a polis structured so as to insulate them

---

46. Ibid., 1386a19–23.
47. *Myth and tragedy*, p. 34.

from these "unnatural" happenings.[48] In every tragedy there is thus a hidden comedy, at least in the modern sense of that term.

Pity thus makes tragedy "safe for human consumption" – especially in Aristotle's conception of the human. For pity to be a possible emotional response to a drama, even the most horrific reversals must have an inherent logos. Of course, Oedipus is going to be taken by surprise but, from Aristotle's perspective, the audience is reassured that the reversal is the outcome of a particular blindness on his part, not a surd eruption of meaningless devastation. In this way he attempts to domesticate surprise. For consider what sorts of experiences might lead us to conclude that human destructiveness lay beyond the bounds of logos. It would seem to be that despite our best efforts to understand, human destructiveness repeatedly takes us by surprise. After each outburst we may retrospectively try to offer an account, but we find that this does nothing to insure us against future surprise. This, it would seem, is the phenomenology we should expect if human logos is inadequate. Precisely because logos cannot grasp human destructiveness it will forever be surprised by it. Of course, there can never be a definitive proof that destructiveness lies beyond logos's pale: there may forever be the hope that an account lies just around the next corner. But the enduring repetition of surprise may eventually suggest that there is something about human destructiveness that lies beyond logos. This lends added poignancy to the spectacle of Oedipus working out his own surprise. On the one hand we can imaginatively enact our own susceptibility to surprise; on the other, we defend against it by seeing Oedipus use logos to arrive at his surprise and by taking up the position of an omniscient audience who knows all along what is going to happen.

It is, I think, by including pity as a tragic emotion that Aristotle fails to provide a sufficiently robust test of his conception of human nature. For if tragedy is meant to test the limits of human destructiveness, all destruction which lacks logos is thereby eliminated from the realm of the human. All human attacks on logos must themselves manifest logos – otherwise, they will not be counted as human. Tragedy thus "legitimates" the ability of logos to account for human destruction, because it ignores any destruction that does not fit. Of

---

48. Ibid., pp. 26–7; J-P. Vernant, *The origins of Greek thought* (London: Methuen, 1982). Tragedy could thus be viewed not as representing an attack on logos, but as offering a critique of an earlier, flawed attempt at logos.

course, I do not think one can *prove* that Aristotle begged the question: one person's "begging the question" is another person's "internal legitimation." From Aristotle's perspective the point of tragedy is to test logos *from the inside*: to move around within the domain of logos, explore its outer reaches, and see how far destruction can go while still remaining intelligible. Aristotle obviously does not think he begs the question by citing pity as a tragic emotion. Pity is there precisely because Aristotle wants to secure the autonomy of human nature. Humans are the unique animals whose task it is to determine their own nature through debate, legislation, education and other cultural activities, for instance tragedy. These activities all occur within the polis, which is itself a creation and manifestation of human logos. In feeling pity, an audience of citizens set their own outer bounds on what counts as human. Aristotle thus legitimates the ability of logos to account for human destruction – at the cost of excluding unintelligible horrific destruction from the domain of the human. By contrast, Plato and Freud are less interested in human autonomy and more interested in pursuing the darker threads of human behaviour, even if that points beyond the bounds of intelligibility. They thus have a more inclusive conception of human nature; and they are willing to countenance the thought that certain forms of human destruction are brute attacks upon logos, which themselves have no logos at all.[49]

Those of us who find Aristotle's account of tragedy flat-footed and would like an account which allowed tragedy to explore this darker conception of human nature might try eliminating pity as a tragic emotion. But we need to recognize pity's central theatrical value: it keeps the audience emotionally connected to the dramatized events. Too closely connected, perhaps, but Aristotle is certainly right that some balance needs to be struck between an audience's sense of dread and its sympathetic emotional involvement. The possibility of tragedy obviously relies on a delicate balance of conflicting emotional currents; but it remains completely unobvious what that balance is. It is beyond the scope of this paper to lay down an alternate set of abstract conditions; and that is just as well, since I do not know what I would propose. But, in any case, I think the strategy for anyone who wants to probe the possibility of pitiless tragedy is to investigate those extant tragedies for which pity seems inappropriate. Aristotle

---

49. See Bernard Williams's fascinating discussion in *Shame and necessity* (Berkeley: University of California Press, 1993), e.g. pp. 164–6.

focused on Oedipus, and Freud has brought to our attention deep reasons why we might take Oedipus to be "like us." But need we feel pity for Medea or Antigone? Might not our awe, our wrenching upset and terror, come from a profound recognition that they are not "like us"?

Aristotle's reluctance to countenance the opacity of *human* destruction is, I believe, the central failure in his account of tragedy. In reflecting on this failure, I think we may gain insight into certain strengths and weaknesses of his ethical realism. Aristotle's ethics is an attempt to work out the idea of autonomy, subject to the constraints of outlook of a brilliant philosopher of mid-fourth century Athens. His hope is for meaningful and rich human existence inside the polis, a social structure that is at once a manifestation of reason and transparent to reason's inquiry. Precisely because humans are to work out their own nature by reasoned debate inside, Aristotle has to exercise care about who is allowed to participate. The ethics represents Aristotle's attempt both to contribute to and anticipate the outcome of that debate. His account of tragedy is an attempt to reclaim the opacity of human destructiveness: to lend it intelligibility and thereby confer upon it some political value.

If one feels disappointed by Aristotle's lack of breadth, that is likely to be for one of two reasons. Either: like Plato and Freud, one places less significance on autonomy and greater significance on exploring the darker realms of human existence. One is, as it were, willing to accept that humans are not rational animals: and insofar as they lack rationality, it is not obvious that they should be autonomous. Or: one does value autonomy, but is disappointed with the severe social restrictions placed on those who were allowed to exercise it. This, I think, would be the most widespread source of disappointment today. It is, after all, difficult to read Aristotle's discussions of slaves and women without discomfort.

These may be reasons for disappointment. But we use them simply to dismiss Aristotle at our peril. By the standards of his social world Aristotle was not a bigot or a crank. He did not think that Athens was a perfectly ordered polis, but it provided the framework within which he made the adjustments he thought necessary to craft a just society. That is, the world in which he lived provided a framework for and constraint upon his philosophical imagination. Is that not true of us all? The point is not to forgive Aristotle for living twenty-odd centuries before the Enlightenment, but to recognize that his is a creditable attempt to articulate and legitimate an idea of autonomy, subject to the constraints of his social world. So described, could we hope to do more? If his constraints now appear too constrained, that should caution any of us who wish to formulate an ethics in which autonomy or virtue plays a significant role. The virtues, notoriously, are legitimated internally: a coward, for instance, cannot see the value or the pleasure inherent in brave acts. But how, if we have acquired a purported virtue and are enjoying the distinctive outlook that virtue permits, can we avoid complacent smugness? How, that is, can we avoid dismissing any challenge to our virtue as a brave person dismisses a coward's demurrals? From within the perspective of the alleged virtue, it is not at all clear how we might come to recognize that our perspective was distorted by illusion. This problem has not yet been sufficiently addressed by those who wish to revive a broadly Aristotelian approach to ethics.

As for autonomy, any ethical system that values it will place restrictions on who is allowed to exercise it. There will always be a question whether those restrictions are legitimate. Certainly, one does not automatically purchase sufficient inclusiveness by saying that autonomy should be exercised by any rational being. Aristotle, as we have seen, thought that any fully rational being should be a citizen, but that did not prevent him from having a restricted view of who counted as capable of sufficient rationality. There will always, then, be a question of social inclusiveness. Similarly, there will also be a question of psychic inclusiveness: are the parts of our psyche which make the decisions sufficiently inclusive that the decisions are genuinely an expression of ourselves? Or do we beg the question by simply refusing to countenance the excluded bits as parts of ourselves? These are serious questions and it is difficult to know how to answer them. The reflections of this paper suggest that any attempt to offer an internal legitimation of an ethical system that values autonomy will be in danger of ignoring the very challenges it should take seriously. This is an occupational hazard of internal legitimations, to be sure. But we overlook that hazard at the risk of being overtaken by horrific surprise, the very surprise it was the aim of tragedy to depict.[50]

---

50. I would like to thank Rudiger Bittner, Raymond Geuss, and Malcolm Schofield for making very helpful comments on a previous draft. I owe a special debt to Cynthia Farrar and Bernard Williams for helping me to re-think a fundamental assumption of the paper.

STEPHEN HALLIWELL

Tragedy, reason and pity: a reply to Jonathan Lear

STEPHEN HALLIWELL

Since I cannot hope to examine all the strands of argument in Jonathan Lear's fascinating paper, I intend principally to address myself to his central concern with the potential challenge posed to philosophical reason by the nature of tragedy. I shall follow his own procedure to the extent of offering first a few remarks on Plato, before considering some of the ethical implications of Aristotle's perspective on tragedy. About Lear's contention that Aristotle uses tragedy to test, and in some sense to validate, the limits of his concept of practical reason, I shall say a little in the later part of my comments. But my reaction to that complex point is necessarily guided, and will be chiefly communicated, by the modifications that I shall propose to the details of Lear's case. Most of my commentary will consist of respectful dissent from Lear's position; I hope that this will at any rate promote some clarification of what is at stake in this important area.

Why have philosophers so often interested themselves in tragedy? In the context of ancient Greek culture, at least, the necessary beginning of an answer to this question is the observation that philosophy and tragedy were, or could be perceived as, rivals – rival claimants to the deepest insights into, perhaps even the ultimate truth about, the human condition. As seen from philosophy's point of view, this rivalry was of a peculiarly threatening kind. It was not just that tragedy could be thought of as expressing one (or maybe more than one) alternative vision of human experience. There is a sense in which tragedy presented such potent and disturbing images of the field of this experience that it might, if taken with the fullest seriousness, crack the very foundations, the essential rationality, of philosophy itself. While philosophers might seek to establish that man is a political animal, or has an immortal soul, or requires virtue for real happiness, tragedy was capable of enacting for its audiences, and making them emotionally absorb, the idea that man is a tragic creature and that happiness is unattainable. There might be, and indeed have been, philosophers who could concur with this idea. But neither Plato nor Aristotle belongs in that category. For them, there was a fundamental choice of strategy in the face of tragic drama's cultural influence: they could either renounce it altogether, or re-interpret it so as to effect its compatibility with their own intellectual and ethical frameworks. That Plato was compelled to take the former approach, and that Aristotle chose the latter, is tolerably uncontroversial. But their attitudes to tragedy have extensive ramifications: and as Jonathan Lear's paper greatly helps us to understand, these ramifications at every point impinge reciprocally on the significance of both philosophy and tragedy.

In Plato's case, Lear sees the repudiation of tragedy as stemming from a troubled sense of the existence of violent, destructive forces in the psyche, which lie beyond the explanatory power, although not the repressive control, of reason. These forces are those that come to dominate, and thereby to corrode, the tyrannical soul. The tyrannical soul actually lives out the lawless desires, the shamelessly omnivorous appetites, which in most other souls remain in a repressed state that can find expression only in dreams. Lear quotes the remarkable passage near the beginning of *Republic* IX which pictures the emergence of such dreams from the recesses of the mind: as reason sleeps, the wild, bestial and somewhat id-like element in us comes to life with a raging lust to commit the most heinous of deeds (incest, indiscriminate murder, cannibalism). This passage justifies Lear's claim that the *Republic* diagnoses the presence of an ineliminable yet intractably irrational component at the bottom of the embodied psyche. It is extremely plausible, moreover, that Plato's imagination in this passage has been partly coloured by the material of tragic myths such as those of Oedipus and – probably even more so – Thyestes, although the context contains no explicit reference to tragedy. It is, however, the next and crucial step of Lear's argument that I cannot endorse. For he goes on to suggest that it is precisely the lawless desires of *Republic* IX that, in Plato's judgement, tragedy helps to unlock and release. According to Lear's reading, tragedy "stirs up the emotional and appetitive parts [of the soul] . . . and thus encourages the audience to act out on the political stage the destructive impulses acted out in the theatre" (p. 71).[1]

The first part of this claim is uncontentious, but the inference that follows it receives no support from, and in my view clashes directly with, Plato's most extensive remarks on tragedy in the last book of the

---

1. The passage in Book IX is also connected with Plato's view of tragedy by T. Gould, *The ancient quarrel between poetry and philosophy* (Princeton: Princeton University Press, 1990), pp. 29–30, 215–16.

Republic.² In *Republic* X, there is no hint at all that tragedy's paradigmatic concern is with the display or encouragement of "destructive impulses." On the contrary, the kernel of tragedy is located in the dramatization of acute suffering, and its effect upon an audience is analyzed wholly in terms of the arousal of intense "sympathy" (the now much-weakened English derivative hardly captures the force of the Greek verb, *sumpaschein*) and pity. Besides, while the drive to sympathetic pity comes from the lower mind, it has nothing like the blind and at least semi-unconscious impetus that Lear well describes, in the case of the tyrannical soul, as "desire lurching out of control." Far from inhabiting only our darkest dreams and the souls of tyrants, the urge to pity that tragedy stimulates has the power to overcome the waking minds of "even the best of us".³

There are admittedly some parallels of language and imagery between Book X's discussion of tragedy and the account of lawless desires in Book IX; both contexts use typically Platonic metaphors from physical appetite and quasi-animal strength to characterize the nature of desire.⁴ But these parallels concern the dynamics, not the contents or objects, of the respective desires, and they cannot obscure the differences between the destructive cravings of the imagination's dream-world and, on the other hand, the "surrender" to profoundly compassionate instincts that takes place in the soul's response to tragedy.⁵ If, as we surely must, we take *Republic* X as our best guide to the Platonic critique of tragedy, we are bound to conclude that what is repudiated by Plato is tragedy's unregenerate attachment to embodied human value – the very opposite, in other words, of irrational destructiveness. It is exactly because tragedy draws on and solidifies the values of personal bonds, and therefore vindicates the experience of loss and suffering as the truest diminishment of the human, that

---

2. Lear also cites *Republic* 568b for tragedy's legitimization of tyranny; but Plato's slightly casuistical point there is the very different one that outright praise of tyranny is sometimes voiced in tragedy.
3. *Republic* 605c10, with c6–8.
4. For the range of such language, including some traditional antecedents for it, see my commentary, *Plato Republic* 10 (Warminster: Aris & Phillips, 1988), notes on 605b3–4, 606a3, 606a5. Gould (ibid.), p. 30, places too much weight on the repeated imagery of "waking" the desires.
5. "Surrender" is Plato's own term at *Republic* 605d3; I use "instincts" to represent the point which Plato makes by categorizing the feelings in question as "natural" (606a5).

the principles of Platonic logos require its suppression. It is the psyche's addiction to pity that Plato rightly recognizes as grounding the Greek tragic tradition. And it is this addiction, not the very different impulses that break out within the monstrous life of the tyrannical soul, that forms both the psychological and the cultural nub of Plato's objections to tragedy.

On this reading, tragedy is dangerous to the ideals of philosophical reason, as Plato construes them, precisely because of its deep and tenacious humanity – its capacity to compel a close imaginative involvement in the sufferings of other beings, and to make us believe that such suffering tells us something supremely important about the world. That, in part, is why Plato wrote the *Phaedo*, in order to dramatize in the sharpest contrast the roots of a tragic vision and his radical alternative to it.[6] The *Phaedo* re-imagines Socrates' death, and thereby redefines the significance of what could count, on a tragic view, as extreme waste and affliction. Plato feels a vital need to contest tragedy's status on its own imaginative and myth-making territory. When we reach Aristotle, no trace of such a need remains.

Jonathan Lear offers an interpretation of Aristotle's attitude to tragedy that rests on the proposition that "Aristotle insists on the inherent rationality of tragic mythos", and which argues that the motivation behind this insistence was a desire to put tragedy to work "in the self-validation of logos" (p. 76). About the rationalizing thrust of the *Poetics*' treatment of tragedy, I am in total agreement. The treatise repeatedly asserts the principle of excluding "irrationality" (*alogon*) from the structure of dramatic action, and its central concept of the "complex" plot seems expressly constructed so as to emphasize the revelation of intelligible meaning, of a terrible but coherent logic, within the causation of tragic suffering. Lear is also surely right to say that the intelligibility prescribed by Aristotle's theory is a matter of "the humanly explicable" (p. 78), and to draw a contrast between this level of understanding and the sense of a more-than-human significance which is projected by a play such as Sophocles' *Oedipus Tyrannus*. However, in developing a case for judging that Aristotle effectively denies the possibility of tragic opacity, Lear's argument moves from this metaphysical point to a psychological focus upon the phenomenon of human destructiveness and violence. In doing so, I

---

6. See my article, "Plato and Aristotle on the denial of tragedy", *Proceedings of the Cambridge Philological Society* 30, 1984, pp. 49–71, at 55–8.

believe that it misidentifies the kind of opaqueness that Aristotle's theory is designed to eliminate from tragedy.

Aristotle codifies the archetypal model of tragedy as a great and ethically portentous transformation in human fortune. The transformation must be such as to arouse pity and fear (in a traditional formula to which I shall shortly return), and this condition entails that there must be essentially undeserved suffering at the heart of the ideal tragedy. This at once makes it difficult, I think, to approach Aristotle's reading of tragedy as a philosophical response to human destructiveness – as an attempt, in Lear's words, "to establish the adequacy of logos to account for even the most destructive aspects of human nature" (p. 76). Even in *Poetics* 14, where the patterns of tragic action are most explicitly formulated in terms of destructive actions between close kin, Aristotle's position steers away from plots based on full cognizance, and gives a strong preference to deeds performed in ignorance (or, best of all, averted just in time). Despite some notorious interpretive problems in this chapter's apparent recommendation of Euripidean melodrama, its underlying concern is consistent with the work as a whole, and that concern is not primarily with the motivation of tragic agents, but with the larger shape of events in which the agents unwittingly help to implicate themselves. The focus of Aristotle's theory of tragedy, that is to say, is fixed not upon the psychological springs of destructiveness, but upon configurations of events in which agency encounters its own limits, and by which extreme transformations in human fortune are brought about.

If we were to test this theory against either of the two works that the *Poetics* repeatedly cites as its paradigm tragedies, Sophocles' *Oedipus Tyrannus* and Euripides' *Iphigeneia in Tauris*, the conclusion we should be warranted in reaching, I believe, is that Aristotle's rationalization of tragedy is a denial not of the psychologically unfathomable, but of metaphysical or (more appropriately, in this context) religious opacity. Neither in these nor in most other surviving plays are we confronted by incomprehensible human motivations or the emergence of irrational destructiveness from the psyche. Crucial moments of psychological obscurity do unquestionably occur in Greek tragedy, in works such as Aeschylus's *Agamemnon* and Sophocles' *Ajax*, but it is extremely doubtful whether this factor can be regarded as central to the genre in the same way as the enigmas, ambiguities and outright mysteries of the religious frame of reference. Moreover, most cases of human violence in the extant plays derive either from intelligible if harrowing motivations (which could in principle be encompassed by the categories of Aristotelian ethics), or else – and sometimes simultaneously – from god-induced frenzy (which points to a different source of difficulty from the object of Lear's analysis). Aristotle's *Poetics* might perhaps be faulted for taking insufficient account of tragic destructiveness, but to question whether its postulates can cope with the darkest possibilities of the human mind is, I submit, to apply to it criteria that can hardly have struck Aristotle as a paramount challenge within the Greek tragic tradition.

One aspect of the difference between Lear's argument and my own, on this point, is that, when Lear characterizes tragedy's test to ethical reason as a matter of its "representations of attacks on [the] elementary bonds" (p. 76) of the polis, I would prefer to shift the emphasis much further towards tragedy's display of the *vulnerability* of these bonds. In that respect I think that Aristotle's theory is less of a failure than Lear suggests, since I take the *Poetics* to answer faithfully enough to the fundamental weight of tragic suffering. Where Aristotle's normative re-interpretation of tragedy loses close contact with the traditions of the genre, in my view, is in the secularizing force of the rationality that it imposes upon tragic plot-structures.[7] For most of Greek tragedy, human vulnerability and suffering (as well as some kinds of human violence) are a religious problem, and a problem ultimately impervious to the methods of reason: in the thought of one of Aeschylus's choruses, the will of Zeus is like a forest through which run only dark and impenetrable paths (*Suppliants* 88–90, = 93–5). It is this religious mentality that gave Plato a major ground for repudiating tragedy (including Homer),[8] and it is this same outlook which I believe that Aristotle rationalistically suppresses in the *Poetics*.

While, therefore, Lear and I are agreed that tragedy does in some sense test the limits of logos, my main disagreement with him is that where he regards Aristotle's treatment of tragedy as an attempt to show the power of reason to comprehend even extreme human destructiveness, I regard it rather as an attempt to preserve the intel-

---

7. I argue this point more fully in *Aristotle's poetics* (London: Duckworth, 1986), pp. 202–237. On Greek tragic religion, see my article, "Human limits and the religion of Greek tragedy", *Journal of Literature and Theology* **4**, 1990, pp. 169–80.
8. Plato arraigns Homeric and tragic conceptions of divine injustice and inscrutability at *Republic* II–III, especially 379a–383c; he also alludes to such ideas in book X, when he refers to the "indignation" (i.e. against alleged divine injustice) shown by typical tragic characters (604b10, e1–2).

ligibility of the causes of suffering at the point where agency intersects with contingency. This means, furthermore, that the threat which Greek tragedy potentially poses to an ethics such as Aristotle's is smaller on my reading than on Lear's. For as I see it, Aristotle faces tragedy as an exploration of the severest dangers that the world contains for human agency, and thereby for the chances of a happiness that can be ethically sustained by practical reason. If his theory departs from the worldview of the tragic tradition, it does so by neglecting a set of religious beliefs that his own philosophy could give powerful arguments for rejecting. On Lear's reading, by contrast, a grave misgiving is directed close to the core of Aristotle's model of the mind. It is evidently a large question how far Aristotelian psychology has the means to stave off the anxieties that Lear has formulated, partly with the help of Plato and Freud, about the limits of reason. I would draw attention here only to the lack of any *prima facie* difficulty for Aristotle in acknowledging, as he actually does in his remarks on bestiality in the *Ethics*,[9] the kind of meaningless irrationality that Plato had identified in *Republic* IX: it is, after all, a tenet of Aristotelian politics that, without the forms of life incorporated in the polis, human beings become "the worst of all creatures."[10] Be that as it may, the main doubt I have emphasized is whether Aristotle was, or could have been, conscious of the psychological challenge adumbrated by Lear as one that was posed to his ethical convictions by Greek tragedy as such.

Because I disagree with Lear's perception of irrational human destructiveness as a salient preoccupation in Greek tragedy, I inevitably part company too with much of what he says about the status of pity and fear in Aristotle's theory. What most needs emphasizing here, I think, is that Lear implicitly treats tragic fear as almost exclusively *self-regarding*. He correspondingly supposes that everything said about fear in *Rhetoric* II.5 is directly applicable to tragedy, whereas I would wish to contend that *Poetics* 13 refers to an imaginative fear that is principally sympathetic and focused on the dramatic character(s) – hence the definition, "fear arises for/regarding [*peri*] a person who is like us" (*Poetics* 1453a5–6). If fear is part of the experi-

---

9. See *Nicomachean ethics* 1148b19–24, 1150a1–8, where the examples include cannibalism (as at *Republic* 571d2–3), and where the bestial man is utterly lacking in reason.
10. *Politics* 1253a33.

ence of imaginative sympathy, as the traditional coupling of these emotions suggests,[11] then its force becomes entirely complementary to that of pity, and the tension that Lear appears to find between the two emotions will not exist. Conceived in this compound manner, tragic pity-and-fear will thus represent an aesthetic response which pulls us entirely inwards, so to speak, towards the exposure of vulnerability and suffering, simultaneously expressing a recognition of human value and a sense of shared humanity with the sufferer – precisely the reasons for Plato's strong renunciation of the experience of tragedy.

When Lear suggests, then, on the basis of the *Rhetoric*'s account of the passions, that tragic pity is a kind of barrier against raw terror, this presupposes the normal, self-regarding force of fear. Accordingly, where Lear discerns a reason for treating the fear that accompanies pity as a limited, "domesticated" version of the emotion, I prefer to note a further reason for treating it as a largely imaginative and other-regarding response to tragedy.[12] If we applied the psychological analyses of *Rhetoric* Book II without qualification to the experience of tragedy, we would indeed have to count pity and fear as standing in a relationship of some tension: in the *Rhetoric*, Aristotle is unequivocal that pity can be driven out by fear,[13] whereas the *Poetics* repeatedly links them (in traditional fashion, as I have mentioned) without any hint of incompatibility. The difference is explicable only, I believe, by the assumption that tragic fear is focused upon, and elicited by and for, the prospective sufferings of others. Tragic fear must certainly connect with, but it does not predominantly express, what we fear for ourselves.

If that is correct, tragic fear is not so much a distinct impulse as a kind of index of the intensity of the impulse to pity, a symptom of the powerful pull of the sense of shared humanity which Aristotle expresses by the requirement that the objects of sympathetic fear must be "like us."[14] Lear makes this requirement part of the basis for

---

11. For the earlier coupling of pity and fear see especially Gorgias *Helen* 9, Plato *Ion* 535b–e.
12. Lear links tragic fear at one point (p. 79) with imaginative identification, but he otherwise seems to count fear as essentially self-regarding.
13. *Rhetoric* 1386a21–23: the term *deinon* used there is also used in the *Poetics*, at 1453b14 and elsewhere.
14. The condition of likeness applies equally to pity, as a comparison of *Rhetoric* 1383a10 and 1386a24 shows.

his claim that tragedy, on the Aristotelian interpretation, is a psychologically "safe" experience – one that is insulated both from the most appalling suspicions about our own nature and from the worst conception of human vulnerability. I suspect that there must be a level on which this claim is justified, but that it may turn out to be the level on which it is practically inconceivable that we could have *any* experience, through the mediation of an art-form, which was describable as a nakedly unconsoling admission of the worst that could be imagined.[15] It may be, in other words, that Nietzsche's famous aphorism, "we possess art lest we perish of the truth",[16] has a clearer, or more necessary, applicability to tragedy than to anything else. Indeed, one might venture to say that the view of tragedy that Lear ultimately ascribes to Aristotle has a structural parallel to Nietzsche's own view of Greek tragedy itself: in both, we are saved from gazing into an abyss of irredeemable terror (whether that lies inside or outside the soul) by the workings of an illusion. In Aristotle's case – if this is not too drastic a statement of Lear's critique – that illusion may be nothing less than the foundation of his entire ethics.

If the difficulty of imagining a tragic art entirely without a layer of psychological protection or consolation provides a partial defence of Aristotle against Lear's charge, albeit one that makes him rather incongruously rub shoulders with Nietzsche, I would now like briefly to indicate an alternative and more positive direction in which the arguments of the *Poetics* might be ethically developed. This involves seeing pity and fear as the basis of an experience that, although it perhaps cannot altogether "test the limits" of either practical reason or Aristotle's conception of human nature, does open up the perpetual possibility of significant revisions within ethical thought and feeling. If pity, as Plato and Nietzsche both insistently recognized, is an intrinsically powerful dissolver of psychological self-sufficiency, then it possesses a correlative capacity to create an expanded awareness of humane and ethical affinities, and to override the sharp-edged criteria of likeness and difference that may operate in ordinary social life. Thus, when Lear suggests that what matters in an audience's

---

15. Even Schopenhauer's pessimistic account of tragedy does not posit such an experience, since it entails some kind of aesthetic consolation in the turn towards resignation.
16. *The will to power*, W. Kaufmann & R. J. Hollingdale (trans.) (New York: Vintage Books, 1968), p. 435, §822.

response to tragedy is whether it *takes* a character to be "like" itself, I would prefer to follow Plato's insight into tragedy's ability to induce "surrender" to its exhibitions of suffering.[17] Pity, on this reading, is a force that can surprise, compel and reshape the ethical imagination. Far from tending, as Lear suggests, to allow "idealized self-images to go unchallenged" (p. 80), the tragic impulse to pity is one that, by engendering a response to the extreme afflictions of others, has the potential to contribute to the tacit redefinition of an audience's moral identity. Some such idea, I want to maintain, lay close to the heart of the Greek tragic tradition, and was accordingly perceived as basic to the nature of pity by both Plato and Aristotle.

One representative aspect of this Greek tradition – a tradition in which, as both philosophers rightly agreed, Homer was the essential precursor of Attic tragedy – will serve to make my point concisely for me in this context. It is crucial to the Greek experience of tragedy that it is capable of encompassing, and indeed accepting at its centre, an exposure to the sufferings of characters who do not simply match the status of the male-citizen theatre audience of the polis: above all, female and non-Greek characters. In some of their most extraordinary efforts of imagination, Homer and the tragedians deliberately dramatize the potency of pity as a moulder of perceptions of human value in situations where such characters are involved. This is a thread that runs, to name only some obvious instances, through the encounter between Achilles and Priam in *Iliad* 24, the mythologization of Xerxes' and his people's tragedy in Aeschylus's *Persians*, and the treatment of Hecuba and her companions in Euripides' *Trojan women*. In these and in many other contexts, the Greek tragic tradition discerns in compassion the power to expand and *transform* the apprehension of others as "like ourselves." From this perspective, pity need not simply answer to a preconceived sense of identity and affinity; it can implicitly impinge upon an audience's self-image, by eliciting feelings, and therefore judgements, which cut across the practical norms of political and social life.

But even if what I have just said is true of the tragic tradition as a whole, is it true of Aristotle's own theory of tragedy? I do not want to claim that we can give an unproblematic answer to that question, not

---

17. From this Platonic perspective, I do not understand Lear's claim that pity "guarantees" our ability to pull ourselves back from involvement in tragedy. Pity is not voluntary.

least because the *Poetics* resolutely declines to pursue the ethical implications of its arguments in any detail. But I think it would be unfair to Aristotle to rule out an affirmative altogether. The conception of pity found in both the *Poetics* and the *Rhetoric*, and the stress placed on pity in the former, is demonstrably in tune with older and widely attested Greek attitudes to tragedy. Besides, Aristotle's theory of tragedy does not closely specify the limits of what it means for characters to be "like us":[18] indeed, the phrase appears to mark a condition whose status is psychologically descriptive rather than normative. In that sense the theory surely does allow for, even if it does not spell out, a range of ethically imaginative relationships between the audiences and the agents of tragedy. By the same token, it leaves room within the experience of tragedy – an experience that Aristotle hardly seems to confine to the polis of the ideally virtuous or practically wise – for serious adjustments in understanding the intricate criss-crossings of agency and contingency, knowledge and ignorance, deliberation and misfortune, external goods and virtue. It is not clear to me that the *Poetics* circumscribes this possibility by the assumption that the male citizen spectators of tragic theatre respond on the basis of an exclusive and predefined self-image of their own moral identities.

I agreed earlier with Jonathan Lear that Aristotle's view of tragedy insists on a rationality that necessarily excludes certain kinds of inexplicable atrocities. I have disagreed with him, however, about the major source of opaqueness in the Greek tragic tradition and about the centrality to that tradition of the consequences of human destructiveness. If, then, what Lear calls the "pitiless tragedy" of human destructiveness has a claim on our attention, as it may well have, we must seek it in places other than the religious drama of Greek antiquity. But I end by surmising that the fundamental test posed by such an alternative tragic vision (or, indeed, by its philosophical and psychoanalytical equivalents) is one that imperils not just the realism of Aristotelian ethics, but the possibility of ethics in any readily recognizable form at all.

---

18. Lear (p. 79) quotes *Rhetoric* 1386a24–27, where several criteria of likeness are mentioned: there Aristotle's concern is with the norms of psychology in rhetorical contexts such as political assemblies, but his remark still gives us some idea of how various might be the factors that would allow or invite us to perceive tragic agents as "like us."

Outline of a response to Halliwell
JONATHAN LEAR

Above all, I would like to be brief. The point of these remarks is to let an interested reader know how I would go about fashioning a response to Professor Halliwell's thoughtful comments. Professor Halliwell challenges a number of interpretations I have made of relevant texts; and while I think textual interpretation of great importance, I also believe that in the parry of criticism and defence of one's interpretation, one can get distracted from the philosophical points at issue. So I should like to begin with what I take to be Halliwell's most significant philosophical criticism of my paper: his remarks on pity. Pity, in Halliwell's vision, has the power to expand one's moral vision, to make the audience emotionally susceptible to imaginative possibilities that might hitherto have lain beyond their ken, "to contribute to the tacit redefinition of an audience's moral identity" (p. 94).

My response is: that's very nice, if true. But what if it isn't? How would we ever know, especially if we are spending our philosophical time telling ourselves self-satisfied stories about the redemptive power of pity? That is, shouldn't we be concerned that this conception of pity's ethical potential might not itself be part of a misleading self-image of who we are and what is possible for us? And, if we are concerned, how could we responsibly go about exercising that concern? I suppose this is part of a larger worry that might roughly be put as follows: might not ethical life, at least as Aristotle understood it, be bad for you and for those around you? And if it is, how could one ever tell? Aristotle is so eloquent on how, say, the courageous person's perspective is unavailable to the coward. From a cowardly perspective, the courageous act will appear reckless and foolish; and thus the courageous person does well to ignore the coward. That is straightforward. Indeed, the point can be so moving, it can blind us to the following question: how do "virtuous" people know that they might be dismissing someone, as they dismiss the coward, who might have something to teach them about re-orienting their world view? Aristotle paid little more attention to women and slaves than he did to cowards; and he thought he was right to do so. Here it becomes sickeningly easy to see how the "virtuous person's distinctive outlook" can degenerate into smugness and complacency. Here it obscures what a genuinely ethical life might be like. This is an issue, of utmost importance, raised *by*

Aristotle's ethics: one question I wished to explore in my paper was to what extent one might see the issue as raised *within* it.
Now I shall make some brief comments on specific criticisms:

1. *Metaphysics, psychology and ethics* There is nothing in my paper that seeks to deny that Aristotle's rationalization of tragedy is directed primarily at denying metaphysical or religious opacity. But that metaphysical stance will, for Aristotle, obviously have psychological and ethical consequences; and it is some of those that I wished to explore in this paper.
2. *Irrational destructiveness vs preserving intelligibility where agency intersects with contingency* This seems to me to be a false dichotomy. Of course, to be treating the issue as an intersection with contingency, rather than with the religious *alogon*, is to be treating the issue in a secularized, and thus debased, form. But whichever form of intersection one chooses, there will be psychological and ethical manifestations of that intersection. So what, from a metaphysical perspective, is the intersection of two realms – the human–political and the religious–opaque – may well from an ethical and psychological perspective manifest itself as extremes of human destructiveness.
3. *Fear and pity as complementary* I agree. The "tension" I spoke of is a tension of complementarity. I do, by the way, use the *Rhetoric*'s account of the emotions to shed some light on the imaginative fear in the audience of a tragedy. But that should not suggest that I believe there are no issues of nuance or interpretation. The claim that I believe that "everything said about fear in *Rhetoric* II.5 is directly applicable to tragedy" (p. 91) is overstated.
4. *"We possess art lest we perish of the truth"* The idea that tragic art might save us from "gazing into an abyss of irredeemable terror" (p. 93), that it provides "a layer of psychological protection or consolation", is an interesting one. But it is not, I believe, the question at issue. The important question in this context is whether Aristotle gives us a satisfying account of our own experience of tragedy. Whatever protective function art may (or may not) possess with respect to the truth, has Aristotle adequately captured that art? I suspect that the answer to that question is "no." The problem with Aristotle's account, I believe, is not that it adequately captures tragedy's protective function, but that it disguises tragedy's lack of protection. We might paraphrase

Nietzsche and say that, for Aristotle, "we possess a philosophical account of art lest we perish from the truth of art."

5. *The interpretation of* Republic X   I refer readers to my article, "Inside and outside the *Republic*" (*Phronesis* **37**, 1992, especially section 5). Halliwell's point looks strongest, in my opinion, when one takes *Republic* X in isolation – "as the best guide to the Platonic critique of tragedy" (p. 87) – whereas my interpretation depends on weaving that book into the argumentative contexts of the entire text.

Aristotelian ethics and the "enlargement of thought"

SABINA LOVIBOND

In considering the topic of Aristotle and moral realism, I have found myself drawn to the question of how, if at all, current "realist" views in ethics can find support in the ethics of Aristotle. In order to make any progress with this question, we obviously need a working definition of "realism", and for present purposes I shall assume – however contentiously – that there is no compelling reason to mistrust the close conceptual link that exists pre-philosophically between "reality" and "truth." In other words, I shall leave undisturbed the apparently naïve notion that, when we succeed in saying something true, we thereby succeed, regardless of subject matter, in recording an aspect of reality. In contrast to those who regard the former kind of success as merely a preliminary qualification for realism in a "discourse" or class of statements,[1] I shall be content to understand as "realism" a position that maintains simply that statements of the relevant class are truth-evaluable and that some of them are actually true.[2]

Next, we need to review the defining features of an "Aristotelian" ethics. If I were to lay claim, on my own account, to a position of this kind, what elucidation could I be expected to offer? In the first place, I would have to advance something corresponding to Aristotle's view that human nature – the answer to the question "What is it to be a human being?" – determines the human *energeia*; that is, that it fixes what we can count as fully successful human functioning. In mentioning "success" here I would have to think of myself as having

---

1. See e.g. C. Wright, *Truth and objectivity* (Cambridge, Mass.: Harvard University Press, 1992), esp. pp. 199–201.

introduced a value term, so that *successful* human functioning assumed the status of a goal that all members of the species would set before themselves in so far as their judgement was not impaired. (I am abstracting for the moment from the fact that for Aristotle himself this goal is not equally within the reach of the leisured and the labouring classes, of men and women, and so forth.) Secondly, I would have to retain the thought that human beings are by nature "rational" and "social"; that is, that successful human functioning means, among other things, participation in the life of a community and in some sufficiently varied sample of the sorts of conversation carried on within human groups. Thirdly, I would have to regard as

---

2. Cf. *Essays on moral realism*, ed. G. Sayre-McCord (Ithaca: Cornell University Press, 1988), p. 5. Note that by a "statement of the relevant class" I mean one expressing ontological commitment to some item or items purportedly referred to by the distinctive vocabulary of that class of statements: otherwise the proposed characterization of realism could be challenged by pointing to statements in which that vocabulary is used within the scope of a negative operator. For example, it has been put to me that theological discourse might contain statements satisfying both the conditions I have mentioned (e.g. "God does not exist", "Smith is not an unholy person") without there being any theological reality. However, if there is no such reality, then expressions like "God" and "unholy" will lack reference. Hence statements (or apparent statements) in which they occur will be construable as expressing genuine thoughts (and hence as truth-evaluable) only in one of the following ways: either by analyzing such expressions in terms intelligible to the atheist (i.e. recognized by him/her as having sense), in which case the relevant statements will cease to be distinctively theological; or by virtue of some such device as Gareth Evans' "game-to-reality shift" (G. Evans, *The varieties of reference* (Oxford: Oxford University Press, 1982), pp. 370–71), i.e. by representing the sample negative claims as denials that in "quasi-understanding" certain sentences ("God exists", "Smith is an unholy person") one would be entertaining a true proposition. Again, this would not itself be a theological thought; if there is no theological reality, all that will be available to those wanting to "talk about God" will be the opportunity of conniving in a certain shared practice of *fictional* (i.e. make-believe) reference.

The objection might also be raised to this conception of realism: how small a number is meant by "some"? Would I, for example, qualify as a moral realist if I believed there was just one moral statement (in the sense explained above) that was determinately true? I am not sure whether this state of affairs is coherently imaginable, but perhaps one should in any case grasp the nettle and answer "yes": such a realism might be of vanishingly small practical interest, but then it seems quite plausible on general grounds to say that the human significance of realism about a given subject matter will depend on the degree of determinacy attributed to the subject matter itself.

an indispensable condition of such participation some measure of the specific kind of competence whose full realization is described by Aristotle as *phronesis*, "practical wisdom" – the ability to appraise and act upon particular situations in a way that is conducive to the creditable overall conduct of life. And in order to maintain a recognizably Aristotelian position I would have to have not just a formal but a substantive conception of *phronesis*: I would have to see it not as mere technical competence in the attainment of subjectively determined goals, but as competence in realizing a particular kind of life, namely one informed by a correct sense of value. Hence I would have to think that there was such a thing as correct judgement about the ethical, and that the exercise of such judgement was a (partial) expression of the capacities of human beings *qua* human.

Finally, my credentials as an "Aristotelian" would rest on my endorsement of a certain idea of how *phronesis* is acquired. Aristotle holds that this particular "intellectual virtue" includes within itself the cognitive element or "right rule" necessary to each of the virtues of character, which are held together by their common dependence on this element (*Nicomachean ethics* VI.13, esp. at 1144b32–1145a2; references to Aristotle hereafter will be to the NE unless otherwise indicated). For him, therefore, our progress towards *phronesis* is constituted (or "formally caused") by such progress as we may make in respect of the latter virtues. Now, his account of how we acquire the virtues of character invokes the idea of a process of ethical formation (Greek *paideia*, German *Bildung*) whose purpose is to instil dispositions to take pleasure and displeasure in the appropriate kinds of object (1104b11–13; cf. *Eudemian ethics* 1221b33). Taking as given the universal tendency to pursue whatever counts, for the subject in question, as pleasurable (a propensity that follows from the desire to enhance vital functioning; cf. 1153b25–32, 1175a18–19), Aristotle argues that *paideia* should not seek to eradicate this tendency but should use it as a fixed point around which to organize the desired systematic changes in individual motivation.[3] As learners, we are called on to become progressively more emancipated from the crudely physical conception of pleasure and displeasure. In keeping with Aristotle's threefold taxonomy of value (1104b31) – which is also, of course, an order of rank – we have to advance first of all from

---

3. Cf. M. F. Burnyeat, Aristotle on learning to be good, in *Essays on Aristotle's ethics*, A. Rorty (ed.) (Berkeley: University of California Press, 1980), esp. pp. 79–80.

an impulsive (*kata pathos*, 1095a8) to a prudent habit of behaviour (this being, presumably, the limit of *paideia* for those who will always need external incentives to morality: 1179b7–16); then – if we have it in us – beyond *mere* prudence to the attempt to realize ethical value, *to kalon*, for its own sake. These more sophisticated objects of pursuit, which become ours only in a culturally mediated way,[4] nevertheless present themselves to us (once they are ours) as sources of pleasure in their own right (cf. 1105a1); the pleasures they offer are available only to those who have reached the appropriate stage of ethical formation (cf. 1173b28–31).

There is no phrase in Aristotle's Greek that corresponds exactly to the "moral reality" that features in some contemporary philosophical writing. However, Aristotle has no difficulty in principle with the thought that there are truths about the subject matter of ethics – in particular, about worthy and unworthy objects of pursuit. For example, he says in the context of a certain evaluative question, namely whether pleasure is a good, that "what everyone agrees upon, we call true (or: we declare to be the case, *einai*)" (1172b36–1173a1).[5] He holds, further, that *phronesis* is "a reasoned and *true* state of capacity to act with regard to human goods" (1140b20–21, trans. W. D. Ross; cf. 1142b33), and that this capacity, which relates to the kind of practical concerns that cannot be brought within the scope of a *techne* (cf. 1140a30), is the mark of those who have the "eye of experience" and therefore "see aright" (1143b13–14); such people also supply a paradigm of the "perception" (*aisthesis*) that determines whether a certain response to a given situation would or would not be within the limits of the "mean" (1109b20–23). In fact, they provide the "yardstick and measure" (*kanon kai metron*) of ethical value (1113a33), just as under the more general designation of "good men" they are our guide to what is truly pleasant (1176a17–19).

---

4. This claim calls for refinement as far as *to sumpheron* (the expedient) is concerned: non-human animals must learn from experience a great deal that has survival value, but this learning is not "culturally mediated." However, *human* prudence encompasses much more than the prudence of other species, requiring as it does a grasp of concepts such as those of health, money, various kinds of social relationship, etc.
5. Note that I do not read this sentence as an expression of the ("idealist") view that *the fact that everyone believes that p makes it the case that p*. "What everyone agrees upon, we call true" is a phenomenological remark (and a hard one to disagree with, at that), not a metaphysical one.

These passages suggest a view within which the intellectual virtue of *phronesis* – the quality that sums up the outcome of a successful upbringing – constitutes, as it were, our central piece of evidence for the objectivity of the ethical. To begin with, they reflect a certain feature of social experience, namely that what compels our initial recognition of ethics as a subject matter is the encounter with a particular kind of authority. From the standpoint of the learner, the status of (say) one's older male kin as *phronimoi* (practically wise) – at least in relation to oneself – is a fact that one grasps in advance of any real understanding of what it is that a *phronimos*, as such, is competent to observe or to make judgements about. Evidently there is something that is disclosed to (all and only) the possessors of *phronesis*, and in the consideration of which one may hope, in time, to be able to join them; one presumes that they are not just engaged in an elaborate word-game. But in the first instance it is the simple fact of moral authority that one has to accept.

I spoke just now of a feature of social *experience*, but it seems to me that at the theoretical level also – if "theory" is not too heavy a word for an account of ethics whose declared aim is to stay close to common beliefs (cf. 1098b9–12) – the figure of the *phronimos* will be important. I think in fact that this figure will be more central, for the purpose of assessing the present position as a *realist* one, than any of the ideas that form the stock-in-trade of metaphysical debates about realism (e.g. "mind-independence", "recognition-transcendence", "explanatory potency"). It is not that the realist credentials of my putatively Aristotelian view (which I will from now on refer to as "ours") cannot be discussed with reference to these ideas; it is simply that such resources as we have for attaching to our view the various "realist" characteristics identified in the technical literature seem to depend on a prior ontological commitment on our part to the quality of *phronesis* (or to its equivalent in our own philosophical idiom), and on a willingness to recognize actual persons as at least approximating towards the possession of this quality. The point can be put more concretely by saying that if we have a use for talk about *correct* moral judgement (the kind of judgement that we can point to as an adequate representation of reality from the perspective of moral concern), this is due to our having received a certain amount of instruction in distinguishing correct from incorrect, in the course of which our attention has from time to time been directed to particular examples of correct judgement. Without such a background, it would be as idle to talk about "correctness" in ethics as it is in, say, doodling. But ethics is saved from this kind of subjectivity by the actual existence, within the social environment to which our theory relates, of certain habits of judgement to which morally competent adults themselves defer. These habits of judgement provide the standard against which individual affective (including ethical) responses to particular situations are assessed for appropriateness; that is, they determine a quasi-perceptual *norm* analogous to the perceptual norms which dictate, for instance, what colour it is right to describe something as having.

But the *phronimos* can provide a conceptual anchor for moral *realism* only in so far as the theorist consents – with Aristotle – to take this figure at the value placed on him[6] by his own community: to accept him as one who sees aright, makes correct judgements, and so forth. And it is a commonplace of recent ethical writing that this attitude of acceptance is hard to sustain under modern, not to mention "postmodern", conditions. The problem posed for moral realism by the reflective awareness of cultural difference has been a staple theme of European philosophy since the age of Romanticism, and it remains one of the most valued resources of anti-realist argument, surfacing, for example, in J. L. Mackie's "argument from relativity"[7] or in Bernard Williams' thesis that reflection can destroy ethical knowledge.[8] More topically, materialist scrutiny of various institutional settings of knowledge production has prompted the debates we so often see trivialized under the heading of "political correctness". These debates themselves are, no doubt, simply an expression of what Hegel called the "principle of the modern world" which "requires that what anyone is to recognize shall reveal itself to him as something entitled to recognition";[9] an expression, that is, of the disposition to call into question the moral credentials of all self-styled authorities. Hence the disorientation they induce belongs to the same genus as that which powers the "argument from relativity", namely a loss of conviction that we know, concretely, who exemplifies *phro-*

---

6. Given Aristotle's stated views about the evaluative significance of femaleness (e.g. *De gen. anim.* 775a15 or *Politics* 1260a7–31), I have not found it appropriate to use gender-neutral language in expounding him.
7. J. L. Mackie, *Ethics: inventing right and wrong* (London: Penguin, 1977), pp. 36–8.
8. B. Williams, *Ethics and the limits of philosophy* (London: Fontana/Collins, 1985), p. 167.
9. G. W. F. Hegel, *Philosophy of right*, T. M. Knox (trans. & ed.) (Oxford: Oxford University Press, 1952), p. 294; addition to para. 317.

nesis. A standard response to this loss of conviction is the retreat to an attitude, at least for theoretical purposes, of knowingness or "irony"[10] – although this does not necessarily preclude a willingness to "speak with the vulgar"[11] about substantive questions of value.

The significance of these obstacles to identification with any specific embodiment of *phronesis* is that, if the realist qualifications of an Aristotelian ethics have to be explained by reference to the *phronimos* and to the process of ethical formation that produces him, then the more seriously we take such obstacles, the less we shall see in Aristotle as an inspiration to contemporary moral realism. Supposing, therefore, we admit the existence of a process of moral formation as envisaged by Aristotle, it remains to consider how far this process is capable of bringing it about that there *is*, as far as we are concerned, anything deserving the name of "moral reality." Is the idea of ethical formation adequate, in default of clear paradigms of what the formative process aims at, to support this kind of superstructure? For example, can people living under conditions of cognitive disorientation think of themselves as engaged in the truth-directed (and so, by my standards, distinctively realist) exercise of self-criticism and self-correction?

It may be helpful here to look more closely at the semi-technical notion of "modernity" associated with Hegel. Modernity in this sense is the phase of history in which individuals have come to transcend their social roles – to be able to reflect on the local systems of convention into which they have been initiated and to evaluate those systems by standards not wholly internal to them. For Hegel this "principle of subjectivity", i.e. the expectation of individual citizens that the institutions regulating their existence should be such as to meet their own standards of rational defensibility, was what constituted the decisive difference between ancient and modern political societies;[12] whereas for some present-day Aristotelians it is not so much an achievement as a symptom of cultural perversity – that is, of the misguided refusal of Enlightenment rationalism to accept that moral traditions come

---

10. Cf. T. Nagel, *Mortal questions* (Cambridge: Cambridge University Press, 1979), p. 23; R. Rorty, *Contingency, irony and solidarity* (Cambridge: Cambridge University Press, 1989), esp. ch. 4.
11. R. Rorty, "Feminism and pragmatism", *Michigan Quarterly Review* 30, 1991, p. 237: "Although practical politics will doubtless often require feminists to speak with the universalist vulgar, I think that they might profit from thinking with the pragmatists" (i.e. with the "ironists" of *Contingency, irony and solidarity*).

ready-equipped with all necessary means of self-criticism and self-transformation.[13] Now, consider again the condition of disorientation that consists in our not being able to locate in our own social surroundings any particular habit of ethical judgement possessing the exemplary status of *phronesis*. With the Hegelian conception of modernity in mind, we can see this as a distinctively "modern" condition in that what makes the location of *phronesis* problematic is the impossibility – now that all social practices have to be able to justify themselves before an independent "tribunal of reason" – of taking any embodiment of moral rationality at its own valuation. Each of us, or rather every reasonably sane human product of modernity, is conscious of having too much experience of the sudden encounter with intellectually unassimilated "difference", and of exposure to critical appraisal from this or that "different" perspective, to be drawn into attributing actual existence to the *phronimos* – at any rate, if the latter is supposed to be exempt from such encounters by virtue of his supremely adequate *paideia*. So if by an "Aristotelian" we mean someone who makes *phronesis* the beginning and end of their moral epistemology, then it would seem that under "modern" conditions the attempt to define oneself as an "Aristotelian moral realist" is doomed to lead either to bad faith (in the form of a regressive and cliquish vision of "community"),[14] or to scepticism and moral paralysis. However, what does deserve investigation is the possibility of bringing together, first, the Aristotelian idea of *proficiency* in moral judgement as something derived from successful *paideia* in a specific community (where "proficiency" is to be understood, for the moment, in a straightforwardly behavioural sense), and, secondly, the "modern" habit of recourse to universalistic criteria in order to determine

---

12. Cf. M. B. Foster, *The political philosophies of Plato and Hegel* (Oxford: Oxford University Press, 1935), ch. 3. The idea is not that in the ancient world there was no questioning of social convention or of political authority, but rather that the modern world is characterized by forms of organization that provide space for such questioning (for example, the substitution of party politics for stasis, i.e. civil strife).
13. Cf. A. MacIntyre, *After virtue* (London: Duckworth, 1981), esp. chs 5 and 18.
14. Thus, MacIntyre, *After virtue*, p. 245: "What matters at this stage is the construction of local forms of community within which civility and the intellectual and moral life can be sustained through the new dark ages which are already upon us." (This is offered as the fruit of an attempt to "[restate] the Aristotelian tradition ... in a way that restores intelligibility and rationality to our moral and social attitudes and commitments." – ibid., p. 241).

whether a given positive morality is worthy of acceptance. This possibility is the one I want to explore in the remainder of the chapter.

An Aristotelian ethical theory, as characterized at the outset, comprises (what I propose to call) both a foundational and a non-foundational element. The latter consists in what the theory has to say about the acquisition of the moral virtues, and of the intellectual virtue of *phronesis*. This is "non-foundational" in the sense that it does no more than remind us of what goes into the making of an ethical subject whom *we ourselves are prepared to describe* as *phronimos*: it assumes, but does not solicit by argument, our adherence to an existing moral consensus that determines the particular list of qualities a morally admirable person will have, who counts as having a grasp of the "starting-points of action" or as possessing the "eye of experience", and so on. (Aristotle indicates as much in his remarks about the dependence of moral philosophy on its students' having received an appropriate upbringing, and about the accountability of the subject to "reputable opinion".) However, even if our access to this consensus is through initiation into the ways of a particular social world, this does not mean that we have to resign ourselves to the thought that our acceptance of the prevailing scheme of values is a mere historical accident. In fact, once we have actually attained in some measure to the putative quality of *phronesis* and are in a position to reflect (with Aristotle) on the processes that have brought us to this point, no such resignation is necessary. For the theory contains a foundational element too, in the guise of a general account of human capacities and of the constraints these place on what we can recognize as a good life for human beings.

Although I agree with the standard contemporary view that the theological ideas informing Aristotle's own treatment of the foundations of ethics – the hierarchically organized cosmic household (*Meta.* 1075a11–23), the god who furnishes the universe with an object of desire (*Meta.* 1072b3) – are of historical interest only, I think contemporary moral realism has good reason to aspire to be "Aristotelian" in a looser sense. This alternative way of appropriating Aristotle would preserve the method of immanent (phenomenological) description of the ethical habit of mind – the "non-foundational" element – but, in contrast to some recent anti-Enlightenment philosophies that seem content to throw in their lot uncritically with *local* forms of life, it would acknowledge the legitimacy of the wish to have "our way of life", our conception of *phronesis*, displayed not just as a brute cultural datum but as something with a rational claim on us. In seeking to meet this wish it would echo, in some as yet unspecified way, the foundationalist theme in Aristotle.

It may seem premature to start talking about "foundationalism" simply in virtue of the need we feel for an escape route from our inherited morality. A familiar, and correct, comment that may be made at this point is that "moralities" in the positive sense (or at any rate those current in developed, pluralist societies) contain their own critical resources and can therefore address their own deficiencies without benefit of any absolute, supra-cultural standard against which to measure themselves.[15] Doesn't this suggest that in the mood just characterized we may be in danger of committing ourselves to something decisively discredited by the naturalist turn in epistemology – namely, the idea of an ahistorical "Archimedian point" from which any rational appraisal of existing institutions ought to proceed?

The warning should not go unheeded; but it seems to me that too few of those who reject unreconstructed "foundationalism" succeed in distancing themselves adequately from the relativist alternative. To be sure, the idea of the Archimedian point must be rejected by anyone who wants their ethical theory to be consistent with a view of the human species as continuous with the rest of the natural world, and with it must go any idea of an alternative, as far as our moral thinking is concerned, to the kind of "situatedness" that consists in having *some* determinate sociocultural origin. But to concede this is not yet to fall back on the kind of critical thinking that is "situated" in the sense of being deliberately restricted to the working-out of a perspective recognized by its occupants as being just one among many (for example, that of Richard Rorty's "liberals").[16] It is not yet to submit to the demand that we think within the conceptual or evaluative horizon proper to any one group whose particularity, relative to some wider domain, we ourselves can recognize.[17] And if to be a "foundational-

---

15. Cf. S. Benhabib, *Situating the self: gender, community and postmodernism in contemporary ethics* (Cambridge: Polity, 1992), p. 227, who cites M. Walzer, J-F. Lyotard, and R. Rorty as advocates (along with herself) of "situated criticism." MacIntyre too qualifies for inclusion in this list in so far as he holds that "a [moral] tradition is sustained and advanced by its own internal arguments and conflicts" (*After virtue*, p. 242). The title of the present paper was suggested by chapter 4 of Benhabib's book.
16. Cf. R. Rorty, *Contingency, irony and solidarity*, p. 196.

ist" is simply to aspire to think in a way that is not, in this stronger and voluntarily parochial sense, "situated" – i.e. if it is a matter of holding ourselves accountable not just to those within some arbitrarily determined community that is supposed to be "ours", but to anyone with whom we are capable of establishing communication – then the disjunction "relativist"/"foundationalist" is after all one with respect to which we have to take sides, and the "foundationalist" side of it is the right side to be on.

In order to substantiate this claim, we should begin by taking seriously the idea that local conceptions of *phronesis* can be evaluated by reference to the norm of *a way of life appropriate to human beings* in virtue of our specific characteristics. Without entering into discussion of Aristotle's "intellectualism" (i.e. of the primacy he eventually gives to the life of contemplative over that of practical reason) we can note that one of the most important types of "realism" in current moral and political controversy shows an obvious debt to the Aristotelian assumption that there is, at any rate, some such thing as a distinctively human *energeia* (mode of functioning).[18] This realism rejects the view that, since values and meanings are "socially constructed", we cannot legitimately pronounce on what may or may not be detrimental to the wellbeing of people whose social environment is radically different from our own; it maintains that, on the contrary, we can sometimes say with confidence that the conditions of life of some group of people are such as no *human being* should have to suffer, or that *human* capacities are being wasted or spoilt under a given social order.

No doubt there is much to be learned from the attempt to state explicitly what we consider to be the universal preconditions of a satisfactory human existence.[19] But even without embarking on this constructive philosophical task, we may still find ourselves committed to an attitude that can equally legitimately be described on negative

---

17. Cf. B. Williams, Wittgenstein and idealism, in his *Moral luck* (Cambridge: Cambridge University Press, 1976), esp. pp. 151–2.
18. Cf. N. Geras, *Marx and human nature: refutation of a legend* (London: Verso, 1983), pp. 112–15; M. Nussbaum, "Nature, function and capability: Aristotle on political distribution", *Oxford Studies in Ancient Philosophy*, supplementary vol., 1988, pp. 145–84; M. Nussbaum, "Human functioning and social justice: in defense of Aristotelian essentialism", *Political Theory* **20**, (1992), pp. 202–46.
19. See for example M. Nussbaum's "thick vague conception" of the human form of life ("Human functioning and social justice", pp. 216–23).

grounds as "universalist." We shall find ourselves so committed if we refuse to acknowledge any *a priori* limits – limits motivated by theoretical opposition to "grand narratives", the Enlightenment, utopian politics, etc. – to the "community" from which rational criticism of our conception of *phronesis* can issue.

This attitude is both faithful and unfaithful to the spirit of Aristotle. On one hand, it preserves the Aristotelian thought that attempts at critical thinking are idle (because merely subjective) except in so far as they orient themselves towards some actually existing paradigm of sound judgement; that is, it continues to picture moral enquiry as involving processes of selection and discrimination carried out by finite individuals within their own historical setting. But it departs from Aristotle in that it no longer assumes these processes to enjoy the support of a *canonical* "practical wisdom" – a consensus as to who counts as a "reasonable man [sic]" – but sees them instead as going forward on the basis of provisional and tentative hypotheses about what deserves to take on the status of *phronesis*, here and now, in relation to our own thinking.

Our question was whether a view of ethics that makes the virtue of *phronesis*, as concretely realized in certain individuals, the enabling principle of our belief in real moral properties and obligations can accommodate this departure without giving way to scepticism. I believe there is reason to hold that it can. For the relevant differences between pre-modern and modern social conditions are best understood not in absolute but in relative terms. To begin with, even a classical Aristotelian ethics requires us, as recipients of *paideia*, to place our trust in the veracity of a (substantive) habit of evaluative thought whose correctness cannot be rationally demonstrated to someone not already initiated into basic sympathy with it. Anyone may agree verbally that the *telos* of life is "doing well" (*eupraxia*), but this will not have the same practical implications for them as it does for the Aristotelian *phronimos* until they have been won over to the same ethically informed conception of *eupraxia* that he possesses. John McDowell has pointed out on Aristotle's behalf that

> if someone really embraces a specific conception of human excellence, however grounded, then that will of itself equip him to understand special employments of the typical notions of "prudential" reasoning – the notions of benefit, advantage, harm, loss and so forth – according to which (for instance) no

payoff from flouting a requirement of excellence, however desirable by [natural as opposed to ethical canons of value], can count as a genuine advantage; and, conversely, no sacrifice necessitated by the life of excellence, however desirable what one misses may be by those sorts of canons, can count as a genuine loss.[20]

Such understanding, however, has a cultural basis, the presence of which is not to be taken for granted in any given case; and this is a thought that has to co-exist, for the Aristotelian, with the belief that someone in whom the basis is lacking (i.e. who has not "embraced" the relevant conception of *eupraxia*) is missing out on features of the world to which a better endowed and/or better educated person would be sensitive. In other words, we find here a combination of *ontological commitment to a domain of fact* with *acceptance that the facts in question will not be equally accessible to everyone*; if you like, a realism unabashed by the experience of failure to persuade.

Perhaps this attitude is not particularly heroic in a socially homogeneous setting where we can expect a high degree of like-mindedness about evaluative as well as other matters from the people with whom we come into contact. Clearly, it demands more coolness of nerve in proportion to the difficulty of ascertaining, in any given case of evaluative disagreement, that we understand our opponents better than they understand themselves; and when conjoined with disrespect for the seriousness of this difficulty, it is a failing. Suppose we agree, however, that even where the extension of the concept *phronimos* (or equivalent) is, culturally speaking, at its most stable, there is going to be the occasional argumentative *impasse* about evaluative and, more particularly, practical questions. Such situations will present us with the following options: either conclude that there is no "fact of the matter" where the disputants were seeking one and that all views about the disputed question are equally correct or incorrect (i.e. the sceptical option); or be prepared to discount one of the competing positions as epistemically inferior to the other (i.e. the option of saying that ethical discourse exerts what Crispin Wright has called "cognitive command").[21] Now unless we are inclined *a priori* towards scepticism, the occurrence of an argumentative *impasse* has no auto-

---

20. J. McDowell, "The role of eudaimonia in Aristotle's ethics", in *Essays on Aristotle's ethics*, A. Rorty (ed.) (Berkeley: University of California Press, 1980), p. 369.
21. C. Wright, *Truth and objectivity*, p. 144.

matic tendency to precipitate us into it:[22] other things being equal, we find it natural to try to rank cognitive subject positions in point of authority, either on a critical or (at worst, so to speak) on an uncritical basis.[23] But then the question arises: why shouldn't this work of negotiation and selection, with its inbuilt capacity to protect our realist assumptions from the potential sceptical threat posed by the experience of "arguments breaking down",[24] be just as feasible in principle under conditions of disorientation as it is under those of tradition and hierarchy? After all, the relatively uncontroversial extension of the concept of *phronesis* in Aristotle's social world could not relieve individuals, in their ethical capacity, of the burden of exercising judgement as to what the *phronimos* would say about this or that concrete situation (cf. 1106b36–1107a2, read in conjunction with 1109b20–23; also 1137b19–24 and context on the related quality of *epieikeia*, "equity"). In so far as Aristotle was telling his audience that they had to be prepared to resolve uncertainties of this kind to the best of their ability *en passant*, he was asking them to accept the fact that not all questions about the legitimate range of application of an ethical concept are settled in advance, even for someone whose usage sets the standard for mastery of that concept.[25] And from this formal point of view our own position is no different from theirs: what sets us apart

---

22. This is not to say that such episodes are necessarily devoid of epistemological significance. Cf. J. Annas & J. Barnes, *The modes of scepticism: ancient texts and modern interpretations* (Cambridge: Cambridge University Press, 1985), p. 162.
23. S. Freud, *New introductory lectures on psychoanalysis* (London: Penguin, 1973), p. 96, may shed some light on the uncritical mode of ranking: "[The super-ego] is also the vehicle of the ego-ideal by which the ego measures itself, which it emulates, and whose demand for ever greater perfection it strives to fulfil. There is no doubt that this ideal is the precipitate of the old picture of the parents, the expression of admiration for the perfection which the child then attributed to them."
24. Cf. P. Foot, "Moral arguments", in *Virtues and vices* (Oxford: Basil Blackwell, 1978), pp. 96–109.
25. This fact persists unaltered even if the knowledge such a person possesses about the meaning of terms such as "just", "brave" or "generous" is available in the guise of an explicit definition. For "definition is of the universal and of the form" (*Meta.* 1036a28–29); as such, it cannot contain within itself a rule for the correct subsumption of particulars under the universal in question. (That is why "if language is to be a means of communication there must be agreement not only in definitions but also (queer as this may sound) in judgements": L. Wittgenstein, *Philosophical investigations*, G. E. M. Anscombe (trans.) (Oxford: Basil Blackwell, 1967), Pt. I, para. 242).

is simply the more problematic and inconclusive character of our ethical formation.

There is a further reason to resist the view that under conditions of disorientation it is impossible to sustain the conviction that our ethical judgements can (sometimes) achieve truth. Again, this takes the form of a reminder that our own ethical formation – the problematic and inconclusive affair just mentioned – has an important structural feature in common with the more manageable one envisaged by Aristotle. This feature consists in the fact that for us, as for the classical Aristotelian subject, the organizing principle of *paideia* is the need to acquire habits of evaluative judgement – and, *pari passu*, motivational dispositions – that are progressively more independent of immediate stimulation.

It is this principle that governs the development from a system of practical concerns focused exclusively on current physical and/or emotional needs (*to hedu*), via one in which such needs are ordered and controlled by a strategy for their efficient longer-term satisfaction (*to sumpheron*), towards the ultimate destination of an ability to be moved to action by what is not even in one's long-term personal interest, where "interest" is understood in a sub-ethical way (i.e. to be moved by the notions of *to kalon* and *to aischron*). The application of the principle is perhaps easier to recognize at the earlier of these stages – one learns to forgo immediate pleasure for the sake of a more solid good – but provided we can be convinced that there is such a value as *to kalon*, and that practical conflicts can occur in which this value deserves to take precedence over expediency, we shall see the same principle in action at the point where agents have to learn to do violence to their own (sub-ethical) interests in the service of the virtues. This learning process can be equated from one point of view with the construction of an individual will, according to the archaic conception of "will" recently explained and endorsed by Bernard Williams:[26] not an inherently moral capacity, but a capacity to refuse the solicitations of feeling in order to carry out *whatever* course of action one may think best after deliberation. (Such a capacity will of course be *contingently* supportive of morality, i.e. it will be so on condition that the learner comes to accept the primacy of *to kalon* where the latter's claims conflict with those of other values.)

---

26. B. Williams, *Shame and necessity* (Berkeley: University of California Press, 1993), ch. 2.

Now, it seems to me that an "Aristotelian" ethical theory, meaning one that gives to *phronesis* the sort of centrality I have described, can adjust itself to the demands of modernity by renewed reference to this principle of emancipation from the immediate. Admittedly, the adjustment depends on giving the principle an unorthodox application, since it asks us to consign to the status of (relative) immediacy the very thing that originally figured as the *telos* of our emancipation from the immediate – that is, a sensitivity to the claims of *to kalon* as construed by our local community. But the more abstract ideal of *not being unduly ready to accept the apparent good at face value* remains in force. Someone who successfully completes Aristotle's form of ethical *paideia* acquires a standard – namely, that of compatibility with the demands of *to kalon* – by which to identify as not really worthy of pursuit what may have appeared worthy from some less adequate perspective, e.g. that of instinct or of (mere) prudence. Analogously, someone who projects the principle governing this *paideia* into the new context created by modernity acquires a standard by which to criticize, in turn, the adequacy of the perspective that their local upbringing has taught them to think of as that of the virtuous person.

Here too Williams' recent work offers a point of reference, this time in the form of the "abstracted, improved, neighbour lodged in one's inner life"[27] – the figure whose imagined reactions of scorn or indignation can deter us from a contemplated course of action. Can this image be placed at the service of a moral realism built around the notions of *phronesis* and *paideia*, yet sensitive to the "modern" demand for an account of moral consciousness that will not condemn us to "social heteronomy"?[28] With the latter demand in mind, it is time to see whether we can characterize the "abstracted, improved, neighbour" in terms of a more exacting rationalism than the one available directly from Aristotle.

I suggested earlier that, so far as we are concerned, what is most readily acceptable in the ethics of Aristotle is its non-foundational component, while the foundational component marks the site of a theoretical problem to be solved according to our own lights. Now, the occurrence of the term "heteronomy" is an invitation to seek guidance at this point from Kant, and in particular to recall his list of the "maxims of common human understanding." These are: "(1) to

---

27. Ibid., p. 98.
28. Ibid.

think for oneself; (2) to think from the standpoint of everyone else; (3) always to think consistently."[29] It is the second maxim, which Kant calls that of "enlarged thought", that is of most interest here. In itself this maxim simply expresses the general principle that in the critical appraisal of our own judgement we must try to accord recognition to every possible point of view from which it might be regarded; it tells us not to overvalue the immediate (the obvious aspect of things) at the expense of the remote. However, the paths of "enlarged thought" now diverge. If we continue, with Kant, along the rationalist track, we shall make certain exceptions to the requirement of identification with *every* point of view – exceptions reflecting the idea that what commands respect as an "end in itself" is *rational* nature, i.e. not any old manifestation of the subjectivity of a natural being that is also (in some degree) rational, but just those that are free from hostility to the work of reason – in this case, the co-ordination of different individual wills.[30] On the other hand, we may decline to enter this qualification to the universalist demand and thus commit ourselves, instead, to an empiricist model of practical rationality in which every subjective preference is treated as a brute fact equally entitled, so far as its content is concerned, to influence deliberation.[31]

Although Kant and Aristotle have standardly been portrayed as representing opposed positions in moral philosophy,[32] I believe it is the former (Kantian) and not the latter (empiricist) course that offers the prospect of a modernist "enlargement" of the notion of *phronesis*.

---

29. I. Kant, *Critique of aesthetic judgement*, J. C. Meredith (trans.) (Oxford: Oxford University Press, 1952), para. 294.
30. Cf. O. O'Neill, *Constructions of reason: explorations of Kant's practical philosophy* (Cambridge: Cambridge University Press, 1989), pp. 19–20; also Kant, *The metaphysical principles of virtue*, tr. J. Ellington (Indianapolis: Bobbs-Merrill, 1964), p. 46: "If it is to be my duty to promote happiness as my end, then it must be the happiness of other men whose (*permitted*) end I thereby make mine too" (my emphasis).
31. See e.g. R. M. Hare, *Moral thinking: its levels, method and point* (Oxford: Oxford University Press, 1981), pp. 109–110 and context: "I can see no reason for not adopting the same solution here [sc. in cases of conflict between the preferences of two or more persons] as we do in cases where our own preferences conflict with one another."
32. This portrayal no longer finds automatic acceptance. See e.g. T. Engberg-Pedersen, *Aristotle's theory of moral insight* (Oxford: Oxford University Press, 1983), ch. 10; A. W. Moore, "A Kantian view of moral luck", *Philosophy* **65**, 1990, pp. 297–321; R. B. Louden, *Morality and moral theory* (Oxford: Oxford University Press, 1992), ch. 6.

ARISTOTELIAN ETHICS & THE "ENLARGEMENT OF THOUGHT"

For *phronesis* is a normative concept – that of excellence or correctness in practical judgement (NE 1140a25–28, b4–6). And when it comes to continuing our ethical formation beyond the limits of a local culture, the way to preserve this element of normativity is to ask ourselves whether there is some other perspective, itself unobjectionable, from which our own way of going on looks like a proper object of scorn or resentment, and which we have failed to take into account. Only where this distinctively ethical question receives the answer "yes" do we find ourselves exposed to the demand for self-reconstruction – or as Aristotle might have put it, to the *pathos* or quasi-*pathos* of shame (*aidos*), which he regards as appropriate to a state of incomplete formation (since it makes us receptive to moral guidance, and hence capable of improvement: 1128b16–21). However, whereas Aristotle associates such incompleteness firmly with youth, and regards shame as unsuitable in an older person (who should have had time to eliminate any cause for it), a formative process that takes place under conditions of disorientation cannot guarantee ever to make the learner safe from unfamiliar kinds of critical gaze; although we can still hope to gain in ethical competence by submitting to this process, the requirements of "enlarged thought" are such as to prevent anyone from emerging definitively (even if "definitively" never really meant more than "for practical purposes") from the position of the learner. This is not a flaw in the account of moral rationality now being developed, but a feature it has to have in order to display the fallibility – the merely provisional character – of even our best warranted conceptions of *phronesis*.

But how are we to tell whether there is anything "objectionable" about a given perspective from which we ourselves may be open to objection? If this question is unanswerable, there will be no way to distinguish cases where the hostile judgement expresses a point of view with which we are implicitly identified from those where it expresses one that we have discounted.

One possibility would be to answer the question on formalist lines. An "unobjectionable" point of view would then be one informed by the intention to take all points of view into consideration *in so far as they were themselves informed by this same intention*; or in other words, what would demand respect would be a habit of practical thought that was "universal" in the sense of *respecting all other subject positions from which the demand for "universal" thinking was acknowledged*. Against this approach, though, there is the standard criticism of

Kant's ethics, which claims that without a tacit appeal to existing (substantive) values he cannot explain the nature of the constraints on what maxims we "can" universalize.[33] If there is merit in this criticism, then we shall make only limited progress by saying that an "unobjectionable" moral point of view, and hence one that can set itself up in legitimate opposition to our own, is simply one that meets these constraints.[34] What we must fall back on, therefore – and here Aristotle can again be our guide – is a policy of deciding by reference to their *content* which moral positions have to be taken seriously as potential sources of *aidos*-provoking, and hence educative, condemnation of our own conduct or character. The question for a conscientious ethical reasoner would then be the entirely open-ended one: is my present position *flawed* in some way not immediately apparent to me, but capable of becoming apparent on closer inspection?

It may appear at first glance to follow from this suggestion that no reasonably confident adult will ever have to face the demand for significant self-reconstruction, since the force of such demands, issuing as they do from a point of view significantly different from his or her own, can never be felt by the person in question; or conversely, that since their force *can* be felt, they cannot issue from any point of view different enough to enjoin change. I believe, though, that this appearance is misleading, for as Williams has noted:[35]

> It is a mistake to take that reductive step and to suppose that there are only two options: that the other in ethical thought must be an identifiable individual or a representative of the neighbours, on the one hand, or else be nothing at all except an echo chamber for my solitary moral voice . . . The internalised other is indeed abstracted and generalised and idealised, but he is potentially somebody rather than nobody, and somebody other than me.

What makes possible the continuation of *paideia* beyond the stage of "social heteronomy" is our disposition to place an abstract, idealized other – but one abstracted from information that we possess

---

33. See Hegel, *Philosophy of right*, para. 135 (including Remark).
34. We encounter here the problem of the "fanatic" familiar from Hare's work prior to his rapprochement with utilitarianism: see Hare, *Freedom and reason* (Oxford: Oxford University Press, 1963), ch. 9.
35. Williams, *Shame and necessity*, p. 84.

about *concrete* human realities[36] – in the role established by our early attachments, namely that of the subject of a gaze that provokes shame and the need for a renewal of self-love. It is this disposition to measure ourselves not just against the figure of the *phronimos* as locally construed, but against that of a *phronimos* putatively liberated from the various defects of the local mentality, that allows us to attach sense to the notion of truth (as opposed to conventional acceptability) in moral judgement. In other words, it is the enlargement of the Aristotelian scheme to include a post-conventional phase of *paideia* that brings this scheme into line with contemporary (or "modern") requirements for a realist position in ethics.

Meanwhile, who is the "idealized" other – or rather, how do we determine what such a being might think? On the general question of criteria for sound ethical judgement, the message of Aristotle – as of any other theorist for whom ethics is a matter of giving articulate and coherent expression to an existing moral consciousness – is that the philosopher, as such, has no special expertise. It may be worthwhile, though, to shift the emphasis of the previous paragraph and to point out that *deciding* whether or not I am justified in discounting any given instance of "neighbourly" censure, whether concrete or abstract in provenance, is a cognitive activity of *mine*. It is my capacity for seeing how things relate to the overall good – i.e. my practical reasoning powers, so far as these go – that I bring into play in making the decision. So it is my actual *ethos*, i.e. whatever has resulted from the particular ethical formation I have undergone to date, that supports any judgements I may make as to when I may need to submit to further formation, and of what kind. In this sense, *phronesis* is self-regulating – not just in the setting of a local and (relatively) terminable *paideia*, but also in that of a cosmopolitan and (relatively) interminable one. And this means that a view of ethics that incorporates a commitment to recognition-transcendent moral truth need not be as epistemologically barren as critics have sometimes claimed. For if my conception of the ideal *phronimos* – that is, my substantive conception of what would and would not be acceptable to this person – is arrived at critically or negatively, by a process of checking for error in successive new positions that come to my attention, then the inherent incompleteness of that conception will be a consequence of the fallibilist thought that I cannot say categorically that what now appears

---

36. Cf. Benhabib, *Situating the self*, ch. 5.

to me to be error-free will always continue to appear so. And more to the point for a defence of realism, *we* – meaning the totality of moral enquirers – cannot say this either; hence the substantive mind-set of the ideal *phronimos* is something that transcends not just my individual "recognitional" capacities, but our collective ones. The idea of recognition-transcendent truth in this strong (but not hyperbolical) sense hangs together with that of possible future revisions of opinion, and so with an acceptance of change.[37]

References

Annas, J. & J. Barnes. 1985. *The modes of scepticism: ancient texts and modern interpretations*. Cambridge: Cambridge University Press.
Benhabib, S. 1992. *Situating the self: gender, community and postmodernism in contemporary ethics*. Cambridge: Polity.
Burnyeat, M. F. 1980. Aristotle on learning to be good. In A. Rorty (1980), 69–92.
Engberg-Pedersen, T. 1983. *Aristotle's theory of moral insight*. Oxford: Oxford University Press.
Evans, G. 1982. *The varieties of reference*. Oxford: Oxford University Press.
Foot, P. 1978. *Virtues and vices*. Oxford: Blackwell.
Foster, M. B. 1935. *The political philosophies of Plato and Hegel*. Oxford: Oxford University Press.
Freud, S. 1973. *New introductory lectures on psychoanalysis*. London: Penguin.
Geras, N. 1983. *Marx and human nature: refutation of a legend*. London: Verso.
Kant, I. 1952. *Critique of aesthetic judgement*, tr. J. C. Meredith. Oxford: Oxford University Press.
Kant, I. 1964. *The metaphysical principles of virtue*, tr. J. Ellington. Indianapolis: Bobbs–Merrill.
Hare, R. M. 1963. *Freedom and reason*. Oxford: Oxford University Press.
Hare, R. M. 1981. *Moral thinking: its levels, method and point*. Oxford: Oxford University Press.
Hegel, G. W. F. 1952. *Philosophy of right*, tr. T. M. Knox. Oxford: Oxford University Press.
Louden, R. B. 1992. *Morality and moral theory*. Oxford: Oxford University Press.
MacIntyre, A. 1981. *After virtue*. London: Duckworth.

---

37. I am grateful for comments on an earlier draft of this paper to Robert Heinaman, Stephen Williams, and members of the "B" Club at the University of Cambridge.

Mackie, J. L. 1977. *Ethics: inventing right and wrong*. London: Penguin.
McDowell, J. 1980. The role of eudaimonia in Aristotle's ethics. In A. Rorty (1980), 359–76.
Moore, A. W. 1990. A Kantian view of moral luck. *Philosophy* **65**, 297–321.
Nagel, T. 1979. *Mortal questions*. Cambridge: Cambridge University Press.
Nussbaum, M. 1988. Nature, function and capability: Aristotle on political distribution. *Oxford Studies in Ancient Philosophy*, supplementary vol., 145–84.
Nussbaum, M. 1992. Human functioning and social justice: in defense of Aristotelian essentialism. *Political Theory* **20**, 202–46.
O'Neill, O. 1989. *Constructions of reason: explorations of Kant's practical philosophy*. Cambridge: Cambridge University Press.
Rorty, A. (ed.) 1980. *Essays on Aristotle's ethics*. Berkeley: University of California Press.
Rorty, R. 1989. *Community, irony and solidarity*. Cambridge: Cambridge University Press.
Rorty, R. 1991. Feminism and pragmatism. *Michigan Quarterly Review* **30**, 231–58.
Sayre-McCord, G. (ed.) 1988. *Essays on moral realism*. Ithaca: Cornell University Press.
Williams, B. 1976. Wittgenstein and idealism. In his *Moral luck*, 2–39. Cambridge: Cambridge University Press.
Williams, B. 1985. *Ethics and the limits of philosophy*. London: Fontana/Collins.
Williams, B. 1993. *Shame and necessity*. Berkeley: University of California Press.
Wittgenstein, L. 1967. *Philosophical investigations*, tr. G. E. M. Anscombe. Oxford: Blackwell.
Wright, C. 1992. *Truth and objectivity*. Cambridge, Mass.: Harvard University Press.

Pitfalls in doing post-Hegelian ethics with Aristotle: a reply to Sabina Lovibond

TROELS ENGBERG-PEDERSEN

In a 1992 review article in the *Times Literary Supplement* on the present state of moral philosophy, Martha Nussbaum made the following claim: "This [meaning the present one] is one of the few periods in the history of Anglo-American moral philosophy when close historical scholarship [namely, scholarship concerned with the virtue theories of Plato, Aristotle, and the Hellenistic thinkers] has proven a leading and creative force in the field as a whole."[1] Sabina Lovibond's paper fits Nussbaum's description exactly, not because it is itself a piece of close historical scholarship, but because it presupposes that scholarship and then uses Aristotle to address central contemporary issues.

The paper is stimulating and I am in sympathy with her attempt to develop the notion of an "enlargement of thought." Here, however, I see my main task as being (constructively) critical in helping us towards reaching some kind of reasoned view on Aristotle and (modern) moral realism. Indeed, stimulating as Lovibond's paper is, it is also very courageous and even bold. She wishes to defend a form of moral realism that combines insights from Aristotle and Hegel while overcoming any tension between these two philosophers by bringing in a third major contributor, Kant, and then by combining the insight derived from Kant with another one to be found in (of all people) Bernard Williams! The canvas is broad and one needs a steady hand to keep the whole thing together. In the end, I shall argue, it cannot be done.

---

1. *Times Literary Supplement*, no. 4657, July 3, 1992, p. 10.

A basic problem relating to Lovibond's Aristotelian *persona*

Lovibond obviously does not wish to engage in Aristotelian exegesis. What Aristotle himself meant is not at issue. That is fine and I have absolutely no quarrel in principle with the kind of thinking-on along basically Aristotelian lines that Lovibond undertakes. In a modern philosophical context one must surely be allowed to make whatever independent use one can of ideas derived from any philosopher, including Aristotle – as long as certain conditions are fulfilled. Thus, it must be entirely clear, first, that one is not in fact doing exegesis; secondly, that the project is to be independently evaluated in terms of its own intrinsic coherence and the illumination it yields; and thirdly, that one might skip any reference to the theory's pedigree – in this case "Aristotelian."

This, however, is where my problems with Lovibond's project begin. For as we shall see, these conditions appear not to be fulfilled. What she does is to construct a certain *persona*, an "Aristotelian" faced with modern issues. This person is identified as one who adopts four positions that serve to define "an 'Aristotelian' ethics" (p. 99). The first two are well known and fairly obvious. There is first the idea that human nature fixes what we can count as normal and successful human functioning. Secondly, there is the idea that human beings are by nature rational and social. The last two features of the four focus on *phronesis*, "practical wisdom" or "moral insight." One is that human beings *qua* human have the ability to appraise particular situations in the light of an overall conduct of life as being either conducive to it or working against it. The other is that *phronesis* is a competence in realizing a particular kind of life, namely one informed by a correct sense of value. In other words, there is such a thing as correct judgement about the ethical, and *phronesis* is such a judgement.

These four positions are evidently meant to capture essential features of the ethics of Aristotle, the philosopher, himself. Equally obviously they should express the "Aristotelian" theory that Lovibond herself wishes to endorse. But the overlap between Aristotle and Lovibond's "Aristotelian" theory is not complete. For the major part of her argument is taken up by an attempt to develop a perspective on moral thought (and hence the activity engaged in by the *phronimos*) that incorporates vital elements from broadly modern perceptions that were first formulated by Hegel. Moreover, Lovibond even states explicitly that when she brings in this perspective she is no longer faithful to "the spirit of Aristotle" (p. 110).

So Lovibond's own "Aristotelian" theory both is and is not Aristotle's. It probably aims to stay as close to Aristotle as possible, but when necessary it is also prepared to leave him behind.

As I said, there is nothing wrong with this in itself. But it means that the fact that a given idea was Aristotle's must not be allowed to figure *anywhere* in the argument for Lovibond's *reconstructed* Aristotelian position. Once she has taken that single, vitally important step away from presenting Aristotle's theory to presenting her own, no matter how "Aristotelian" in inspiration, she is bound to argue her case on her own, in complete independence of what Aristotle may have thought on the particular issue.

As I see it, Lovibond does not sufficiently live up to this demand. Thus, when we look more closely at her arguments I think we must conclude that she moves too unselfconsciously for comfort between finding shelter in the shadow of Aristotle himself and arguing independently for some of her positions, primarily those acknowledged by her not to be originally Aristotelian ones. And even here she seems too prone to think that if a position can in some way be shown to follow along basically Aristotelian lines, then by the same token it has been shown to be most likely *right*. To my mind that just will not do.

The issue should be clear enough. Had Lovibond adopted a completely Aristotelian *persona* in such a way that it would genuinely count whether what "she" said was or was not something Aristotle either himself does say or very likely would say, then *"she"* would not have to argue "her" (that is, Aristotle's) case when that was being confronted with other views. Since, however, she adopts an Aristotelian *persona* of a different kind, one that is also her own, the need to provide *independent* argument lies with *her*.

Lovibond might accept this very simple point but come back as follows: Why should we not take it initially that Aristotle is likely to be right? In other words, the onus of proof lies on those who deny Aristotle's position, not on those who adopt it. But is the argument of *onus probandi* of any use in a case like this? Is it reasonable to claim of any position in this area that it has a favoured status to begin with? I would strongly deny that – even when the authority that is being invoked is that of Aristotle!

Lovibond might come back again as follows: What I claim to be right is not just Aristotle, but Aristotle as reconstructed and as reconstructed in all places where there is a need for that. In principle that would make sense. In practice, however, and certainly in Lovibond's practice, the project remains a highly risky one. If one *starts out* from Aristotle, is it likely that one will *press on* to reconstruct him *wherever* that is needed? Is it not likely that one will be tempted from time to time to stay with an idea of Aristotle's which appears intuitively attractive, just because it is Aristotle's, or at least without giving adequate attention to potential counter-arguments? Similarly, is it not likely that one will *a priori* find non-Aristotelian ideas less attractive, just because one has started out from Aristotle? All through there is a real danger that when it comes to defending a theory which is not meant to be Aristotle's but one's own, one will insufficiently question its Aristotelian components just because one has started out from his theory. To my mind Lovibond does not avoid this danger.

To summarize so far. Lovibond's stated aim is to consider "how, if at all, *current* 'realist' views in ethics can find support in the ethics of Aristotle" (p. 99, my emphasis). Her overall strategic line seems to be this: If she succeeds in defending a reconstructed form of Aristotelianism that incorporates certain (universalistic) features of moral thought that we as moderns find mandatory, then, since Aristotle's theory is a realist one, and since she shall also have succeeded in meeting several modern sceptical arguments against bringing in those features at all, the reconstructed Aristotelian theory supports a valid form of modern moral realism. Against this I suggest that, at the very centre of her undertaking, Lovibond owes us arguments to show why one should adopt Aristotle's position, and its various components, in the first place.

In what follows I shall highlight some sections of her argument, which I take to show that she has not sufficiently liberated her "Aristotelian" *persona* from Aristotle himself. Thus, at one point she is dangerously near to engaging in exegesis of Aristotle (actually in false exegesis) in order to show that something she herself finds interesting (as part of her *reconstructed* Aristotelian position) is to be found in Aristotle himself. But why that turn of the argument? Is it sufficient for an idea to be right that it is Aristotle's? Similarly, on two other occasions where she argues against a certain modern, non-Aristotelian view, the force of her argument seems to derive merely from the fact that it was also Aristotle's. Finally, I shall suggest, just because Lovibond has not adequately liberated her own Aristotle-*inspired* position from Aristotle himself, she fails to consider adequately the *internal* consistency of the position she advocates, irrespective of the extent to which it is backed up by Aristotle.

A fallacious move and the first main argument

A notable feature of Lovibond's paper is that, of the four defining characteristics of an "Aristotelian" ethics, her central interest is in the last two ideas – those focusing on *phronesis* – rather than (as one might have expected) the first two ideas. For instance, she states (quite rightly) that "Aristotle has no difficulty in principle with the thought that there are truths about the subject matter of ethics" (p. 102) and quotes three passages that very clearly support this. But in her original paper Lovibond went on to claim that these passages suggest that the intellectual virtue of *phronesis* is "conceptually prior to that which the *phronimos* ... is competent to observe", and that "For us [namely as putative Aristotelians], moral *rationality* is a more primitive notion than moral *reality*." Although these sentences have been dropped from her paper as published in the present volume, she still says that "such resources as we have for attaching to our view the various 'realist' characteristics identified in the technical literature seem to depend on a prior ontological commitment on our part to the quality of *phronesis*" (p. 103).

Here is a case where, as I see it, Lovibond's interests clash with Aristotle. What the three passages show is, I take it, that Aristotle had what we may call a "robust realist" view of the subject matter of ethics, one that was in no way genuinely worried by apparently conflicting claims in the area of ethics. He would never suggest, indeed he would hardly see the point of suggesting, that moral rationality is a more primitive notion than moral reality, that it is prior to it both conceptually and ontologically. And there is no pressure whatever in the three passages towards moving in that direction. Lovibond, by contrast, finds the idea interesting and worth working on. As it happens, it plays a crucial role in her final argument where she uses the notion of an enlargement of thought (that is, moral rationality) to support moral realism. So: well and good! But why does she attempt to buttress her suggestion by ascribing it (falsely) to Aristotle himself? I can see only one explanation: because she thinks that if she can manage to stay sufficiently clearly within the Aristotelian orbit, even where she incorporates ideas that are not found, just like that, in the philosopher himself, then moral realism will be vindicated – *by Aristotle, the moral realist*. However, the vital underlying premiss has not been argued for (but is simply assumed): *Aristotle was right*.

Consider another example of this unhealthy reliance on Aristotle. After she has identified her own "Aristotelian" position, Lovibond spends some time on developing certain characteristic features of the modern situation, including its Hegelian requirement that any given moral view must be able to meet rational criticism. From then on, the brunt of the paper is taken up with three main arguments by which Lovibond wishes to defend against modern relativistic sceptics the view that we can "have 'our way of life', our [local] conception of *phronesis*, displayed not just as a brute cultural datum but as something with a rational claim on us" (pp. 107–108).

The first main argument brings in what she recognizes as being a "foundational" element in the Aristotelian ethical theory she identified to begin with, the first of its four features, the one concerned with human nature and functioning. This is the feature that insists on giving "a general account of human capacities and of the constraints these place on what we can recognize as a good life for human beings" (p. 107).

In her remarks on this feature Lovibond urges us to take seriously the idea that "local conceptions of *phronesis* can be evaluated by reference to the norm of *a way of life appropriate to human beings* in virtue of our specific characteristics" (p. 109, Lovibond's emphasis). That, of course, sounds Aristotelian enough, but there is no reason *why we* should take the idea seriously in view of the well known extreme difficulty of stating in any interesting way what Lovibond later calls "the universal preconditions of a satisfactory human existence" (p. 109). Instead, there is first a reference to "one of the most important types of 'realism' in current moral and political controversy" as showing "an obvious debt to the Aristotelian assumption" on this score (p. 109). But that seems to make the argumentative circle full: we should take Aristotle's idea seriously because it fits a certain type of modern realism – which is derived from it. Secondly there is a bald insistence that we can "legitimately pronounce on what may or may not be detrimental to the wellbeing of people whose social environment is radically different from our own" and that we can "sometimes say with confidence that the conditions of life of some group of people are such as no *human being* should have to suffer" (p. 109, Lovibond's emphasis). To a very small extent, that is no doubt true. But if it is meant to refer substantively to specific, statable features of life that must be fulfilled by *any* way of life that qualifies for being "appropriate to human beings", the yield of this reference to human nature will notoriously be very small. So much has happened between Aristotle and us over a whole range of phenomena, from changes in material circumstances to shifts in cultural perception, that one cannot just rely on Aristotle here. Instead, one needs to engage and discuss it directly. Lovibond does not do this, and the reason appears to lie in her misconstrual of the argumentative obligations incurred by her adoption of an Aristotelian *persona*.

The second argument: realism unabashed by the experience of failure to persuade

There is somewhat more substance to her two remaining arguments, which focus on what she calls the non-foundational element in her Aristotelian ethical theory, "what the theory has to say about the acquisition of the moral virtues, and . . . *phronesis*" (p. 107). (In Aristotle's own theory, by contrast, it is not at all clear that this element is "non-foundational".) This is where she attempts to defend her proposal that one may combine the Aristotelian specificity of *phronesis* with modern universalism, the idea that we should hold ourselves "accountable not just to those within some arbitrarily determined community that is supposed to be 'ours', but to anyone with whom we are capable of establishing communication" (p. 109).

The first of the two arguments refers to what Lovibond calls a "realism unabashed by the experience of failure to persuade" (p. 111) that she finds in Aristotle, a "combination of *ontological commitment to a domain of fact* with *acceptance that the facts in question will not be equally accessible to everyone*" (p. 111). That is fine as it stands since it describes very precisely the kind of robust moral realism that we do find in Aristotle. However, Lovibond wishes to endorse the idea as her own. And she quotes John McDowell to show that he agrees. However, since McDowell is, to some extent at least, himself influenced by Aristotle, this looks a bit like the circular type of reference we noted earlier.

However, Lovibond does attempt some independent discussion of the issue. She admits that it demands "more coolness of nerve" to insist in the modern situation that "we understand our opponents better than they understand themselves" (p. 111). Indeed, she claims, we must take the difficulty involved in this entirely seriously. Still (so she seems to be arguing) if the strategy of discounting one of two competing positions as epistemically inferior to the other worked in antiquity, then "why shouldn't this work of negotiation and selection . . . be just as feasible in principle under conditions of disorientation as it is [or was] under those of tradition and hierarchy?" (p. 112). In other words, the difference between then and now is not so marked as we may have thought.

But why? Even though the two positions (McDowell/Lovibond's and Aristotle's) are identical in formulation, it seems evident to me that they must be very different in content. Is it not rather clear that very different things will go into the "experience of failure to persuade" in either case? In Aristotle this experience was fitted smoothly into a system (of who had knowledge and who not) that was social and markedly hierarchical. There were those who knew and those who did not. And so much the worse for the latter, who were just "uneducated." *Could* we say the same with any degree of confidence in a modern situation of failure to persuade? Does our lack of a comparable social, hierarchical system to support a certainty unabashed by failure to persuade not make our experience of such a failure quite different from what it was for Aristotle? I emphasize the social differences here between then and now, the far more pervasive democratization of modern Western societies than anything to be found in antiquity, even in democratic Athens. Also highly relevant are the differences with regard to the notion of individual autonomy and self-determination (Hegel again!). These differences are themselves an essential part of the "conditions of disorientation" of which Lovibond speaks. They will surely make an enormous difference to the experience of failure to persuade.

Here too one might mention the modern, heightened perception of cultural differences. We do seem to find ourselves confronted with other general ways of living, in relation to which we find it difficult to get a proper hold on anything that might serve as a criterion for branding them as either better or worse than our own. They are different, very different, but are they better or worse? Just how should we compare them? It hardly matters whether in either of these respects the difference between the ancient situation and the modern one is absolute or only relative. It is, I think, big.

Again, however, the main point is that Lovibond appears to be too wedded to Aristotle himself (as opposed to her own reconstructed Aristotelian position) to engage in substantial discussion and argument where she needed to do that.

The third argument: emancipation from the immediate

Finally there is Lovibond's second argument for the idea that the difference between then and now is not so marked. She suggests that just as there is an idea in Aristotle of "emancipation from the immediate" (namely, *from* perceptions focused on pleasure or immediate satisfaction *via* those focused on the beneficial or longer-term satisfaction *to* those focused on what is morally good), in a similar way we may speak of a more abstract ideal of *"not being unduly ready to accept the apparent good at face value"* (p. 114, Lovibond's emphasis), including the *kalon* as construed by our local community. She notes that this is a somewhat unorthodox application of the principle. However, she develops it in more detail in order to establish a credible form of moral deliberation that remains tied to the perceptions from which the moral deliberator starts, but is also able to engage in a real way with other perspectives, perspectives *from* which the deliberator may then consider his own perspective. For the first part of this she draws on the image recently introduced by Bernard Williams of the "abstracted, improved, neighbour lodged in one's inner life." For the second part she draws on Kant in an avowedly rationalist, genuinely Kantian interpretation of his demand that we think from the standpoint of everyone else.

This section of the paper appears to me particularly interesting, and personally I am in much sympathy with Lovibond's emphasis on our "disposition to measure ourselves not just against the figure of the *phronimos* as locally construed, but against that of a *phronimos* putatively liberated from the various defects of the local mentality" (p. 118). But my worries continue. First, have we not after all moved so far away from Aristotle that the internal coherence of Lovibond's theory, which was elsewhere more straightforwardly Aristotelian (in fact too much so), is in serious danger of breaking down? Secondly, is Lovibond right to say that the modernizing picture of moral thought that she develops supports moral realism? Is the real reason why she thinks this not, once more, that right from the start she has decided to take Aristotle as her guiding figure – and he was a moral realist?

Take the first point. At the very end of the paper, Lovibond states that the picture she has presented is meant to incorporate a strong commitment to recognition-transcendent moral truth, since it implies not only the fallibilist thought that I cannot say categorically that what now appears to me to be error free will always continue to appear so, but also that *we* – meaning the *totality* of moral inquirers – cannot say that. This, of course, is a realist claim, but it is also one that goes *directly* against Aristotle's own moral epistemology. For him, as Lovibond herself quotes elsewhere, "what everyone agrees upon, we call true (or declare to be the case)" (*NE* 1172b36–1173a1). Or as he also says in the *Rhetoric* (1355a15–17): "human beings are by nature sufficiently disposed with relation to the true and most often they reach the truth". This is a simple kind of realism that does not even feel the need for anything like the idea of recognition-transcendent truth. It is therefore different from the kind of realism that Lovibond endorses.

Note then that the kind of epistemological optimism I have just referred to seems to lie behind parts of Aristotle's ethical theory, which Lovibond too endorses, in particular the line of thought that goes into the *ergon* argument (compare Lovibond's first main argument) to the effect that there are statable specific characteristics of human nature that fix what counts as normal and successful human functioning. But then, is Lovibond not committed, within the confines of a single paper, to two different types of moral realism? That is not reassuring. In other words, it seems to me that there is a distinct risk that Lovibond's position will fall apart as soon as one begins to regard it as a position of its own, independently of whether and how it is also (properly) Aristotelian. In developing her own position, Lovibond has not liberated herself sufficiently from Aristotle.

The second point: does Lovibond's picture of moral thought support moral realism? Not just as it stands. The fact that we do play the universalizing game in moral deliberation certainly does not by itself ensure a realist dimension to that exercise. Even if we see truth as a kind of regulative idea implied in the very practice of measuring ourselves against other perspectives, it does not follow that there is such a thing as *the* truth in moral matters as something to be discovered by that kind of deliberation. There is a whole range of positions in modern moral philosophy (from Simon Blackburn to Bernard Williams) that find non-realist ways of accounting for genuine moral reflection, even of a universalizing kind. However, Lovibond thinks that the realist conclusion follows. But again I suspect the reason lies not in her argument but in her set-up. If from the beginning she basically accepts an Aristotelian framework, which certainly is a realist one, and then only wishes to see how it may be upheld in a manner that takes account of later ideas (including the challenge to local views formulated by Hegel), then giving sense (as she calls it, p. 118) to the notion of truth in moral judgement will perhaps be sufficient. But then, as I have insisted, the question becomes that of why one should accept the Aristotelian framework to begin with.

The local character of Aristotle's own moral realism

I have focused these remarks on the lack of independent argument in Lovibond's paper for her reconstructed Aristotelian position. That is at the same time somewhat tedious and absolutely necessary. But let us ask in conclusion: could she have provided convincing arguments?

Perhaps one cannot exclude that in advance. On the other hand, the discrepancy between Aristotle's own moral realism as reflected in his epistemological optimism in ethics and the kind of moral realism that Lovibond envisages towards the end of her paper makes one doubt that the attempt could ever be successful. I suspect that the problem lies in trying to keep together the two halves of an Aristotelian ethical theory as identified by Lovibond, the "foundational" one (cf. the two first defining features) and the one focusing on *phronesis* – *when the latter is being given a non-"foundational"* (and so, I have claimed, non-Aristotelian) *interpretation*. Lovibond is to be commended on the clarity and forthrightness with which she brings in some of the basic differences in what we as moderns are prepared to count as valid justification of a moral position – Hegel's principle of subjectivity and the need for rational, universalizing justification. But when she then goes on to develop her own version of moral deliberation in order to meet Hegel's challenge, she should acknowledge that she has in fact left Aristotle behind. One might say that the difficulty begins very early in her discussion when she takes Aristotle's focus on *phronesis* to imply that moral rationality is ontologically prior to moral reality, in the sense of that which the *phronimos* is competent to observe. Aristotle would have disagreed and this already indicates that there is no valid bridge between Aristotle himself, or a position that is sufficiently close to Aristotle to count as recognizably Aristotelian, and a valid modern form of moral realism. Aristotle and the modern issues are just too far apart.

But of course Aristotle was a moral realist. Indeed, he was a "robust realist" in ethics. As Lovibond herself says, "Aristotle has no difficulty in principle with the thought that there are truths about the subject matter of ethics" (p. 102). He was of course aware that there was contention and disagreement over ethical issues, and more here than perhaps anywhere else. Still, he apparently thought that he could understand well enough all the various things that were said and also explain the apparent disagreements, in other words, solve the various *aporiai* – he could do all this sufficiently well to have felt no need to provide any explicit defence of the view that there are truths about the subject matter of ethics. Aristotle just "saw" that that is so (just as he "saw" it in biology) and went straight on to explain what those truths are. (And let us not forget that, if we wish to be Aristotelian moral realists, we should also be prepared to find some way of endorsing his – very local – accounts of the moral virtues.)

To my mind, that kind of moral realism is no longer tenable, for many reasons, some of which Lovibond has herself expounded very well. Far too many changes have occurred, historically, during those more than twenty centuries in the basic social fabric and the human self-understanding that it engenders to make Aristotle's ethical optimism a viable option for us. Instead, we should read Aristotle, at least when he is addressing substantive ethical and political issues, as a paradigm example of the kind of moral philosophizing or critical reflection that Bernard Williams claimed (in *Ethics and the limits of philosophy*[2]) to be the only legitimate form, reasoning within a tradition. That, by our lights, is what Aristotle did, even though he did not see himself in that way. And it is his enormous power to elucidate and shape the ordinary Greek consciousness to such a degree that it all came to hang together and came to make much internal sense that explains why he makes such interesting reading and continues to do so.

Personally, I believe that we need something in addition to this kind of internal reading of the classics (Aristotle and anyone else). We need the notion that Sabina Lovibond has interestingly begun to develop of an enlargement of moral thought. But I doubt that it can in

---

2. London, Fontana/Collins, 1985.

the end be fruitfully combined with Aristotle's account of *phronesis* and I do not see that it will by itself provide support for an adequate form of modern moral realism.

Aristotle and modern realism

DAVID CHARLES

1. Introduction

1.1 Aristotle in his discussion of what is pleasant, hot and sweet writes:

> It seems in these cases that what appears to the good person (pleasant, hot . . .) is really so. If this is correct, as it seems to be, and excellence and the good person are the measures of each thing, those things will be pleasures which appear so to him, and those things pleasant which he enjoys (NE 1176a15–19).[1]

Nor is this an isolated case. Elsewhere he notes:

> What appears (good) to the good person is truly good . . . for the good person discriminates each thing correctly and the truth in each matter appears to him . . . as the canon and measure of these things (1113a25–33).

In these passages, it appears that Aristotle holds both that the good discern what is good correctly and that they are the measure of what is good. And taken together this encourages the view that he holds the following claim:

☐ [a is good ↔ a seems good to the good].

1.2 This bi-conditional can be understood in a variety of ways. One

---

1. In this paper, all references will be to the *Nicomachean ethics* (*NE*) unless otherwise stated. I shall include the books common to the *Eudemian ethics* and the *Nicomachean ethics* as *Nicomachean*.

account, beginning with the left-hand side (LHS), presupposes an account of what is good given without reference to the right-hand side (RHS). Thus, "goodness" might be the name for a simple non-natural property understood in a way independent of our moral practices of approval and disapproval (as suggested by Moore or, in certain moods, Plato) which is, as a matter of fact, seen by the good person. While this accommodates the possibility of the good seeing what is good, it does not explain in any straightforward way how they are *measures* of what is good. Conversely, one might begin one's account with the RHS of the bi-conditional, and construct a theory of what is good from what seems good to the good. In one version of this viewpoint, one catalogues what we take to seem good to those we take to be good, and bases a theory of what is good on this. But this starting point, while it accommodates the thought that man is the measure of all things in (what I shall call) a Protagorean fashion, does less justice to the idea of the good person as one who sees what is good.[2] Equally, it fails to make proper sense of the ideal we have of aiming to make our thoughts and actions conform to what is good.

1.3 Aristotle, it is generally agreed, wishes to reject both the Platonist and the Protagorean readings of this bi-conditional. What is the nature of his alternative understanding? One view might run as follows:

> What is good is such as to appear good to the good person in a way analogous to that in which what is sweet is such as to appear sweet to the normal healthy observer. The good person is in turn understood as the one to whom what is good seems good. So no priority is given to either the RHS or LHS of the bi-conditional, in contrast to the Platonic or Protagorean reading of this bi-conditional. This view is non-Protagorean because one cannot represent what it is to seem good to the good except in terms which understand their practices as aimed at the good. But it is non-Platonic in that it does not attempt to characterize what is good in terms abstracted from human practices of praise and criticism.

---

2. There is considerable debate as to whether Protagoras himself was in this sense a "Protagorean." In this passage, I will be focusing only on the Protagoras "of legend."

This viewpoint appears to do justice to the idea of the good person as one who sees and measures what is good. Further, it suggests an attractive account of the structure of the *Nicomachean ethics* itself. Its starting point is wellbeing, characterized as a life of excellent activity (I.7, 1098a16–18). What is excellent activity? Activity chosen by the practically wise (II.6, 1106b36ff.). But who are the practically wise? Those who deliberate successfully towards wellbeing (VI.5, 1140a25–28). Thus, the good life is, it appears, characterized in terms of activities chosen by the practically wise, and they, in turn, are characterized as those who see what is good.

This account may appear circular and uninformative. However, for the proponent of the no priority reading, this form of circularity (if such it be) is far from uninformative. He takes it to show only that there is no external viewpoint from which to assess the comparative merits of wellbeing[3] (thus connected with virtue and practical wisdom) with the type of wellbeing favoured by the self-indulgent. Rather, wellbeing itself is to be understood in terms of its connections with these other terms. To break these connections is to give up talk of wellbeing altogether. The circle is not uninformative because it offers much information *en route* about the individual constituents and their interconnection.

In this paper, I shall examine how far Aristotle followed this strategy in the *Ethics*, and whether it provides the basis for a correct understanding of Aristotelian moral realism. I shall argue that, while Aristotle does not accept either the Platonist or the Protagorean understanding of the relevant bi-conditional, his viewpoint differs in certain important respects from that sketched above.

1.4   The idea of a realist mid-position between Platonism and Protagoreanism is an attractive one. In modern times, it has encouraged attempts to characterize moral realism in ways that do not involve classical versions of the correspondence theory of truth, or the thesis that the only genuine properties are those that play a role in the preferred basic scientific theory of the world and its efficient causal interactions, or the claim that the only genuine properties are those that are graspable in ways that do not essentially involve reference to

---

3. In particular, there can be no conception of human function or human nature specified independently of the views of the practically wise, and no set of morally neutral desires whose satisfaction constitutes wellbeing for us.

our particular practices or sensibilities. One impetus, in modern discussions, towards this viewpoint arises from Donald Davidson's writings on truth and interpretation. The understander (or radical interpreter) aims to give a theory of truth for utterances in the language to be interpreted, including such sentences as "This is red" or "This is disgraceful."[4] The relevant T. sentences will include:

"a is disgraceful" is true in L iff a is disgraceful.

The evidence for attributing a theory with these consequences is our success in rendering the speaker intelligible by our lights. This involves making him intelligible or reasonable by reference to features of reality as we see them to be. There is nothing more to there being moral values "out there" in the world than their playing this role in making people intelligible in the best interpretation of this type.

1.5 The precise characterization of this mid-position in both the general and the moral cases is a matter of considerable delicacy. For the sake of clarity, I shall be explicit on several points on which the more cautious may prefer to remain silent.

[A] While neither side of the original bi-conditional can be understood without reference to the other, the LHS is *explanatorily prior* in a certain form of rational explanation in which things merit approbation *because* they are good. [Role of Moral Properties in Rational Explanation].

[B] This objectivity conferring form of rational explanation is legitimate in moral cases where we can construct the relevant explanations from the inside (RHS). This is possible when our practices of approbation themselves contain coherent standards of criticism by which to judge particular reactions as well or ill judged, reasonable or unreasonable, noble or ignoble, etc. When our reactions are able to withstand this type of criticism we are justified in concluding that they are responses to objective properties. If our reactions cohere in certain ways, we will have the basis for a theory of (e.g.) human good and human harm. [Objectivity Secured by the Withstanding of Internal Criticism].

[C] In the moral case, there is no further basis for constructing

---

4. Donald Davidson, *Inquiries into truth and interpretation* (Oxford: Oxford University Press, 1984).

such standards apart from that described in [B]. There can be no theory of the LHS drawn from materials in any way independent of our actual responses to situations. In other cases (e.g. such as those concerning danger or colours) involving similar bi-conditionals, such as

☐ [a is a danger ↔ a merits fear],

an independent theory may be constructed of the LHS involving standards drawn from materials other than our actual or potential reactions, and couched in terms of what is actually life-threatening and what leads to injury or physical harm, etc. This background theory allows us to classify our fears as "unmerited" when we are afraid of what is not, properly speaking, dangerous. By contrast, in the moral case, there can be no theory of the human good which is, in this way, independent of our practices of approbation because we lack a reaction-independent theory of what the relevant properties are. All we have to go on is our reactions, and standards of criticism based on them. Approbations will be "unmerited" only when they clash with other of our reactions, or do not withstand criticism based on reactions of others.[5] The locus of authority, *the measure*, resides in our reactions (and the standards of reasonableness and nobility they encapsulate), not in an external theory of the good for man constructed from other materials. Indeed, there can be no validation of our moral judgements in a reaction-independent theory of the human good. [No Reaction-Independent Theory of Human Good].

[D] In the moral case, "given a not implausible holism", the relevant moral reactions form a self-contained group distinct from non-moral ones. If so, it follows from [C] that the theory of the human good constructed wholly on their basis will be an exclusively moral one. [No Non-Moral Basis for, or Ingredient in, the Theory of Human Good].

---

5. In the case of colours there may be a reaction-independent background theory, couched in terms of the different ways in which colours affect light, the physiology of our optical systems, etc. There is certainly good reason to believe that Aristotle thought that there is. This background theory would permit us to regard certain colour reactions as mistaken not because they do not cohere with other reactions (as in the moral case), etc., but because we have reaction-independent grounds for taking objects to have a certain colour. While creatures without sensibilities like ours could not grasp what redness is (in the way we do), the locus of authority in determining what is red may lie in some measure with the reaction-independent theory of colour by which our reactions are judged. If this were so, the cases of colour and value would be importantly distinct.

[E] Indeed, our relevant reasons may not even permit the construction of a systematic theory of the human good by reference to which we can endorse our particular reactions as worthwhile or reasonable. The locus of authority resides in our particular reactions to and views about what is reasonable in a variety of cases. A general theory could itself only be validated if it were underwritten by such case-specific reactions. However, in the light of the variety and complexity of the situations we face, there is reason to doubt whether we can construct a general theory of what is reasonable or worthwhile to do. [The Centrality of Case Specific Reactions: Difficulties in the Very Notion of a General Theory of the Human Good].[6]

[F] [A]–[D] address issues concerning the LHS of the bi-conditional

☐ [a is good ↔ a seems good to the good].

There are further consequences drawn by the modern moral realist (MMR) concerning the theory of virtue by a consideration of the RHS. In one such view, the virtuous are essentially those to whom what is good seems good. Their virtue consists in their having the right beliefs or intuitions, which in turn explain their appropriate actions in response to situations and properties. Desires, or any other reactive states, which may play a role in the explanation of these actions, are determined in their nature and content by the nature and content of the relevant moral perception or intuition.[7] If the moral fits together as the self-contained unit described in [D], the virtuous agent's actions will be explained fundamentally in terms of their response to the moral (and only the moral) features of the situation, and all other responses are "silenced." The self-controlled, by contrast, are aware of other non-moral but still desirable features of the situation, but keep their focus clearly on the moral goal and act accordingly. By contrast the akratic, when tempted, lose their clear grasp on what is good, and as a result fail to act accordingly.[8] [The Centrality of Belief in Action Explanation].

---

6. This claim might be supported by the role given to *nous* in seeing what to do in particular situations (1143b12–15, 1144b9–12).
7. Desire, if needed at all, is a necessary step between belief/intuition and action, but the size and direction of this step is itself determined by the size and direction of the initial belief step.
8. Desire may, in certain cases, play a further background role as a causally necessary condition for (e.g.) the onset of faulty perception in the case of *akrasia*, or as the cause of the presence of the non-silenced values of the self-controlled. But it is not constitutive of virtue that one has right desires. The virtuous is understood fundamentally as the one who knows what is good.

DAVID CHARLES

[G] Since for my modern moral realist the primary task is to make sense of the mature native's utterances and concepts in the process of radical interpretation, he begins with the native, and ourselves, at the conceptual level, and is not concerned to understand how we (or they) initially acquired the relevant concepts. For some, any such concern may appear to be an attempt to do what is impossible, "to dig below conceptual bedrock" in the vain hope of vindicating our concepts "from the outside." But in any event such a project is unnecessary because our understanding of truth and objectivity does not require, according to my MMR, this type of foundation. We begin with the concepts we employ to make ourselves and others intelligible, and these provide all the materials needed for a full understanding of objectivity. [The Conceptual Thesis].

I shall take a position that includes all these claims as my paradigm of modern moral realism, and shall argue that Aristotle was not in this precise form a modern moral realist. Within this position, [A]–[C] are the basic claims, while [D]–[F] are further proposals. However, I shall begin by discussing [D], [F] and [G] both because of their intrinsic interest and because of the light they throw on [B] and [C]. ([E] is a background concern throughout the paper). My understanding of this viewpoint has been gained mainly from a series of illuminating and justly influential articles by John McDowell on Aristotle and moral realism.[9]

1.6 While this position is interesting and radical, it faces several problems. I shall focus only on two.

[I] Can it sustain, via claims [A]–[D], an adequate account of moral objectivity or moral truth? One way to raise the difficulty runs as follows. In addition to the bi-conditional with which we began:

---

9. John McDowell's relevant papers include the following: "Are moral requirements hypothetical imperatives?", *Proceedings of the Aristotelian Society*, supplementary vol. LII, 1978, pp. 13–29; "Virtue and reason", *Monist* LXII, 1979, pp. 331–50; "The role of eudaimonia in Aristotle's ethics", in *Essays on Aristotle's ethics*, A. Rorty (ed.) (Berkeley: University of California Press, 1980), pp. 359–76; "Non-cognitivism and rule-following", in *Wittgenstein: to follow a rule*, S. Holtzman & C. Leich (eds) (London: Routledge & Kegan Paul, 1981), pp. 141–62; "Values and secondary qualities", in *Morality and objectivity*, T. Honderich (ed.) (London: Routledge & Kegan Paul, 1985), pp. 110–29; "Some issues in Aristotle's moral psychology", in *Ethics*, S. Everson (ed.) (Cambridge: Cambridge University Press, 1996). For a related but somewhat differing approach, see several D. Wiggins papers in his *Needs, values, truth* (Oxford: Oxford University Press, 1987), pp. 87–214, 313–56.

☐ [a is good ↔ a merits approbation],

there appear to be a range of similar but less appealing bi-conditionals:

☐ [a is a humorous situation ↔ a merits laughter]

☐ [a is a divine object ↔ a merits worship]

☐ [a is a magical object ↔ a merits the respect due to magical objects]

☐ [a is a yummy object ↔ a merits approval as something to eat or as something to be called "yummy"].

If (as is plausible) one is drawn to regarding at least some of these in a projectivist spirit, what (if anything) distinguishes that case from the valuational one? What is it about the type of meriting in the one that is absent in the other? Are there rational grounds for accepting one bi-conditional of this form as the basis for an account of the objectivity of moral discourse while rejecting another as the foundation of the objectivity of magical or even "yummy-ness" directed discourse?

It might seem that in some of these cases one could make the utterer's attitudes intelligible as responses to properties in reality (e.g. by attributing to her second sight or the ability to discern what is really tasty or magical), especially if we share their responses ourselves. Further, there may be internal consistency in what we reasonably judge to be humorous, magical or yummy, and in certain cases convergence between different judges. If so, we could construct and argue for a reaction-dependent theory of what is yummy or magical. But in that event, can anything be reasonably regarded as a projection or the result of "mere sentimentalism"? The MMR needs to show how, in general terms, the relevant distinction is to be drawn once we abandon the demands for a reaction-independent theory of what is yummy and for an objectivity conferring mode of acquisition of the relevant concept.

[II] Does the MMR offer a plausible account of moral psychology, moral conflict, education and achievement in claims [F] and [G]? Is it embedded in an adequate moral psychology?

I shall not attempt to establish that the MMR cannot successfully answer these questions in the affirmative. My goal in this paper is limited to examining how far Aristotle's own view approximates to that of the MMR, and trying to understand where the differences (if any) lie. Towards this goal, I shall not argue directly against the MMR interpretation of Aristotle, but rather try to develop an alternative reading of parts of his account.

2. Was Aristotle a modern realist? (1) Claims [D] and [F]. Non-moral elements in Aristotle's account of the human good. The explanatory role of desire

2.1   I shall begin my investigation with the view of moral psychology advanced by my MMR.

In the view under consideration, Aristotle's courageous person emerges, in the light of the moral holism implicit in [D], as a military saint: one who feels no fear because he realizes that even death in the context of battle for a worthwhile cause is not a *moral* harm (given his notion of the moral). If fear is conceived as pain or disturbance occasioned by the perception of something bad or harmful as coming one's way, the courageous feel none – because in the circumstances they (correctly) see no *bad* or *harm* approaching, since for them the only bad or harm is moral bad or moral harm.

2.2   There is, apparently, a conflict of evidence in Aristotle's own writing on this issue. On occasion he writes as if the courageous feel fear and pain:

> (1) 1115b10–13: "The courageous person is as undaunted as a human can be. On the one hand, he will fear such things, but as he ought and for the sake of reason he will remain."
>
> (2) 1117b7–11: "Death and wounds will be painful to the courageous person and unwelcome, but he will remain . . . Indeed, the more virtue he has, the more he will feel pain at the prospect of death."

There are, however, several passages that suggest an alternative account.

> (3) 1115a32–33: "The courageous person is fearless in the presence of a brave death."
>
> (4) 1117a17–19: "It is the mark of a brave person to be fearless,

i.e. unmoved in unforeseen dangers."

The second set of passages appears to require that the courageous man feels no fear, while the first (at least) allows that he may do so.

2.3 Fortunately, the appearance of conflict is superficial. In 1117a17ff., Aristotle qualifies fearless by "unterrified" – which suggests that "fearless" means not "without any fear at all" but "undaunted or unmoved by fear." Similarly, in 1115a32–33, "fearless" is compatible with the immediately subsequent passage if it means "undaunted or not deterred by fear." This person will be as unterrifiable as a person can be. Elsewhere, Aristotle describes the courageous "as in general fearless", "being such as to never feel fear or only slightly and reluctantly and seldom, and with regard to things that are of magnitude" (*EE* 1228b4–8). Here, *being fearless* is clearly consistent with feeling some measure of fear for appropriate objects.

If this is correct, there is no Aristotelian requirement that the courageous person be the military saint. He can feel fear for objects it is reasonable for us to fear (but not (e.g.) mice, 1149a7–8) provided that his fear is not so great as to make him daunted by fear, and so incapable of remaining steadfast without the pain of fear as his predominant or only sentiment (1104b5–8). Thus, Aristotle's courageous person may withstand fear rather than serenely dispensing with it (1115b12, 1117b9). Since fear is conceived as a reaction of pain to something harmful which is seen as imminent (*Rhet.* 1382a26–30), what is feared is death in the coming battle, not death in the abstract. The courageous may fear death and wounds in this struggle here and now. And this seems to be a welcome consequence as it makes courage an accessible human virtue – not one confined to the military analogue of the saint.

2.4 The courageous person described in 1117b7–15 is particularly interesting:

> Death and wounds will be painful to the courageous person and unwelcome, but he will remain ... And whoever has a greater share of the whole of virtue and is more happy (*eudaimon*), the more he will be pained at death. Such a man is particularly worthy to live, and he will be deprived of the greatest goods and he knows this, and this is painful. But he is not the less brave, but perhaps is more so since he chooses nobility in war instead of these things.

This person is contrasted with those who are less courageous because they have less to lose. For they are ready for dangers, and exchange their lives for small gains (1117b17–20). The first person prefers one great heroic noble action to many lesser ones (1169a24–25).

There is no indication in this passage that the courageous see no harm in the death, wounds or hardship they face. These are painful to them precisely because there is so much of value in their lives: virtuous activities across a wide dimension, including friendship, intellectual excellence, etc. If there is harm here, the notion of "harm" is not confined to moral harm, but includes the diminution or destruction of other forms of worthwhile activity. Indeed, the notion of "harm" cannot refer only to moral harm if it is correct to insist that in facing death in a good cause the courageous realize that no moral harm can afflict them.

2.5 Aristotle could, of course, have easily written as follows: "In cases of danger, the courageous man is aware of the loss of things which are in the abstract valuable, such as life and health. However, he does not see their potential loss in this context as something to be feared, for he realizes that, from the moral perspective, no harm can come to him by acting courageously. So considerations pertaining to life or health count for nothing with him then. He faces the possibility of his death in this cause without fear or struggle, indeed serenely."[10]

But there is reason to believe that it was no accident that he did not

---

10. See John McDowell's characterization of the courageous person in "Are moral requirements hypothetical imperatives?", pp. 27–8. In McDowell's view, while Aristotle's truly courageous feel no fear, they may regret the fact that their life may come to a premature close or that they are confronted with this choice. However, this projected loss of life or health should make no valuational impact on their actual deliberation in the situation of danger. Thus, they should not regret losing their lives now in this way in this context. Indeed, if they do feel regret about this death, it is a mere psychological effect, cut off in this context from its appropriate valuational basis. (Compare the type of "squeamishness" experienced by the utilitarian acting against (e.g.) his intuitions about justice under the dictates of the utilitarian principle). However, although some courageous agents may be completely without fear (as Aristotle allows in *EE* 1228b4–8), it is hard to believe that this can be a prerequisite, or the one ideal form, of courage in his account. Similarly, even if some may regret death "in the abstract" while not regretting dying now in this cause, this mode of thought cannot be demanded of all courageous agents. (Compare the man pained at *the* death and *the* wounds he faces by staying at his post (1117b7–11). He appears not to be worried about death "in the abstract", but about *the* death that is upon him). In my view, Aristotle is correct to be more liberal in these two requirements than McDowell's characterization allows.

describe the courageous in this way, but speaks throughout of fear and of
  (a) his loss as painful (1117b13) (as are the labours he endures – 1117b3–5),
  (b) his realization that he is being deprived of goods as why it is painful (1117b12–13), and
  (c) his choosing nobility in war *in place of* the other goods (1117b14).

The pain in question presumably arises from his knowledge that he may soon be deprived of the greatest goods (1117b11–13). Most likely it is a component of his fear of the dangers that now confront him (*Rhet.* 1382a26–30). But even if it were the expression of a form of regret separate from fear, it appears to be directed towards dying and being wounded now (*the* death he faces, not death in general, 1117b11). If there is fear and regret of this type, the courageous are not represented as serene. Further, the last phrase (c) is used elsewhere to depict conscious choice between goods and harms: what should be chosen in place of what, and what should be endured instead of what (1110a28–31, 1116b20). Should I endure maltreatment rather than do some injustice? Should I prefer death to dishonour? This appears to be Aristotle's terminology for comparing goods and evils, not that for noting that one option in this case, involving death, has nothing bad or regrettable about it. It seems that the courageous, with good lives and much to lose, are represented as comparing in deliberation the value of a heroic death in a good cause with the value of what they will give up, and doing so from a viewpoint that permits them to weigh together a wide range of perfectionist goods. (See also 1169a21ff.: "they choose one fine action rather than many indifferent ones.") For them, this death is more choiceworthy than safety achieved by cowardly flight (1116b20), because dishonour is more to be feared than the death they face.

2.6 The painfulness of heroic action reflects the presence of goals that are not specifically moral ones. A wider conception of wellbeing and benefit appears to be at work than one confined to moral good and harm. Other values – intellectual, prudential and social (such as those focused on honour) – properly make their impact in deliberation (contrary to the moral holism implicit in claim [D] above). Further, these values seem to be choiceworthy along the same general dimensions as the narrowly moral ones, since they are all elements in wellbeing as Aristotle presents it (I.7, 1097b1–5). There is no indication in these passages that the non-moral goods are seen as choiceworthy by the courageous in some radically distinctive, incommensurable way.[11] To be a military saint is not, in this view, a human ideal, but one that is above us, perhaps fit for the gods (of a given kind), but not for us because it abstracts too far from things we have reason to fear. Nor is it one to which the human ideal approximates, because it also ignores the significance of the complex range of abilities (intellectual and social) whose exercise, in Aristotle's view, comprises human wellbeing, and which generate the conflict intrinsic to the human virtue of courage (cf. 1115b26–28, 1145a21–23). A background theory of human nature is making an impact in his characterization of the deliberation of the practically wise, which separates it from that of the super-hero (or elsewhere the bestial).

2.7 It might be thought that this discussion of courage shows only that Aristotle's view of wellbeing exceeds the narrowly moral (pace thesis [D] in 1.5), and that this has little bearing on the other more basic thesis of the MMR. However, if temperance resembles courage (as Aristotle suggests),[12] his temperate agents need not be saints either, untroubled by genuine temptation when the time comes to act temperately. For both courage and temperance are forms of maximal self-control with regard to objects that we have reason to fear or desire, given our natures. Indeed, if the analogy is maintained, the temperate and the self-controlled may share the same valuational

---

11. Aristotle's form of choiceworthiness seems to embrace the moral and non-moral alike. Indeed, there is reason to doubt that he operated with a clear or motivated distinction between the two; his notion of "excellent activity" as introduced in I.7, 1098a16–18, clearly spans intellectual and moral virtue. For a contrasting view, see John McDowell's exclusively moral reading of this passage in his contribution to this volume. The evidence adduced in favour of attributing to Aristotle some form of radical incommensurability thesis appears weak. See my discussion of it in *Aristotle's philosophy of action* (London: Duckworth, 1984), pp. 133–5. McDowell's understanding of the Aristotelian courageous or virtuous agent may depend on his discerning in Aristotle's writings the idea of radically distinct types of choiceworthiness along incommensurably different dimensions. In my view (as argued above), there is no need to introduce this hypothesis to understand either Aristotle's account of virtue or the phenomenon itself. The onus lies on those who support this exegetical hypothesis to produce further direct evidence in favour of it.
12. Both are described within the unifying theory of the mean, subject to the qualification noted in III.12. I have discussed this comparison, and Aristotle's account of courage, in greater detail in *Aristotle's philosophy of action*, pp. 170–77.

appreciation of the situation, and differ only in that (as Aristotle remarks, 1146a12–13) the latter have (e.g.) excessive counter-desires that result in their doing the right action with some degree of reluctance – or at least being such as to enjoy overall acting against their better judgement in acting intemperately (1152a1–3). There is no indication that their excessive desires for permissible goods need change their valuational assessment or make it different from that of the virtuous. This makes Aristotelian temperance, like Aristotelian courage, a less demanding and more humanly accessible virtue, and shows how other factors may play a constitutive role in determining the moral quality of our characters and actions. For possession of right desire, as well as correct valuation, appears to be constitutive of virtue. If so, Aristotle's descriptions of courage and temperance indicate not only that the notion of wellbeing is not a narrowly moral one, but also that factors apart from belief, such as strength of desire, play an independent but still constitutive role in accounting for the nature of human moral virtue. And this runs contrary to claim [F] of the MMR.

3. Was Aristotle a modern realist (2)? Moral education, moral decline; claims [F] and [G]: "non-conceptual" elements in Aristotle

3.1   To acquire virtue, according to my MMR, is to acquire the ability to see what is intrinsically worthwhile, to be "initiated into" a conceptual space in which what is actually good seems good to you. The process of initiation could be effected either by encouraging the child to admire the good acts others point out as being such, or by training her to take delight in certain circumstances (in a way that does not involve any appreciation on her part of the concepts in question). In the first case, the child acquires a grasp from others of the concepts of virtue. In the second, her training is akin to the setting up in an animal of a trained behavioural response to certain cues. In neither case could the child justify her acquisition of, or adherence to, particular moral claims by reference back to what was involved at the pre-conceptual stage. Indeed, in the former there is no step outside the conceptual at all; one simply accepts on authority one's instructor's concepts. In the latter there is a pre-conceptual stage, but it is merely a causal ingredient in the acquisition of virtue and is not itself a justifier. One cannot provide a justification for one's acceptance of one moral claim rather than another on this basis. And this will remain so, even if the process of initiation is a lengthy one, made up of behavioural training and of conceptual instruction by others.

3.2 This account overlooks one central strand in Aristotle's account of moral education. In his view, before acquiring the ability to see (*nous*) what is intrinsically worthwhile in given situations, one flounders guided by natural virtue alone (1144b5ff.). At this stage one lacks the full concept (*noema*) of justice – despite one's desire to do what is just. But Aristotle holds that "virtue either natural or trained is the teacher of correct thinking about the goal" (1151a16–19). Teaching implies an element of rational persuasion by the faculties invoked at the pre-conceptual stage. But this possibility is precluded in the view set out in 3.1.; for that leaves no room for any pre-conceptual stage, other than that constituted by blind motivational states induced by Pavlov-style habituation, which cannot themselves be rational teachers. Indeed, the view is constructed to rule out, or at least count as unnecessary, any suggestion of rational grounding in pre-conceptual states (see claim [G] above).

3.3 How does natural or trained virtue play a teaching role in the acquisition of correct conceptual moral thinking in Aristotle's account? He repeatedly compares the acquisition of virtue with the acquisition of a skill (1103a31–32, b6–8). In the latter case, the process involved is described with greater care. Below the level of skill, there is an earlier level of experience (*empeiria*) where proper concepts of (e.g.) illness-types and condition-types are absent. Here one can say that *this* medicine works for *this* condition, but will lack a theoretical grasp on what the condition actually is (*Meta*. 981a10–12, *An. Post.* 100a5). It is a major step to go beyond this to grasp the proper concept (*noema*) of a specific kind of illness (universally described), or to see this case as an example of it. In the acquisition of virtue a similar story can be told. At the level of experience one can see that particular cases resemble one another, but still lack a fully conceptual thought about their value; for one cannot characterize (e.g.) justice in ways that go beyond pointing to particular examples, or saying that *this* is like *that*. If one uses the term "justice" at all, one only employs a proto-concept and one's grasp on it is dependent fundamentally solely on one's ability to spot similarities between cases, an exclusively case-orientated discriminatory capacity. Aristotle compares the person of experience with inanimate agents in that the former has been trained to respond without knowledge in given ways to objects presented to them, whereas the latter respond through nature (*Meta.* 981b2–5). In the same spirit he notes that animals who live by imagination share in experience to some small degree (980b25–27). Thus, at this basic level our experience consists in an ability to act differentially on the basis of what is perceptually given and does not require any properly conceptual abilities (e.g. to fit together concepts in a way essentially governed by rational constraints: see §4.5 below). For the latter are not in Aristotle's view abilities we share with animals. If so, this basic level may be seen as radically pre-conceptual, and not merely as the home of (e.g.) indexical concepts governed by the same rational constraints as apply to concepts in general. For the latter will be beyond the reach of animals.[13]

3.4 What is the role of desire and pleasure in this picture? Aristotle emphasizes that it makes all the difference to one's final moral state that one initially takes pleasure in acting justly (1105a5–6). Indeed, virtue springs from pleasures and pains and is destroyed by them (1105a14–16). This might seem to suggest a very different picture from that sketched in 3.3, one in which agents see, at the initial stage, two cases as similarly (e.g.) yummy because both are enjoyable or painful in the same way – in which their perception of similarity is essentially mediated by finding one way of acting pleasant or another disagreeable. In this account, the construction of one's concept of *good action* will essentially refer back to what was initially found pleasant or attractive. And it is these non-cognitive feelings, thus characterized, to which we will be sensitive in constructing our concept of the good. The latter will be based in this way on the non-cognitive feelings of pleasure we happen to have at the earlier stage.[14]

3.5 However, this view of the role of desire and pleasure, while it gives a place to a pre-conceptual stage, also seems to misdescribe Aristotle's views. Its major weakness is that it undermines the analogy on which Aristotle insists between learning to be (e.g.) just and acquiring skills such as house building or flute playing, in which pleasure and pain play no intrinsic mediating role. In the light of this analogy, Aristotle should be taken as giving pleasure a different explanatory role (or roles) from that proposed in 3.4. As he insists elsewhere, if one takes pleasure in a given form of activity, one gets better at seeing what is good in any field of skill or virtue (1175a31–36). This is as true of building as of acting courageously or justly. If one finds acting justly irksome, one will lose – in practical matters – one's ability to see what is right to do (1140b17–19). The person who does not take pleasure in acting justly is open to moral decline or subversion. By contrast, one who enjoys acting justly will become a

---

13. The issues here are complex and deserve extended separate treatment. A few reminders may help to indicate the general framework of Aristotle's account of imagination (*phantasia*).

(i) Imagination is a capacity we share with animals, who lack belief and reason (*de Anima* 427b9–11).
(ii) Imagination serves for us as an input to a thinking, concept applying, reasoning system (*de Anima* 432a9–14).
(iii) Imagination accounts for our (and animals') ability to respond differentially to situations on the basis of retained perceptual experience (re-presentations) (*de Anima* 429a5–8).
(iv) Imagination in our case is radically belief- and reason-independent, as things can go on looking one way to us, even when we know that they are in reality different (*de Anima*, 428b3–6).

The person or animal guided by imagination and experience may have information about objects and properties, but not of the type governed by constraints applicable to conceptual thought, which connect it with reasons, judgement and generality. Informational contents are not graspable apart from perceptual experience and need not be combinable with all other concepts we possess. Nor need they be rejected if they represent objects in ways we know to be misleading. This type of informational system appears more primitive and basic than that involved in conceptual thought. Although its contents are truth assessable (*de Anima* 428a3-4, 12–13), the point of this system is to produce successful action for its possessor. Indeed the notion of truth applicable here is not the full-blooded one that is a property of conceptual thoughts (*de Anima* 432a12–15).

There are striking similarities (and differences) between this account and the one sketched by Gareth Evans of informational, but non-conceptual, content in *Varieties of reference* (Oxford: Oxford University Press, 1982), pp. 103–104, 124, 158. Evans' theory has been developed and modified by John Campbell, in "Conceptual structure", in *Meaning and interpretation*, C. Travis (ed.) (Oxford: Oxford University Press, 1986), pp. 159-74; Adrian Cussins, in "The connectionist construction of concepts", in *The philosophy of artificial intelligence*, M. Boden (ed.) (Oxford: Oxford University Press, 1990), pp. 368-440; and Christopher Peacocke in *A study of concepts* (Cambridge, Mass.: MIT Press, 1992). Evans' account is criticized by John McDowell in *Mind and the world* (Cambridge, Mass., Harvard University Press, 1994). If I am correct, Aristotle, so far from being a forerunner of McDowell's on these issues, is in fact a proponent of the very views he attacks. It lies outside the scope of the present paper to consider the force of McDowell's criticisms when directed against Aristotle's actual position. For a pioneering discussion of Aristotle's view, see Richard Sorabji's *Animal minds and human morals* (London: Duckworth, 1993), pp. 30–40.

"four-square" moral agent – with that combination of right desire and true perception required for acting well. Thus, pleasure and pain play a causal role in the acquisition of virtue, and their contribution is not wholly determined by conceptual or pre-conceptual cognitive responses to the situation. In some cases the fit between cognitive and pleasure/pain response is less than perfect – and this accounts for the nature of the distinctive failures of the *self-controlled* (*enkrates*) and the *akratic*, even if they have acquired proper moral concepts (contrary to [F]).[15] The self-controlled, unlike the virtuous, would not be disgusted if they were to act against their better judgement (1152a1–2). And this chink in their armour is what makes akrasia possible for the lapsed *enkrates*.

3.6 Natural or trained virtue involves a way of seeing individual cases as similar analogous to the mode of apprehension of the person with experience (who has not yet acquired a skill). In order for these perceptions to "become one's own" and to be integrated into one's own value system and practices, pleasure and pain may be required. But in neither case is the detection of similarity itself essentially mediated by whether the actions in question strike one as enjoyable or disagreeable. The relevant experiences are typed by similarities in what is perceptually given and not (even in part) by our pleasure-based reactions to them. For there may be considerable heterogeneity in our pleasure/pain reactions to what is perceived as similar. Indeed, this is precisely what distinguishes the naturally virtuous from those prone to self-control or vice. Further, the virtuous themselves may vary from time to time in how far they enjoy acting generously. This pre-conceptual stage's role as "the teacher of [correct] thinking about

---

14. The types of pleasure and pain here seem to be as described in *Rhetoric* II's discussion of the emotions where (e.g.) pain is compared to disturbance (a favoured medical condition in Aristotle's theory; cf. *Rhetoric* 1378a30ff., 1380a1, 1382a21–22). Although such pleasures and pains are caused by beliefs, they appear to be internal medical conditions not essentially characterized in intentional vocabulary.
15. The requirement that one gets better at making discriminations in activities one enjoys does not require that one enjoys doing the relevant activities for their own sake. Thus, one might enjoy spotting what is just in order to predict what just people will do, perhaps even in order to frustrate them (or as an agreeable, sociological study). So it does not follow from this requirement that only the just, with the right motivations, will unerringly spot what is just. They might achieve their success for different reasons. On these issues, see my *Aristotle's philosophy of action*, pp. 182ff.

the goal" consists in its providing similarities or exemplars that are more deeply understood by the developed moral agents. They learn in this way that there are genuine distinctions to be discerned, and aim to ensure that their concepts are sensitive to them. In this way they seek to keep faith with their earlier pre-conceptual experiences of objective features of the world. In other cases, such as those of the *humorous* or the *yummy*, their experiences would be unified by a different type of similarity itself partially or wholly constituted by their pleasure-based response to situations.

3.7   The sentimentalist was correct, in Aristotle's view, to emphasize the role of our emotional responses at the pre-conceptual level, and to see the importance at this stage of pleasure/pain or other non-cognitive factors. But he erred in thinking that introducing these conditions undermined the basic role played by our pre-conceptual, but still cognitive, ability to spot similarities in the world. My MMR makes an equal but opposite mistake. In his recoil from the sentimentalist viewpoint, he sees no independent role in justificatory explanation either for a pre-conceptual level of response or for the pleasure/pain combinations found there. Aristotle, if I am correct, gives both these features a central role without making the further sentimentalist claim that the pre-conceptual detection of relevant moral similarities is to be understood in terms of our having certain similar non-cognitive reactions of pleasure or pain. The latter certainly play (at least) a causal explanatory role in Aristotle's account of the acquisition of human virtue, since they are both essentially involved in natural and trained virtue. Further, since natural and trained virtue are both said to be teachers of virtue, the pleasure they essentially involve appears to have an additional justificatory role in sustaining our commitment to the noble, and in ensuring that we see its point. For the latter may depend on our keeping faith with our earlier cognitive detection of similarities *and* our non-cognitive reactions to them. (I return to the latter point in 4.9). But even if this is so, moral concepts such as those of justice or courage will differ fundamentally from those for which the sentimentalist story is appropriate (such as those of the *amusing* or the *yummy*). For in the latter, but not in the former, the perception of similarity itself is essentially dependent on our non-cognitive reactions to situations.

3.8   There could, perhaps, be creatures for whom "initiation into moral concepts" did not involve a pre-conceptual stage of this type, and so did not require their taking enjoyment in the right way. Perhaps they were born saints, or had the ability to grasp moral truths, given some background behavioural training or through Platonic recollection and immediately silence their other inclinations. Perhaps they just believed what they were told on authority, and on this basis alone zero-rated their contrary desires. But their moral practices would differ from ours, at least to the extent that their point would be distinct if theirs (unlike ours) is not rationally grounded in any way in what they find agreeable or pleasant at the pre-conceptual stage. If so, their success (if such it be) would not be a human one, and could not constitute a human ideal (in Aristotle's view). They would be more like idealized sages or Socrates' internal *daemon* than human agents with our conception for wellbeing. Indeed, this is why such people can strike us as unnervingly cold, indeed eerie. In our case, practical success consists in grasping the truth in agreement with right desire (1139a29–31). This is a substantial achievement for humans – one that lies beyond some who are correct in their judgements (like the self-controlled and the akratic). In the case of the machine men described above, neither the stability of moral perception nor any part of its justification depends on their finding acting in this way agreeable or a source of delight or pleasure. There are no causal or rational constraints on the nature of their moral development arising from what, given their natures, they enjoy doing. They would be unmoved by such considerations, serene and in some way god-like, because for them pleasure plays no role in rendering stable their commitment to virtue. For human virtuous agents, by contrast (on Aristotle's conception), if pleasure is not an added attraction in the good life, this is because the life of virtue already contains it (1099a16–17). In our case, what is agreeable given our natures plays an important role in rationally constraining what can count as human wellbeing. This, no doubt, is why he was concerned to plot the main virtues on a register of human emotions with their attendant pleasures in the theory of the mean. For his virtuous agent is not just the knower (of classical intuitionist writers) or the Kantian rational being governed solely by an *a priori* moral law, but rather a human person with the complex character, needs and desires we possess.

3.9 A theory of human nature (as it might be described somewhat grandly) has played two roles in this account. In 2.1–2.6, it played a constraining role suggesting that a certain purely moral conception of wellbeing, in the case of courage, is not a genuine human ideal. For this required human beings to downgrade (in the relevant situations) other commitments and sources of delight that make their human lives worthwhile. In 2.6–3.8, it explained why certain other aspects of human virtue are essentially as they are – involving both trained perception and appropriate desires and emotions; for both are required to understand the achievement of the virtuous, and the failures of the self-controlled and the akratic. In this, aspects of human nature limit humanly achievable conceptions of what is good for man, and explain why our moral virtues are as they are. In the latter case, what is presupposed is *inter alia* a rudimentary explanatory theory accounting for our acquisition of moral concepts at the pre-conceptual level. This account, common to various fields of human activity, is not itself a reaction-dependent one. Rather, it is founded on an explanatory reaction-independent theory of human nature, as this is involved in the acquisition and retention of virtue (akin in certain respects to the earlier theory of danger and physical harm).

Reference to our natures explains one difference between truth in practical and theoretical matters. As Aristotle remarks in *de Anima* (431b10–13):

> what does not involve action – the true and the false – is in the same category as the good and the bad: but they differ in that one is without qualification, the other is for someone.

What is good or bad, is good or bad *for* something – and this is involved in the case of practical matters. Truth (in other areas) is unqualified. Human practical truth is truth about what is good for humans, with their distinctive desires and excellences, while theoretical truth is about matters (such as astronomy or mathematics) not so related to our or anyone's distinctive natures.[16] The practically wise human is said to discover what is good for humans, not fish (1141a22–26). This claim is unintelligible without reference to our complex natures, emotions (*pathe*), theoretical intellect and moral character acquired as we acquire it (1178a15–21). In this, as argued above, success for humans essentially involves achieving certain desiderative as

---

16. Practical truth, thus understood, can be absolute truth about what is good for A's. It does not require any additional relativization of the truth predicate. Human practical knowledge grasps what the absolute truth is about what is good for humans and not for fish, etc.

well as intellectual states, where the relevant intellectual state is concerned with what is good for creatures with desiderative as well as intellectual abilities. A background theory of human nature plays a role in constraining the preferred account of human good, and in showing what is needed for us to be properly virtuous.

This account gives some insight into what was wrong from Aristotle's viewpoint with Plato's account of moral virtue. It attempted to represent what is good in a way that did not regard it as radically nature-dependent. What is good for humans differs from what is good for fish, even if they share similar colour perception (1141a22–25). What is needed is a background theory of what is good for humans to sustain this account. Plato (and Socrates) erred in not embedding their view of the moral agent as the knower in a plausible *explanatory* account of our acquisition of moral concepts or of our human natures. If so, Aristotle's rejection of Platonism does not commit him to regarding a theory of what is good for man as a creation of our own moral reactions and of criticisms internal to our moral practices.

4. Was Aristotle a modern realist (3)? Claims [B] and [C]

4.1 The direct evidence for construing Aristotle as an advocate of claims [B] and [C] of 1.5 is not strong. While Aristotle holds:

☐ [a is good (without qualification) ↔ a seems good to the good]

this appears to be a consequence of the good person's ability to see what is the truth in each case. She can thus be the *canon* and *measure* because what is good (without qualification) seems good to her. Thus, she may be epistemically a good guide to what is good, and not, as indicated by [B] and [C], a constitutor of what is good.[17] Elsewhere, Aristotle comments on Protagoras' measure doctrine in similar terms (*Meta.* 1053a31–b4):

> knowledge also we call a measure of things and perception too because we get to know something by them, since they are the measured rather than the measurers ... Protagoras says, "man is the measure of all things", as if he said "the knowing man" or "the perceiving man" – because these have the faculties which we say are measures of their objects. Although Protagoras says

nothing of value, he appears to say something exceptional.

The thought that knowledge or perception is the measured rather than[18] the measurer suggests that they are to be assessed in terms of whether they match up to reality, and does not license the thought that our theory of the relevant properties is itself based solely on our reactions. Further, Aristotle does not think that our account of all we know or perceive is to be secured as objective from the inside only because it withstands internal criticism from other of our reactions. There is nothing in the claim that the good person is the measure of the good which requires the attribution to Aristotle in the moral case of claim [C] proposed by my MMR.

The structure of the *Ethics* can similarly be interpreted without commitment to a radically reaction-dependent theory of the human good. Wellbeing consists in excellent activity, and this in turn is "determined by reason *and* in the way in which the person of practical wisdom would determine it" (1106b36–1107a1). However, the latter sentence may be understood, in the light of the earlier comment in *Meta.* X.1, as saying only that the person of practical wisdom gets it right about which ratio defines the mean. If so, the practically wise will be good judges rather than constitutors of what is excellent activity. There is nothing to exclude the possibility of a reaction-independent account of the human good which would provide an independent theory of the LHS of the following bi-conditionals:

☐ [a is good for man ↔ a seems good to the good man]
☐ [a is good for man ↔ a merits approbation from men]

The relevant question can now be raised fairly sharply: how far

---

17. In III.4, the argument appears to run as follows.
  1 [the good person sees what is true in each case].
  From which we can infer
  2 [a is good ↔ a seems good to the good].
  Further,
  3 [a seems good to the good ↔ a is good for the good].
  Hence, 1 and 3 yield
  4 [a is good ↔ a is good for the good].
  No doubt, in this passage Aristotle is focusing on what is good *haplos*, and not on what is good for someone (e.g. the sick). In this argument, 2 is a consequence of 1, rather than vice-versa. Paula Gottlieb discusses this argument in detail in "Aristotle and Protagoras: the good human being as the measure of goods", *Apeiron* **XXIV**, pp. 25-45, 1991.
18. Similarly if *"mallon"* is translated "more than."

does Aristotle find a way of articulating a theory of *what is good for humans* which is independent of our reactions, in the way in which a theory of danger is independent of our reactions of fear? At the very minimum he needs to establish that there is such a reaction-independent theory, and, more ambitiously, one that shows preference for the life of virtue over the life of self-indulgence. It might perhaps be ceded in the light of sections 2–3 that Aristotle does indeed develop a theory of human nature which constrains our conception of human wellbeing and explains why certain features of human virtue are as they are. But this theory, it will be claimed, does not determine the central constituents of what is good for man (in Aristotle's account). Rather his specific claims, within the parameters set by this background theory, depend essentially on our reactions to certain situations or people, and the standards we construct on this basis. There is no further material provided by Aristotle for a fully articulated theory of the human good. On this view, at the level of rational, conceptual thought about the good, we are confined (according to Aristotle) to internal criticism of the type outlined by the MMR.

4.2 Throughout the *Nicomachean ethics* Aristotle is concerned to trace and develop an analogy between theoretical and practical knowledge. Both grasp the truth in their respective areas (1139a29–31; cf. 1140a10, b4–6), and involve truth-based reasoning from starting points to conclusions that can be represented in syllogistic form. In both, the starting points are universal claims. In this Aristotle simply assumes that there is truth in practical matters that corresponds to theoretical truth. But is he entitled to this assumption? Further, does he provide in both cases for a reaction-independent theory of the objects and properties involved? Aristotle does not confine practical truth to the ethical domain, but detects it also in (e.g.) the medical. Thus, if he can establish a reaction-independent theory of health, and show that human wellbeing is relevantly similar, he will have vindicated these assumptions.

4.3 Aristotle's appeal to theoretical knowledge is important for a proper understanding of the *Nicomachean ethics* for several reasons. Since he holds on perfectionist grounds that theoretical knowledge is the paradigm case of intrinsically desirable activity (the exercise of our highest virtue, the one we share with the gods, etc.), he can establish the intrinsic desirability of the exercise of practical knowledge in the virtuous life by showing that the latter activity resembles the former. This equips him with a measure of intrinsic desirability not specifically tied to ethical virtue (but which also applies to intellectual excellence, as was noted above in 2.6), and offers him a possible way to argue for the intrinsic desirability of ethical virtue. Thus, he has a foothold external to the ethical by which to measure its desirability, but not one that need take us outside the human domain.[19] If he is to achieve his goal, he must establish that there are similar reasons for accepting truth in practical as in theoretical matters. This requires him to show that our acquisition of knowledge is strongly similar in the two cases, and that both involve a similar grasp of truth. If he can do this, he will show there can be a reaction-independent theory of human good and human health, as well as of natural kinds. In this paper I shall focus on the latter two requirements, and not consider further the focal role of intellectual contemplation in the *Nicomachean ethics* in vindicating the desirability of the ethical life.

4.4   What grounds the claim to truth in theoretical knowledge? In NE VI, Aristotle develops his analogy by reference to the *Analytics*, and it is there we should look for an outline of his account of theoretical knowledge.

There are three relevant stages in his account of theoretical knowledge, which emerge if we consider his description of our coming to understand the first principles of a science. In this we will be following his suggestion that our grasp of ethical concepts is somewhat analogous (cf. VI.1, 1143b1–5). In the *Analytics*, the procedure runs as follows:

---

19. Indeed, one of his major strategies in the *Ethics* is to argue that since intellectual contemplation has a paradigmatic role in wellbeing (and human wellbeing), practical knowledge, which is strongly analogous to theoretical contemplation, must also be an element in human wellbeing. Thus, theoretical contemplation is the focal case of human wellbeing, and practical knowledge is itself an element in human wellbeing because it closely resembles theoretical contemplation. Other elements in the good life may also resemble theoretical contemplation in that they are excellences in their differing fields (e.g. friendship, good looks, health). There is no need in this view to treat practical wisdom as necessary for successful contemplation, or to see the virtues as being in any way instrumental to the pursuit of *theoria*. The gods are the paradigm case of wellbeing because – given their natures – they can engage in *theoria* the whole time. No human – however ideally circumstanced – could achieve this. The best life for a human depends on how far human nature can be stretched towards *theoria*, given the moral and other constraints that arise from our natures. For a somewhat contrasting viewpoint, see G. Lawrence's "Aristotle on the ideal life", *Philosophical Review* CII, 1993, pp. 1-34.

Stage I   We grasp the concept, e.g. the concept of *man* or *monad* (*An. Post.* II.19).

Stage II   We come to know that the concept picks out a genuine kind that figures in appropriate explanations.

Stage III   We come to know that certain concepts mark a starting point – something that occupies a position from which one can organize other parts of the relevant subject matter in a systematic and intelligible way.

If concepts that we acquire pass the test at stage II, we know that they are objectively valid and pick out elements or kinds in reality. If they achieve the condition set at stage III, we know that they pick out basic kinds or objects. It is possible to acquire concepts at stage I which are not, in fact, objective concepts (e.g. that of *goat-stag*, or of *cloak – de Int.* 9); but these will be shown to be such because they fail to fit into an organized body of science in the ways indicated in II and III.

4.5 [I]   In Aristotle's account, mastery of concepts for kinds such as *man* requires (very roughly) the thinker to be causally affected by kinds in the world when his thinking faculty is functioning as it should. What makes a given concept the one it is is the "assimilation" of the thinking faculty in appropriate circumstances to the kind.[20] Mastery of genuine concepts (non-indexical ones) goes beyond what is involved at the earlier stage of experience (*empeiria*) with its dependence on seeing similarities between particular cases and its quasi- or proto-concepts of the type we share with the animals (see 3.3). It involves (what I shall call) a rational and context-independent grasp of (e.g.) *man as a given kind of animal*, which registers its connection with other kinds (animals/fish, etc.) and which is the starting point for proper skills and knowledge. We saw this model at work in Aristotle's discussion of illness and medical conditions above (3.3). In both cases, our grasp on the concepts develops from context-dependent reactions to particular cases by reflection on what is *common* to the particular cases and on how the kind, so picked out, relates to other kinds: its position in an explanatory network. In these cases, concept mastery requires interaction in the proto-skilful, experiential, way with the kind which is the causal originator of the relevant thought-

---

20. On this, see my paper, "Aristotle on names and their signification", in *Language*, S. Everson (ed.) (Cambridge: Cambridge University Press, 1994), pp. 37–73.

producing process (cf. perceptual model applied for universals, *An. Post.* II.19). Genuine kinds are precisely those that explain our mastery of concepts in this way. If we are to talk intelligibly using concepts of this type, some of them must refer to genuine kinds in reality (although we need not know which). Aristotle sought to apply this model of concept acquisition in the theoretical, medical and ethical spheres. He argued that the starting point for moral reflection lies in our grasping what is the courageous, generous or cruel thing to do (1143b1–5). If (as argued above) the same basic model of human concept acquisition applies in all three cases, Aristotle has similar grounds for similarly thinking that in each we are in contact with properties (e.g. generosity) for which we can construct similar reaction-independent theories. Each set of concepts starts on equal terms, tracking similarities in the world as we find it. Aristotle offers no ground, at this stage, for regarding the ethical alone as directed to properties for which we can only construct a reaction-dependent theory. Things would have been different if at this stage our mastery of the relevant concepts depended on a grasp of similarities itself essentially mediated by pleasure and pain, as in the case of our grasp of the yummy or the humorous. But this is not so for the ethical terms now under consideration (see 3.6 above). Nor are they all complex in the way that "goat-stag" is.

4.6 [II] How do we know that we are talking intelligibly in using a particular concept thus acquired? In Aristotle's view, to secure the objectivity of discourse about a particular natural kind is to establish that it does in fact fit with other kinds in a type of appropriate explanation, and that the kind itself is an organized unity (even if one does not know what its basic organizing principle is; cf. *An. Post.* II.2, II.8 – establishing the fact: *to hoti*). In this we come to know that we are in touch with genuine kinds and relations. Indeed, we cannot understand the nature of those discoveries except by seeing them as of reaction-independent kinds standing in an objective order. In this reality presses in on us;[21] we begin to construct our reaction-independent theory of the objects or properties involved, as (e.g.) those that stand in a given place in an objective efficient causal order.

In the medical case, Aristotle develops a broadly similar account.

---

21. Compare Wiggins' use of "conceptual realism" in *Sameness and substance* (Oxford: Oxford University Press, 1980), pp. 140ff.

Particular medical conditions are seen to be produced or destroyed by certain sets of causal factors (cf. *Physics* 246b5ff., *Meta.* 981a28ff.). Good human health overall depends on the presence of a set of stable medical conditions in which each organ works harmoniously with others to allow us to function in certain characteristic ways in our environment. Any particular condition is stable only if it is properly related to the conditions that create or destroy it (*Physics* 246b6–8). In this sketch, particular medical conditions are located in a somewhat rudimentary but reaction-independent theory of their creation, maintenance and destruction, and of their teleological role in the human organism.

4.7 [III]   *Establishing the starting points.* In theoretical knowledge (as Aristotle conceives it), to establish something as a starting point depends on coming to grasp, on the basis of experience (1142a15ff.), that it plays a central role in a series of explanations (or demonstrations), which introduces order and point into the field of enquiry that falls under it (*An. Post.* 96b15–25). In constructing a theory of this type we come to realize that certain terms mark out fundamental elements in objective, reaction-independent reality.

In these ways, we establish that particular terms mastered at stage I pick out genuine kinds. Our knowledge rests on our ability to construct on their basis a coherent and organized explanatory theory. That we can do this supports the claim that we are in touch at stage I with a reaction-independent reality.

In the medical case, the relevant starting point is given by the concept of human health and good condition. It is this that gives point and some measure of determinacy to the notion of the proper functioning of particular organs. Against this background, the humans who cannot walk or see are understood to be dysfunctional precisely because they cannot enjoy the use of capacities that are characteristic of healthy, fully functioning, human beings. As Aristotle emphasizes, there is no reason to think that we can give a reductive account of what health or healthy functioning is, or that the concept of health or healthy functioning will be in all respects determinate. However, health, so conceived, is secured as an objective, reaction-independent property because of the explanatory role it plays in accounting for why many different parts of the body are organized as they are (in humans who function well). This is why doctors begin their practical reasoning with premises such as "Since health is so and so, this should be done." It is not that their, or our, ideas of health depend on our views about what is reasonable to do or expect in creatures such as us. Rather, our judgements about what is reasonable to do or expect rest on a more basic understanding of the type of creatures we are, with our distinctive needs and potentialities. And this understanding is underwritten in medical enquiry (at stage III) by the discovery of a successful explanatory account of the human organism, which takes this concept of health as its central feature.

In the case of physical health, we may begin (in Aristotle's approach) with a concept of (e.g.) disease as the phenomenon by which living organisms differ from well functioning members of their species in such a way as to be at a disadvantage with regard to healthy functioning. The notion of healthy functioning may begin with life and fertility ("biological advantage"), but has to be extended to include a wider range of phenomena ("quality of life", absence of pain). When we turn to examples of psychiatric health (which Aristotle briefly discusses in NE 1148b19–34, 1149a10–14), the concept of healthy functioning needs to be further extended to involve (e.g.) well adaptedness in social functioning (e.g. possessing enough autonomy to keep a job, the ability to form interpersonal relations, to plan over time, etc.). Here, well-functioning as a social animal may require that our perception of the world is more or less accurate in certain relevant respects, but also that we are able to achieve a certain pattern of basic human functioning that enables us to use the capacities we possess. It is not, it appears, that our ideas of psychiatric health or illness depend solely on our or our expert's views about what is reasonable to expect in creatures like us, still less on whom we might expect "to turn up as out-patients." Rather, our judgements appear to reflect a more basic understanding of the type of creatures we are, with our distinctive needs and potentialities. In this the case of psychiatric health is not essentially different from that of physical health, at least with regard to major disorders: clinical depression, schizophrenia, anxiety, phobias of various types, anorexia, and so on. In both areas, disease seems to involve an amalgam of pain or distress and loss of appropriate human functioning, understood in terms of a reaction-independent account of the type of organisms we are.[22]

---

22. These issues are discussed by R. E. Kendell in *The role of diagnosis in psychiatry* (Oxford: Oxford University Press, 1975), pp. 9-26.

4.8 How far does Aristotle sustain analogies of stages II and III in the ethical case? When a person acquires *nous* in the practical sphere, she will (*inter alia*) see the interconnections between particular moral concepts (justice, generosity, friendship) and be able to locate particular cases in this wider framework. She goes beyond the stage of being able to recognize (e.g.) particular acts as just or generous to a position in which she can apply the relevant interconnected framework of general value concepts. This is why in the acquisition of *nous*, she comes to have (at least potentially) all the virtues. For the framework she acquires allows her to see that particular virtues cohere with one another (1144b35ff.).[23] Aristotle seeks to develop his analogy with the medical in some detail (*Physics* 247a1ff.). Thus, particular virtues are created and destroyed by a certain set of features, such as pleasure and pain (*Physics* 247a1–3). Similarly, relevant individual states are stable only when they are properly related to the conditions that create and destroy them, and parts are only in this state when they work harmoniously and stably with others to allow the person to function satisfactorily over a long period in their environment. When people acquire *nous*, they will see the relevant interconnections between the relevant virtues, and grasp what the right thing to do is in particular cases from the perspective of the worthwhile life for a properly functioning human being. If the analogy with the medical case is sustained, there will be in both cases a reaction-independent structure whose legitimacy does not rest solely with our judgements of what is reasonable and worthwhile, but is grounded rather in a reaction-independent theory of a properly functioning human, which holds in place our account of the particular virtues (whether of body or soul).

4.9 Does Aristotle establish that there is no less reason to accept a reaction-independent explanatory account of a properly functioning human being in the ethical than in the medical (or we might add the psychiatric) sphere? The relevant starting point for ethical reflection is human wellbeing. As in the case of health, there is no reason to expect a reductive account of what it is to be a properly functioning human. Nor should we expect that our account of wellbeing will be determinate in all respects. Rather, in both cases, the fundamental concept should give point and some determinacy to the account of

---

23. This is why full virtue, involving the range of particular virtues, is not possible without *nous* (1144b14–18).

particular virtues (whether of body or soul), and do so in a way that is systematically revealing of their nature and interconnections.

The conclusion of the famous function argument (*NE* I.7) is that human wellbeing is achieved by those who reason successfully, and display rationally governed excellence. Humans, it is claimed, are such that if they exercise their various reason governed capacities successfully, they achieve in so doing what is good for them to achieve. In this context, the previously introduced and formally specified notion of wellbeing ("whatever it may be") is further refined, in the light of Aristotle's background theory of human nature, to yield the distinctively Aristotelian conception of human wellbeing as paradigmatically a form of reason-based excellence that meets other general requirements: lacking in no worthwhile good (as now constrained by the perspective of excellence), being most goal-like, etc.[24] This claim, which is advanced on general theoretical grounds and is not based on internal criticism of the reactions of particular subjects to particular situations, sets the target for much of the remainder of the *Ethics*.

The Aristotelian conception of wellbeing is of excellent activity, choiceworthy for its own sake in a choiceworthy life. Its paradigm case of this type of choiceworthiness is of excellent (theoretical) rational activity in a life organized around it (1098a16–18). Next best is excellent practical rational activity (1178a9–11). The notions of excellent functioning for a creature with our capacities plays a central role in determining the type of choiceworthy functioning, and in fixing the corresponding notions of harm and disadvantage. But these latter notions have roots in notions such as pain (cf. 1095b31–34), wretchedness and personal misfortune (cf. 1099b3–4, 1101a6–21),

---

24. Aristotle holds that the life of human excellence is the most desirable life available to humans (1098a15–18). On one account, Aristotle begins with a view of the most desirable life independent of the notion of excellence, and then argues that the life of excellence is one that secures such a life. (See H. A. Prichard, "Does moral philosophy rest on a mistake?", in his *Moral obligation* (Oxford: Oxford University Press, 1968).) On one radical alternative, Aristotle begins with the notion of excellence, and then construes what is to be the most desirable life solely in terms of it. (See John McDowell, "The role of eudaimonia", pp. 369–70). The mid position canvassed here takes the relevant notions of benefit and advantage to be understood so that they may involve *both* excellent functioning *and* some prudential value (e.g. pleasure) intelligible in terms independent of excellence. Aristotle's strategy consists in developing a conception of wellbeing that maintains constitutive connections both with excellence and with other goods such as pleasure and social success.

which are not completely transcended in Aristotle's positive account. Indeed, his task is to show that there is a coherent notion of human wellbeing involving excellent as well as pleasurable activity across a range of relevant activities. It is not that the notions of harm and pain are to be understood solely in terms of excellent functioning or vice versa. Rather, his thesis is that both these sets of concepts can be unified in one coherent notion (Aristotelian wellbeing), which gives point to the discussion of individual facets of the good life. I shall seek to exemplify his distinctive approach by considering in outline only a few examples.

In the case of particular virtues (such as courage) Aristotle needs to show that these manifest the type of choiceworthiness captured in his favoured account of wellbeing. He aims to do this by establishing that they essentially involve the exercise of a reason-governed excellence (as defined by "the ratio itself grasped by the practically wise", 1106b35–1107a1, 1115b12–14). For courage, this involves a steady perception of which is the courageous act and a realistic assessment of dangers and risks (1116a2–4, 1117a9–16), together with an appropriate emotional (pleasure/pain) attitude towards courageous acts. The courageous will thus find such acts welcome or even pleasant (1117b1–6, 15–17); they will delight in performing courageous actions, or at least do not do them with unmixed pain or regret (1104b5–6). The case of courage is challenging since it essentially involves a conflict between different goals choiceworthy in the favoured way (1117b9–15, 1169a18–22). Aristotle seeks to show why courage is desirable and why it involves genuine conflict from within the perspective of his favoured conception of wellbeing. He also attempts to make it intelligible how, guided by this perspective, the courageous can reasonably choose to carry out one great and glorious action (or campaign), even if it involves death rather than many less choiceworthy actions over a longer period (1169a23–26). The courageous person's achievement consists not in focusing exclusively on the value of the moral cause, but in seeing many fine things from a perspective in which courageous action, even heroic death, can seem the finest course available to him. ("It is a far far better thing I do now . . ."). This viewpoint (as exemplified by Sydney Carton in Dickens' *A tale of two cities*) is that of the secular hero, not the military saint.

Courage, like other virtues, involves both the ability to see what virtue actually requires in particular situations and an appropriate emotional (pleasure or pain involving) reaction to courageous action.

Thus, courage (as other particular virtues) can be shown to instantiate the Aristotelian ideal of reason-based excellence whose exercise is intrinsically pleasurable (or at least non-painful). Further, such virtues fit together with one another in a way that exemplifies the exercise of practical wisdom, itself a reason-governed excellence (1144b19–21), which defines part of our distinctive nature (1098a5–7) and enables us to avoid harm or injury arising from our own mistakes (1144b8–12). In exercising this virtue, therefore, we achieve a life manifesting the kind of choiceworthiness that, given our natures, it is good for us to achieve.

From the vantage point secured by Aristotle's conception of good human functioning, it is possible to see the point of a wide range of human activity, including (for example) intellectual contemplation and friendship, because both involve (in differing ways) the pleasurable exercise of our reason-based excellences (1170a31–b10, 1177a21ff.). Aristotle's goal is to show that he can non-trivially accommodate within his conception of wellbeing a range of difficult cases: external goods or goods of fortune, certain forms of pleasurable activity, beauty, wealth and honour. He devises a variety of strategies to handle these apparent counter-examples. Some (like wealth, 1099b1–2) have instrumental value, enabling us fully to exercise our rational capacities. Others can destroy our wellbeing by preventing us from engaging in such activity. But pleasure is perhaps the most interesting case. Aristotle seeks to show its close connections (at least in its central cases) with excellent activity (1174b14–24), especially intellectual excellent activity (see also 1177a22–27). These pleasures seem to be taken as paradigmatic because they involve the exercise of our human excellences in a life of Aristotelian wellbeing (contrast the case of the childlike and physical ("slavish") pleasures described in 1177a2–6).

In the case of pleasure, reason-based excellences are taken as paradigmatic, but the excellent use of certain of our other capacities is also given a place (e.g. in perception (1174b20–21, 26–31) and aesthetic appreciation (1175a32–34)). In these cases, a wider range of excellences is given a (non-central) role in Aristotle's account of wellbeing. While for the soul, intellectual excellence is the highest virtue, for the human body, health, strength and beauty (cf. 1099b3, 1140a26–28) are comparable excellences. These are the analogues in their respective spheres (the body) of intellectual excellence in the rational soul (1097a26–30). As a political animal, man's relevant excellence is manifest in good relationships with parents, children, family, friends and fellow citizens (1097b10–14). To be ugly, childless, unmarried or to lack good friends is, on this view, to fail to exercise certain distinctively human virtues (1099b4–8).[25] What distinguishes instrumental or consequential goods (e.g. wealth or honour, the reward of virtue) from those that are intrinsically choiceworthy is that the latter, but not the former, instantiate the ideal of excellence-based activity. Aristotle's aim is to explain what is worthwhile in each of these central cases in a way intelligible on the basis of his fundamental concept of the enjoyable activities of our reason-based excellences. From this perspective, one can see the earlier pleasures involved in natural or trained virtue as important in teaching us the point of rationally based excellence. Their role as persuaders is underwritten by the goals of the ethical life they help to secure (see §3.7).

While Aristotle introduces his fundamental conception of wellbeing dialectically by reference to reputable opinion, he establishes the role of wellbeing thus understood by showing that it can render intelligible the value of other attractive goals in its range in a coherent and unified way.[26] From its perspective, the particular subgoals can be seen to hang together in a non *ad hoc* way that constitutes a coherent and intelligible world.[27] There is a downward, explanatory, road (1095b1) that reveals as intelligibly worthwhile disparate types of activity which had previously seemed individually attractive, but without a background theory of wellbeing to articulate their inter-

---

25. Aristotle also includes good birth in this list (1099b4), as he sometimes counts this as "excellence of breeding" (*Politics* 1283a37). Elsewhere, he classifies good birth as "what follows wealth and virtue", and hence (presumably) not in itself an intrinsic good (*Politics* 1294a21). The latter view may seem somewhat preferable to the reader influenced by the "spirit of modernity."
26. Parts of the *Ethics* are presented within a *dialectically* secured view of human nature in a *scale of nature* reflecting a view about which are the highest capacities (which we share with the gods, etc.: rational activities of a certain theoretical kind) and which are their close analogues (e.g. practical wisdom). But the centre of the argument (on the view proposed) depends on the success of its premisses in rendering intelligible the value of a certain pattern of life and actions (1179a18–24). This test is more authoritative than the opinions of the wise (1179a16–18). For further discussion of this issue, see Robert Bolton's paper, "Aristotle on the objectivity of ethics", in *Essays in ancient Greek philosophy: Aristotle's ethics*, J.P. Anton & A. Preus (eds) (Albany: State University of New York Press, 1991), pp. 7–28.
27. Aristotle was optimistic enough to think that from this perspective one can see the truth in every particular case. But that is clearly a further and more ambitious claim than is required for his main purposes.

connection or point (1097b2–5). We may arrive at our starting point (a particular conception of health or wellbeing) by an upward road beginning with our own experience and reflection on it (as is true in the case of medicine also). But the enquiry is validated by the success of the downward path. From the perspective of Aristotelian eudaimonia (or health), one can (it is proposed) see *the why* as well as *the that*. For this reason, it can be put forward as an explanatory starting point (1095b4–5) in a reaction-independent theory of human good.

Against this background, Aristotle can intelligibly describe us as rationally choosing honour, pleasure, intellect and all of virtue both for their own sake as worthwhile even if no further benefit accrued, and for the sake of wellbeing, because they manifest the type of choice-worthiness characteristic of elements in an intrinsically and non-derivatively worthwhile life (1097b1–5). It is the latter that bestows on the individually desirable activities the distinctive type of underived choiceworthiness we all rationally seek, and not *vice versa* (1097b5–6). The analogy with health is close: we might rationally choose good eyesight or good digestion for their own sake (even if no other benefits accrued), but we also choose them because they contribute to the overall goal of healthy functioning for the whole organism (walking, eye–hand co-ordination, etc.). In both cases, the central concepts (health, wellbeing) give further grounds for regarding already valuable sub-goals as all contributing to the further intrinsic and non-derivative goal of a worthwhile life involving excellent and enjoyable activity for an organism of our type (either in a particular area, or overall – 1140a25–28). Indeed, they give them a unifying point.

Aristotle appears to believe that we could not achieve this degree of unification starting from other basic concepts, such as the wellbeing favoured by the self-indulgent; for there would be goals which this could not render intelligible (e.g. friendship, self-love, courage). This may be why the self-indulgent is represented as at war with himself, without a properly unified practical theory (1166b16ff.). This will be so if the self-indulgent cannot, consistently with being a human being, give up the values and emotions that his basic moral concepts cannot accommodate. But a more basic argument in the *Ethics* consists in Aristotle's attempt to show that a wide variety of intuitively appealing goals can be rendered non-trivially intelligible within the perspective of his favoured fundamental concept. There is thus a parallel pattern of normative justification at work in the cases of health and wellbeing.

4.10 If this is correct, Aristotle is attempting to develop an analogy between practical and theoretical truth in which both are known within successful explanatory schemes of the types indicated.[28] There are, of course, significant disanalogies. Practical reasoning is concerned with what is good for man, and in this sense at least is *anthropocentric*. It is anthropocentric also in being constrained in the ways sketched above (2–3) by our complex nature, with our distinctive emotions, desires and needs. The explanatory interconnections between the properties in the moral or medical case are not, in the main, mediated by efficient causation, but by teleological or more broadly *a priori* relations. But, from Aristotle's viewpoint, the analogies between the cases are sufficiently robust to sustain confidence in the objectivity of moral discourse and the reality of moral properties. They are underwritten by the analogies between explanatory schemes, which in the ethical case render intelligible our reactions to diverse particular cases on the basis of a reaction-independent account of the human good. In this, and in the potential of the general theory to modify our initial reactions, the theory is not itself simply dependent on our reactions and standards of criticism constructed on their basis.

5. Interim conclusions

5.1 On the view outlined in the previous sections, Aristotle supports the LHS of the bi-conditional:

☐ [a is good for man ↔ a seems good to the good man]

in part by a value-laden but reaction-independent theory of what is good for man introduced dialectically but secured by its role in explaining the point of many of the activities we see as valuable. The analogy with theoretical knowledge and with medicine suggests that a similar account of truth can be sustained in this way in all three cases. The knowledge of the good person (like that of the doctor) is

---

28. Aristotle also employs wellbeing outside the *Ethics* in his study of psychological capacities, which he takes as wellbeing-directed. This suggests a richer explanatory theory for the student of human nature who looks at ethical matters. However, I have left these considerations on one side because (i) it is not obvious that the notion of wellbeing is the same in the two cases, and (ii) in the *Ethics*, Aristotle, for the most part, avoids reliance on his scientific doctrines. On this issue, see Bolton, "Aristotle on the objectivity of ethics" (cited in *n*. 26).

the *measure* of truth (although itself more measured than measurer), because it shows that there is reaction-independent truth in the relevant area (and in some cases what that truth is). In a similar way, our grasp of explanatory connections in the theoretical case shows that there is truth of a similar type to be measured there also.[29] The presence of an explanatory scheme legitimizes our grasp of reaction-independent properties, even though no reductive account can be given of what the relevant properties are. Thus, while explanation plays a crucial role in this picture (contrary to the view of my MMR), it is not of the reductive type proposed over the centuries in terms of a value-neutral account of human nature. The analogy Aristotle presses between wellbeing and health (one he shared with Plato in the *Republic*, 443–444) is revealing in its own right. Aristotle appears to envisage or at least allow for a range of kinds of proper functioning relative to different types of goal in a hierarchy (e.g. health, psychiatric health, wellbeing). An Aristotelian argument for the objectivity of the latter notion would be that it is no less objective than that of psychiatric health or health itself. Indeed, it may be hard to sustain the objectivity of discourse concerning psychiatric health without also supporting some measure of objectivity in moral discourse. Both involve negative notions of disadvantage understood in terms of impaired functioning and distress (or pain) at the relevant level and corresponding positive notions of benefit understood in terms of the pleasurable use of the relevant human capacities (e.g. in the psychiatric case, in forming non-stressful personal relations, holding down a job without anguish, etc.). This Aristotelian analogy is worth developing in its own right. It seems to offer a more suitable analogue than those drawn from fundamental physical science for understanding the contested case of the objectivity of the moral.

5.2   In this interpretation, one argument for the objectivity of the ethical is based on the explanatory features discussed from 4.6 onwards, and another is derived from the account of concept acquisition sketched in 4.5 and 3.3. The interest of the view as a whole can be seen if one considers some of the bi-conditionals mentioned earlier, such as

---

29. There is also a further question that Aristotle sometimes asks: "Why is the truth such as to be grasped by our intellect in this way?" His ambitious answer to this, which consists in identifying the world with an intelligible order, or divine mind (*de Anima* III.5), lies outside the scope of the present paper.

☐ [a is a humorous situation ↔ a merits laughter]
☐ [a is a magical object ↔ a merits the respect due to magical objects].

The first example would fail to yield objective reaction-independent truth on this account, because the initial judgements about what is humorous depend essentially not only on reactions to external circumstances but also on our pleasure/pain based reactions to them. The same will be true of many quasi-ethical predicates: "nice", "nauseating", "disgusting", "appalling", "shocking", "awesome", "unsettling", etc. In these cases, as more radically in the case of the "yummy", authority in the application of the predicate remains in large measure with our own non-cognitive, pleasure-/pain-based response to the situations we encounter. Thus, there can be no reaction-independent science of the type described above. If the second example fails to sustain objective truth, this may be because there can be no coherent science of the magical or the divine of the type envisaged in 4.6 onwards. But even if there were a coherent theory of this type, such discourse could fail to be objectively grounded if there is no appropriate analogue of the experiential engagement with the relevant properties and kinds at the pre-conceptual level that partially underpins the objectivity of the ethical concepts. In cases where the only access to the relevant experiences essentially involves the very concepts the developed theory exploits, there is a particular vulnerability to the charge that the whole theory is being kept in place by its own momentum without touching reality.[30] Conversely, in cases where there is a pre-conceptual level of this type, there is evidence for a realism-vindicating, direct engagement with independent objects and objective properties.[31]

---

30. There may also be cases where concepts acquired in the experimental, pre-conceptual, way are shown to be ill founded because the theory in which they fall is itself internally incoherent. This might be true of certain spatial concepts if our basic theories of space were shown to be incoherent.
31. I have gained from discussion of this paper, and related issues, with Bill Brewer, Bill Child, John Campbell, Michael Frede, Bob Heinaman, Jennifer Hornsby, Lindsay Judson, David Pears, Dory Scaltsas, Paul Snowdon, Helen Steward, Rowland Stout and especially Stephen Williams. I was further helped by the constructive comments of Stephen Everson and John McDowell in the Keeling Colloquium in London.

Aristotle and the explanation of evaluation: a reply to David Charles

STEPHEN EVERSON

David Charles' paper is characteristically wide-ranging and philosophically illuminating. It tackles directly the issues that lie at the centre of the contemporary debate over whether our moral judgements are susceptible of realistic construal, and canvasses a daunting variety of texts to elicit an Aristotelian position on this question. Although my reply will, of course, focus on those of his claims that I think should be rejected, this should not obscure the fact that his discussion marks a significant advance in the treatment of Aristotle's account of ethical evaluation.

The paper consists of an exploration of the contrast between what Charles calls "modern moral realism" and what he takes to be Aristotle's method for securing the objectivity of moral judgements. Its core is a discussion of whether, on Aristotle's view, moral properties are to be understood as response-dependent and whether, more generally, this matters for whether we should accept a realistic construal of moral judgement. Before turning to these issues, however, I shall begin, as Charles himself does, by considering what he has to say about the "modern moral realist's" (MMR) moral psychology.

1. According to Charles, if Aristotle subscribes to the position adopted by the MMR, then he will need to maintain that, for instance, the courageous person will be a "military saint" – "one who feels no fear because he realizes that even death in the context of battle for a worthwhile cause is not a *moral* harm."[1] The reason why the MMR requires that, to be courageous, one needs to be saintly in this way is apparently that the virtuous person recognizes only moral goods and moral harms – "since for them the only bad or harm is moral bad or moral harm."[2] This follows from Charles' earlier articulation of the MMR's position, where he gave to the realist the thesis that moral reactions are distinct from non-moral ones and that, given the MMR's cen-

---

1. Above, p. 143.
2. Ibid.

tral claim that there can be no reaction-independent theory of the human good, "the theory of human good constructed wholly on [the] basis [of the moral reactions] will be an exclusively moral one."[3]

Reasonably enough, Charles is suspicious of attributing to Aristotle such a counter-intuitive thesis, and canvasses Aristotle's discussion of courage to see whether he really does expect the courageous person to be entirely unafraid of a noble death. Charles decides that there is no such Aristotelian requirement and so distances Aristotle from the austerity of the MMR's demands on the virtuous agent. However, if the object is to determine whether Aristotle believes that the only goods are moral goods and the only harms moral harms, then this is unnecessary – since it is clear from many places that Aristotle does not subscribe to that view. Most obviously, Aristotle's insistence in NE X that *theoria* is the most valuable activity is incompatible with an entirely moralized conception of what is valuable, if the "moral" is taken to lie with those reasons that are distinctive of practical rather than theoretical virtue. Further, given Aristotle's acceptance that at least some external goods have intrinsic value, this too would prevent his joining the MMR in the moralization of value.[4]

The idea that the only goods are moral goods and the only harms moral harms is highly implausible – indeed, I think, obviously false. Charles, of course, is not committed to the thesis himself, but its implausibility does raise the question of why he should saddle his MMR with it. For even if the "not implausible holism" does deliver a determinate and self-contained set of moral goods (and I am not in fact sure quite how it does this), it does not follow from this that these are the only goods there are – merely that every good is either a moral good or a good of some other sort. A holism that had the effect of denying the existence of aesthetic values seems less than plausible. Certainly, as Charles says, a theory of the human good that is con-

---

3. Above, p. 139.
4. Note that at NE I.7, 1097b2, Aristotle cites honour as something that we choose even if nothing comes from it – and honour, according to Aristotle, is "the greatest of the external goods" (NE 1123b20-21; contrast 1169b9–10). Some, however, have denied that Aristotle allows that any external good has intrinsic value – see, for instance, J. M. Cooper, "Aristotle on the goods of fortune", *Philosophical Review* **XCIV**, 1985, pp. 173–96. For the claim that Aristotle does accept that some external goods have intrinsic value, see, for instance, T. H. Irwin, "Permanent happiness", *Oxford Studies in Ancient Philosophy* III, 1985, pp. 89–124, 1985; and my article, "Aristotle on nature and value", in *Ethics*, S. Everson (ed.) (Cambridge: Cambridge University Press, 1996).

structed *wholly* on the basis of our moral reactions will be an exclusively moral one, but why should the MMR limit the foundations for his account of *eudaimonia* in this way?

The answer to this lies, I presume, in the MMR's explanation of virtuous action. For in the case of the virtuous agent, it is not just that he or she acts according to the dictates of virtue – this is true of the self-controlled or continent agent as well; what distinguishes the virtuous from the continent is that, whereas the latter is "aware of other non-moral but still desirable features of the situation", the "virtuous agent's actions will be explained fundamentally in terms of [his] response to the moral (and only the moral) features of the situation, and all other responses are 'silenced.'"[5] It is this general thesis about the motivation of virtuous agency that requires that the courageous person should feel no fear at the prospect of death in battle, since such a death would not be a *moral* harm. However, the claim that the only goods and harms are moral goods and harms is much stronger even than the claim that the requirements of virtue will, in relevant circumstances, silence all others and is not required to secure it.

Although Charles does not identify his modern realist with any particular contemporary philosopher, he does acknowledge that the MMR's views are closely related to those advocated by John McDowell – and of all the MMR's claims, that moral reasons should silence all others is perhaps the most distinctively McDowellian (indeed the metaphor itself is his). McDowell himself, however, does not support this by denying the value of non-moral goods. So, in his paper "Are moral requirements hypothetical imperatives?", from which the metaphor of silencing is taken, McDowell writes: ". . . part of the point of claiming that the requirements of virtue are categorical imperatives may lie in a rejection of [the] possibility [that they may be outweighed by some other reason]."[6] Rather than seeing this as arising because the reasons for virtuous action always outweigh other sorts of reason, McDowell suggests that it is because "the dictates of reason, if properly appreciated, are not weighed with other reasons at all."[7] Instead, in a situation in which virtue demands acting in a certain way, other, opposing, reasons will not obtain:

---

5. Above, p. 140.
6. "Are moral requirements hypothetical imperatives?", *Proceedings of the Aristotelian Society*, supplementary vol. LII (1978), p. 26.
7. Ibid.

If a situation in which virtue imposes a requirement is genuinely conceived as such . . . then, considerations which, in the absence of the requirement, would have constituted reasons for acting otherwise are silenced altogether – not overridden – by the requirement.[8]

So, the temperate person is "no less prone to enjoy physical pleasure than the next man", but when the pursuit of physical pleasure would count as vicious, "it does not count for him as any reason for acting in that way."[9]

This is not consistent with the view that the only reasons for action are reasons provided by virtue.[10] When the temperate person does pursue physical pleasure, this is not because it is virtuous to do so but because it is enjoyable. What he does not value is physical pleasure in certain circumstances – those circumstances in which it would be vicious to take pleasure in that way. The corollary in the case of courage will be that the courageous person can indeed fear death – regard it as a harm – in most circumstances (he will move out of the way of runaway cars and so on), without having to regard it as a *moral* harm. The courageous man should be fearless in the face of death when to avoid death would be vicious. It is not that in the context of battle death is not a moral harm, but that to attempt to escape death in battle – when this would be to renege on one's duties as a soldier – would be. The virtuous agent does not regard reasons for doing what is morally impermissible as reasons at all.[11]

To show that Aristotle does not accept that all goods and harms are moral goods and harms may distance Aristotle from modern moral realism as it is articulated by Charles, but it does not indicate a divergence between Aristotle and even the most austere modern realists.

---

8. Ibid.
9. Ibid., p. 27.
10. And neither is McDowell's *caveat* on p. 29 that he is not claiming that "clear perception of any moral reason, however weak, silences any reasons of other sorts, however strong." McDowell, at least, allows for the existence of reasons for action other than moral reasons.
11. Charles detects in the MMR's position a possible commitment to the incommensurability of goods (see his §2.6) and rightly distances Aristotle from this. Again, I do not find evidence for this commitment in McDowell's paper – indeed, the thought that the requirements of virtue will, on suitable occasions, silence other considerations suggests that, at least on those occasions, the requirements are quite commensurable with any other reasons for action, since the latter will count for nothing.

Nevertheless, the claim that the brave will be fearless when confronted by death in battle is itself a very strong claim, and Charles provides good reason for thinking that Aristotle would not unhesitatingly accept it. He points to *NE* III.9, for instance, where Aristotle deals with the pain involved in brave actions. So, at 1117a35–b5, Aristotle affirms that the end of courage is pleasant but that this is obscured by the circumstances – as with boxers, their goal is pleasant but the blows they receive are painful. Similarly, for the courageous person, "death and wounds will be painful to the courageous person and unwelcome (*kai akonti estai*), but he will remain because it is noble to do so or because it is base not to do so" (1117b7–9). The brave person may take pleasure in acting nobly, but this will not prevent his feeling the pain of wounds. That sort of pain, of course, is inevitable given the brave person's physiology, but the painfulness of death is not merely physical, even for the brave person:

> And whoever has a greater share of the whole of virtue and is more happy (*eudaimon*), the more he will be pained at death. Such a man is particularly worthy to live, and he will be deprived of the greatest goods and he knows this, and this is painful. But he is not the less brave, but perhaps is more so since he chooses nobility in war instead of these things (1117b9–13).

This sort of pain is the pain of regret. The courageous person does not think that he loses nothing in dying nobly – he accepts that he is harmed.[12]

Although this gives Aristotle a more intuitively appealing position than that required by the austere theorist, it does have difficulties of its own. The great advantage of the austere theory is that it provides a way to distinguish the virtuous agent from the self-controlled agent. If one allows that, like the latter, the virtuous person values what he loses in acting virtuously, it is no longer clear what differentiates virtue from continence. Charles accepts the consequence that "if the analogy [with courage] is maintained, the temperate and the self-controlled may share the same valuational appreciation of the situation", and seeks rather to explain the difference between them by reference to the differing "strength" of their corresponding desires.[13]

---

12. Note that there is no inconsistency between the thought that one is doing or has done *the* right thing (i.e. to deny that the reasons which enter into deliberation are incommensurable) and feeling regret over what has been lost in doing it.

13. Above, pp. 147–8.

The trouble with this is in making sense of the metaphor of desiderative strength. Certainly, the two standard senses in which one might say that one desire is stronger than another seem not to be available here. One can say that a desire for something is strong if one values it highly – so that, in this sense, the akratic's desire to do what is right is stronger than his contrary desire. Alternatively, a desire can be a strong one if it is motivationally effective: in this sense, the akratic's desire to do what is right is weaker than his opposing desire. The first of these senses cannot be employed to explain the difference between the virtuous agent and the self-controlled, since *ex hypothesi* they make the same evaluations of the options. If, however, we take it that the desire of the self-controlled to avoid death, for instance, is motivationally stronger than that of the brave person, it would seem that his desire to act virtuously must likewise be stronger in order to counteract it. This would be an odd claim for an Aristotelian to make.

Now, in NE 1146a9f., Aristotle does say that the self-controlled has "strong and base" desires – a passage duly cited by Charles. What motivates this condition is that self-control is praiseworthy: if the *enkratic* (the continent or self-controlled agent) were controlling good desires, he would not be good, and, if the desires were weak, self-control would not count for much. The enkratic is praiseworthy because he acts against a strong desire not to do the right thing. This, however, is the praise due to the self-controlled and not to the virtuous agent. If the virtuous agent merely possessed weaker desires to do the wrong thing, it is difficult to see why he should be considered more praiseworthy. This problem is removed if we see the very presence of the evil desires as a sign of a defective character – and so the virtuous agent is admirable precisely for lacking them.

This is surely confirmed by Aristotle's having stated just before this that self-controlled and temperate people are distinct because the latter do not have desires that are either excessive or base (1146a11–12). In NE VII.9, to which Charles also refers, this point is made more fully. There Aristotle allows that one can talk of the temperate person's self-control – but this is only because the temperate person and the self-controlled person are alike in that neither is led to act against what is right because of pleasure (1151b34–36). The difference between them lies in that, whereas the continent agent has base desires, the temperate person does not – "the continent does and the temperate person does not have bad desires, and the latter is such as not to feel pleasure contrary to reason, while the former is such as to feel pleasure but not to be led by it" (1152a2–3).[14] The temperate person does not just have weaker desires for pleasure than the continent – in relevant circumstances, the requirements of temperance silence the desire for sex or whatever altogether.

What, then, are we to make of the brave person's regret at dying? If temperance and bravery are analogous, then just as the temperate person's general desire for pleasure is silenced when its pursuit would be vicious, so we should expect that the brave person's general desire to survive will be silenced when to pursue survival would be ignoble. As Charles emphasizes, however, Aristotle allows that the brave person will indeed be pained at the prospect of dying – that is, he will regard it as a harm – even when the death in question is a noble one and it would be cowardly to try to avoid it.

Unlike Charles, however, I do not see that Aristotle maintains this line consistently: rather, he veers between claiming that the brave person will in fact be fearless in the face of a noble death and allowing that he will be pained by the prospect of dying. If it is not possible to reconcile these passages, it is at least possible, I think, to explain why Aristotle should seem undecided on the point.[15] What is important is his underlying insistence on the fact that, although there are some things that are fearful "beyond human nature" (*huper anthropon*, 1115b7–8) and these will be feared by all sane people, "the courageous person is as undaunted as a human can be" (1115b10–11). There are thus *some* circumstances in which even the brave person will be afraid and these will be those that are beyond human nature. Now this would seem to pick up a condition for involuntariness given in NE III.1, where Aristotle has said that someone is excused when he does something he should not, if what leads him to act in this way is such as "to overturn human nature" (1110a23–26). In such a case, the action (or emotion, *pathos*) will not reveal the agent's charac-

---

14. It is open to Charles to challenge the relevance of the last part of this by denying that the differences in what is found pleasurable reflect differences in valuation, but this would be very odd indeed. Both the temperate and the continent have the same physiological mechanisms: if the temperate would fail to get pleasure from particular sexual or gastronomic activity, this must be because his evaluation of the activity blocks the pleasure he would otherwise get.
15. I am not convinced by Charles' attempt to reconcile these claims by taking "fearless" (*adees*) to mean "undaunted or not deterred by fear" rather than "without fear" (p. 144). Aristotle indeed qualifies "fearless" by "unterrified" (*atarachos*) at NE 1117a19, but this too suggests that the brave man is without emotion and not that he has emotion without giving in to it.

ter but merely his (human) nature. The account of voluntariness, of course, is intended to apply not only to actions but to emotions as well, and so it allows that one can excuse someone who feels fear when it would be beyond human nature not to feel fear in that sort of circumstance: such an emotion will be involuntary.[16]

Aristotle's vacillation can thus be explained as arising from the tension that exists between the demands of his general account of virtuous activity and the recognition that virtuous agents will not be able to react virtuously in all circumstances. His initial claim that the brave person will be fearless can thus be seen to reflect his general account of virtue – according to which, considerations of virtue will silence any opposing desires – whereas his acknowledgement that the brave person will regret even a noble death will be motivated by the thought that it may not be possible to be human and to die without regret.[17] In this context, it is worth noting that even McDowell recognizes that his account of virtuous action is an idealized one: "the best we usually encounter is to some degree tainted with continence. But in a view of what genuine virtue is, idealization is not something to be avoided or apologized for."[18] In his less idealistic moments, Aristotle is almost as dubious about the possibility of the military saint as is Charles: his treatment of temperance, however, and his insistence on the principled distinction between the virtuous agent and the merely continent require that the courageous person's attitude to death in battle should not be taken as the paradigm for virtuous activity.[19] One will not be able to determine anything about what it is to be

---

16. For a discussion of this requirement on voluntary action, see my paper, "Aristotle's compatibilism in the *Nicomachean ethics*", *Ancient Philosophy* 10, 1990, pp. 81–103.
17. Compare Aristotle's treatment of the veridical perception of the proper sensibles in *de Anima*: although he begins by saying that it is impossible to be mistaken in the perception of the proper sensibles (418a12), he later qualifies this by saying that such perception is susceptible to the minimum error (428b19). Here too Aristotle begins with an idealization prompted by the support of the general theory of perceptual affection (in standard circumstances, error in the perception of the proper sensibles is impossible) but later nuances this to take into account the nature of what happens in practice (circumstances are not always standard).
18. McDowell, "Are moral requirements hypothetical imperatives?", p. 28.
19. Note that Aristotle's recognition that the brave person may be pained even at the prospect of a noble death forces him at *NE* 1117b15 to qualify his earlier claim (1104b2–9) that what is distinctive of virtuous activity is the agent's pleasure in it (or, at least, freedom from pain). The brave person's regret at dying is not illustrative of the general model of virtuous activity but an exception to it.

virtuous by considering those occasions on which the virtuous person's emotions are the result of his being human rather than his being virtuous. The activity of the virtuous agent is characterized by the absence of desire for non-virtuous alternatives and not by the ability to overcome such desires. The virtuous is not merely less self-controlled than the continent person: he evaluates the world differently.

Thus, both Aristotle and the modern moral realist accept the moralization of value if this is taken to mean no more than that unless one has moral knowledge, one will not be able to acquire a proper understanding of what is valuable and what is not – there will be some goods and harms that one will not grasp. Neither Aristotle nor the modern realist need to be committed to the much stronger claim that, if one lacks moral knowledge, one will have no understanding of what is worth pursuing.

2. As Charles acknowledges, the core of his MMR's position lies not in the moral psychology but in what he has to say about the nature of moral properties. It would be open to a moral realist to deny the MMR's thesis about the categorical nature of moral reasons and still accept his account of what secures the objectivity of moral judgements. That account, as Charles articulates it, is centred on the thought that it is neither possible to grasp moral concepts independently of understanding our moral reactions to things, nor to characterize those reactions other than as judgements that something has the property in question. The properties in question, that is, are response-dependent, but the relevant responses cannot be understood other than as responses to those properties. The objectivity enjoyed by the judgements that objects or actions have or have not the properties in question is guaranteed by the fact that "our practices of approbation themselves contain coherent standards of criticism by which to judge particular reactions as well or ill judged, reasonable or unreasonable, noble or ignoble, etc."[20] Particular judgements can thus be assessed for truth and falsity, despite the fact that one cannot understand what it is for something to have a relevant property independently of its being such as to elicit the judgement that it has that property.[21]

This accords, for instance, with the introduction to a recent anthology of essays concerned with moral realism, in which the author

---

20. Above, p. 138.

claims that "realism [about some subject matter] involves embracing just two theses: (1) the claims in question, when literally construed, are literally true or false, and (2) some are literally true."[22] I take the talk of "literal truth" here to mean just that the truth-predicate, which the contested claims are taken to satisfy by the realist, is the same truth-predicate that any non-contested claim satisfies. Certainly, modern moral realism, as characterized in Dr Charles' paper, is committed to holding both these theses about moral claims – and to doing so without breaking the mutual conceptual links the modern realist allows to obtain between the evaluative properties we ascribe to actions and to objects, and the sensibilities and practices required to understand those ascriptions. Underlying Charles' discussion is a concern that the goals set by the modern realist may be too lax, thereby requiring us to accept a realistic construal of claims for which this is inappropriate. The danger is that one will end up a realist not only about morals but about such less appealing things as the humorous, the divine, the magical and the yummy.

One can, of course, define "realism" as one wishes and, according to one's definition, it may be more or less odd to endorse realism about all manner of things. To give substance to the question, however, it is useful to see the modern realist as maintaining that, once he has shown that some moral sentences are true, no proper distinction in respect of their ability to be used to state how the world is can be drawn between moral sentences and, say, sentences used to ascribe primary qualities to things. As Charles says, modern realism has been concerned to deny that, for instance, "the only genuine properties are those which play a role in the preferred basic scientific theory of the world and its efficient causal interactions" and that "genuine properties are only those which are graspable in ways which do not essentially involve reference to our particular practices or sensibilities."[23]

So, I will take it to be common ground both that there are moral beliefs which are true and that this is something which Aristotle

---

21. See J. McDowell, "Values and secondary qualities", in *Morality and objectivity*, T. Honderich (ed.) (London: Routledge & Kegan Paul, 1985), pp. 110–29, section 3, for the argument that, just because a property is subjective in the sense that it is distinctively phenomenal, it is not subjective in the different sense that unrelativized judgements concerning the possession of that property are not capable of truth and falsity.
22. G. Sayre-McCord, in *Essays on moral realism*, G. Sayre-McCord (ed.) (Ithaca, New York: Cornell University Press, 1988), p. 5.
23. Above, pp. 137–8.

STEPHEN EVERSON

accepts. What is in question is whether more than this is required for a substantive moral realism and, if so, whether we can find in Aristotle reason to think that he would accept that our moral beliefs meet whatever more stringent conditions are put in place. I share Charles' dissatisfaction with the "quietism" of his MMR and agree that this stance is not Aristotle's. As will become apparent, however, I have reservations about the moves that Charles attributes to Aristotle. In the next two sections I shall spell out those reservations and then, finally, I shall suggest an alternative way in which the Aristotelian can meet a recent challenge posed to the would-be moral realist.

4. In Charles' reading of Aristotle, there are two ways in which Aristotle secures the response-independency of our moral beliefs. The first is through Aristotle's account of the acquisition of the concepts that feature in those beliefs, and the second is through the explanatory use to which they are put. I shall discuss the explanatory claims first and then move back to what he has to say about the acquisition of moral concepts.

Looking to see what sort of explanatory role might be played by moral facts is certainly a promising route for the realist to take, for, even if we allow that there are moral facts, it remains open that these are merely the result of our possessing certain norms for belief and assertion when these norms are not themselves regulated by the purpose of describing a reality which is prior to our reacting to it – that, in Crispin Wright's metaphor, such facts "are no more than *shadows* cast by the syntax of our discourse."[24] If, however, it can be shown that moral facts can stand in explanatory relations with other, response-independent, facts, then this will provide them with the desired independence from our moral responses.

The explanatory structure that Charles seeks to uncover in Aristotle is that between particular values and human wellbeing, eudaimonia. He develops this by pressing an analogy between eudaimonia and health. In the case of health, what it is for any particular organ to

---

24. C. Wright, *Truth and objectivity* (Cambridge, Mass.: Harvard University Press, 1992), pp. 181–2. The force of this metaphor should become clearer in the light of §6 below. No offence should be taken at the talk of moral facts here. At least for the sake of this discussion, then, we are accepting that there are at least some true moral beliefs and hence true moral sentences – and I shall take this to license talk of moral facts. That there are facts is simply given by the fact that there are true sentences.

be functioning properly is given determinacy by the higher-level notion of "human health and good condition." One knows, that is, what it is for a given organ to function well only once one knows what role it plays in the proper working of the system as whole. One could not begin by considering the body's organs individually, determine what their healthy state is, and then derive the understanding of a healthy person from this – so that a healthy person would just be one whose parts were functioning as already specified. Rather, one's initial views about the proper functioning of organs will need to be validated by – and can be revised in the light of – a general theory of human functioning, where that theory will itself be secured by its ability to explain why the "many different parts of the body are organized as they are."[25]

Similarly, according to Charles, although someone may begin by identifying particular types of thing as valuable, what will validate this will be the ability to "see the relevant interconnections between the relevant virtues, and grasp what the right thing to do is in particular cases from the perspective of the worthwhile life for a properly functioning human being."[26] Slightly later, he writes:

> While Aristotle introduces his fundamental conception of wellbeing dialectically by reference to reputable opinion, he establishes the role of wellbeing thus understood by showing that it can render intelligible the value of other attractive goals in its range in a coherent and unified way. From its perspective, the particular subgoals can be seen to hang together in a non *ad hoc* way which constitutes a coherent and intelligible world.[27]

The point of the analogy, if successful, is that

> there will be in both cases a reaction-independent structure whose legitimacy does not rest solely with our judgements of what is reasonable and worthwhile, but is grounded rather in a reaction-independent theory of a properly functioning human, which holds in place our account of the particular virtues.[28]

The problem with this is in the need to provide a convincing specification of the standards of coherence and unification. While we can

---

25. Above, p. 162.
26. Above, p. 164.
27. Above, p. 168.
28. Above, p. 164.

make good sense of what it is for a set of beliefs to be coherent, this does not carry over straightforwardly to the case of values. When there is a conflict of beliefs, we know that at least one of the conflicting beliefs must be false – conflict here will arise from inconsistency. While values may conflict in practice, so that in particular circumstances one may not be able to act according to all relevant evaluations, this does not show that any of the evaluations are false or should be given up. Again, just as there is no obvious way in which values can be inconsistent with each other, neither is there any obvious way in which they can entail each other, even in the sense that by accepting one value one should be committed to accepting some other.

It seems that Charles seeks to meet this sort of worry by finding in Aristotle the attempt to ground claims of value in a reaction-independent theory of the human good, which takes the exercise of theoretical knowledge as its paradigm constituent:

> since [Aristotle] holds on perfectionist grounds that theoretical knowledge is the paradigm case of intrinsically desirable activity (the exercise of our highest virtue, the one we share with the gods, etc.), he can establish the intrinsic desirability of the exercise of practical knowledge in the virtuous life by showing that the latter activity resembles the former.[29]

So, practical excellence is similar to theoretical excellence in that it involves the exercise of reason. What, though, of other valuable things, such as the external goods?

Aristotle's goal is to show that he can non-trivially accommodate within his conception of wellbeing a range of difficult cases: external goods or goods of fortune, certain forms of pleasurable activity, beauty, wealth and honour.[30]

Some, according to Charles, are valuable because, like wealth, they allow the exercise of virtue or, like friendship or having children, they "involve (in differing ways) the pleasurable exercise of our reason-based excellences."[31] In the case of pleasure, while the activities of the "reason-based excellences are taken as paradigmatic"[32], the "excellent use of certain of our other capacities is also given a place"[33] – as

---

29. Above, pp. 158–9.
30. Above, p. 167.
31. Ibid. See my paper, "Aristotle on nature and value", (*n.* 4 above) for an attack on this sort of view of the value of personal relationships.
32. Ibid.

examples of which Charles cites perception and aesthetic appreciation. Further, the excellences of the body can be seen to be valuable because they are the "analogues" of intellectual excellence in the rational soul.

The trouble with this is that, for all that has been said, what makes the bodily excellences analogous with the excellences of the soul is just that they are indeed excellences. Once one has accepted that some bodily attribute is an excellence, no more is needed in order to show that it is valuable: if something is excellent, it is thereby worth having. What is needed, if Aristotle is to be seen as following Charles' programme, is for Aristotle to have provided some justification of why various bodily attributes are excellent attributes and to do so by reference to some similarity they have to theoretical excellence. This is not what we find in Aristotle – nor, I think, is there any sign that he would have regarded this lack as a lacuna.

For in his discussion of the value of external goods, Aristotle appears much more blithe than he should do if he had really taken on the task of showing how these, when intrinsically valuable, are so because they are suitably related to reason-based excellences. All he says in NE I.8 is that, in contrast to those external goods that are merely instrumentally valuable, in the case of such goods as friends, children, good-breeding and beauty, we would not say that someone who lacked them is happy. In the case of honour, which Aristotle describes as "the greatest of the external goods" (NE 1123b20–21), this is simply given as one of the things that we choose for itself (NE 1097b2–3).[34]

The analogy with health is not close enough to counter these doubts. The reason why one cannot understand what it is for an organ to function properly without understanding what it is for a person to be healthy is that the organ itself cannot be understood other than as a functional part of the living body. Although Aristotle may allow – explicitly in the *Eudemian ethics* (1216a37–b2) – that the virtues are constituents of eudaimonia, he does not derive from this the consequence that one can only understand either what it is to be just, say, or why justice is valuable if one sees it as a part of wellbeing. In NE I.7, he gives a (not exhaustive) list of those things through which we take

---

33. Ibid.
34. This casts some doubt on Charles' claim (p. 168) that honour, like wealth, is not among those goods that are intrinsically choiceworthy.

ourselves to be happy, and what they have in common is just that we would choose them even if nothing else came of them (1097b2–5). This suggests that the criterion for something's being a constituent of wellbeing is just that it is intrinsically valuable – that is, worth pursuing for itself. Rather than validating the claims that particular types of thing are intrinsically valuable by reference to some theory of wellbeing, Aristotle rather fixes the content of eudaimonia by determining what is intrinsically valuable.

Charles makes the point that the account of wellbeing favoured by the self-indulgent would not serve as well as that favoured by the practically wise in providing a validation of particular values, since "there would be goals [such as friendship and courage] which [it] could not render intelligible."[35] It is not clear, though, that the account of wellbeing accepted by the practically wise can *render* these intelligible – except directly, because of its recognition that they do indeed have value and are worth pursuing. The failure of particular substantive accounts of wellbeing may lie just in the fact that they are overly restrictive. So, an account of wellbeing that neglected aesthetic value would be no more coherent or unified than one that recognized it (perhaps, in fact, less so) – what it would be is defective because it excludes what cannot be excluded if the account is to be comprehensive. To understand this, however, doesn't require a theory of wellbeing but merely the straightforward recognition of aesthetic values for what they are. Once one has recognized this, then one will see that, whatever else someone may achieve, he will not achieve eudaimonia if he remains a philistine. The way to get someone who is aesthetically unappreciative to see that aesthetic activity is indeed valuable is not by making reference to some pre-existing theory of the human good, or by exploring the links between aesthetic and intellectual activity, but by making him look and listen seriously. Experience and training are what are required rather than theory – a point that seems to me a thoroughly Aristotelian one.[36]

5. These considerations make Charles' second route to evaluative objectivity a much more appealing one. By focusing on the parallels between the acquisition of evaluative concepts and that of skills, he is

---

35. Above, p. 169.
36. Part of my disagreement with Charles is due to a different construal of the "*ergon* argument" in *NE* I.7. For this, see my paper, "Aristotle on nature and value" (*n.* 4, above)

able to make a principled distinction between such concepts as those of the humorous or the yucky and those capable of entering into objective evaluations. In the case of both skills and, for instance, the concepts of the various types of virtuous action, the initial ability to recognize the similarity that holds between what falls under the relevant concepts is not acquired in a way that is, as he puts it, "mediated" by the subject's responses of pleasure and pain. In contrast, when one comes to explain how such concepts as the disgusting and the humorous are acquired, it is plausible to think that "similar non-cognitive reactions of pleasure and pain" play an irreducible role in our coming to identify things as being relevantly similar.[37] In the case of objective evaluative concepts, pleasure and pain come into play not by securing a similarity of response to particular cases of some evaluable type but in influencing the direction of the subject's cognitive interests.[38]

Now, I think that Charles' focusing on the acquisition of evaluative concepts, rather than just on, say, convergence of evaluative beliefs, is absolutely right – although I have doubts about the way in which he fits pleasure into the account. Rather than detailing these doubts, however, I shall try to reinforce Charles' strategy by placing these issues within the context of a contemporary debate about the place of moral facts within explanation.[39] Rather than attempting to construct a contemporary realist, I shall take the easier course of using the views of actual philosophers.

A useful starting point is the well known challenge to the realist posed by Gilbert Harman:

> If you . . . see a group of young hoodlums pour gasoline over a cat and ignite it, you do not need to *conclude* that what they are doing is wrong; you do not need to figure anything out, you can see that it is wrong.[40]

We have a case where one is perceptually confronted with an action and thereby comes to believe that the action is wrong. However, in

---

37. Although presumably one would need to make reference to more fine-grained sentiments than pleasure and pain, even if those sentiments are pleasant or painful.
38. So, someone who enjoys a certain kind of activity is apparently likely to take more care to make his judgements about it precise and well informed than is someone who dislikes it. This is the case both for virtuous activity and for other kinds of activity, such as housebuilding.

order to explain how this occurs, according to Harman, there is no need to appeal to any moral properties of the action itself. Whereas, on his view, both the belief that the cat is burning, and the belief that the burning of the cat is wrong, manifest the observer's general beliefs – "Observations are always 'theory laden'"[41], he claims – there is nevertheless a difference between them. Whereas in the case of scientific observation, "you need to make assumptions about certain physical facts to explain the occurrence of the observations that support a scientific theory", in the case of "so-called moral observations", "it would seem that you need only make assumptions about the psychology or moral sensibility of the person making the moral observation."[42]

So, to explain how the subject comes to hold this particular moral belief, "it would seem that all we need to assume is that you have certain more or less well articulated moral principles that are reflected in the judgements you make, based on your moral sensibility." The point here is presumably the following. Provided that someone believes that setting fire to cats is wrong (perhaps because he believes that it is wrong to cause unnecessary suffering to animals and he believes that cats are animals), then if he observes someone setting

---

39. Briefly, Charles thinks that Aristotle cedes ground to the sentimentalist in that, while he allows that our initial responses to actions and occasions of action are fully cognitive, he would regard the realist as erring in seeing "no independent role in justificatory explanation either for a pre-conceptual level of response or for the pleasure/pain combinations found there" (p. 153, above). One worry is whether it is proper to take Aristotle as seeing pleasure as a non-cognitive response rather than itself a form of evaluation. Even if one ignores this worry, however, the role of pleasure in the acquisition of virtue would still not be what the sentimentalist requires. For what is claimed for pleasure is not that it plays any constitutive role in the acquisition or grasp of either concepts or proto-concepts, but rather that it has an effect on how well the agent, as we might say, maintains his moral concentration. Charles contrasts humans with possible "machine men or saints", for whom the stability of moral perception does not depend "on their finding acting in this way agreeable." But if it is possible for there to be agents who can acquire mastery of the relevant concepts without the need for pleasure responses, the sentimentalism canvassed here has less to do with providing a response-dependent account of moral concepts and properties than with emphasizing a perfectly plausible, and no doubt important, thesis about human psychology – that discriminatory capacities that one does not enjoy using are less likely to be used than those that one does enjoy using; and without practice one will become less good at making the relevant discriminations.
40. G. Harman, *The nature of morality* (Oxford: Oxford University Press, 1977), p. 4.
41. Ibid.
42. Ibid., p. 6.

fire to the cat he will believe that the action is wrong. One can explain why the subject should believe what he does about the action he sees without having to credit him with a perceptual sensitivity to any putatively moral properties.

Harman's talk of a moral *sensibility* here, however, masks an inadequate account of moral judgements. For what he leaves crucially out of account are those judgements about particular actions that result not from the application of principles but from the exercise of particular evaluative concepts. For if we are to focus on a class of evaluative judgements that are most plausibly perceptual, these will not be judgements such as "That act is wrong" but rather such as "That act is brutal."[43]

When we seek to explain how the subject comes to believe that the action he sees is brutal, however, it is difficult to see how such an explanation can itself avoid using the notion of brutality, and in two ways. Harman thinks that all that is needed for the explanation is a description of the subject's moral sensibility – but to do this we will need to attribute to him the concept of brutality and we cannot do this without ourselves being able to grasp that concept. Further, unless we can come up with an account of the brutal that will show in other terms what it is for an action to be brutal, then we will not be able to avoid taking the property of the burning of the cat that is relevant to the explanation of the subject's belief to be precisely its brutality. We cannot explain why the subject came to believe that the burning of the cat was brutal without citing either its brutality or those features of the action in virtue of which it was brutal. When we come to explain what it has in common with other actions judged (perhaps under favourable circumstances) to be brutal, then we will need to cite just its brutality.

The idea that this sort of explanation can be used in the service of cognitivism will be familiar from the writings of David Wiggins. Thus, in his paper "Truth as predicated of moral judgements", Wiggins gives the following as one of the "marks" of truth:

> If x is true, then x will under favourable circumstances command convergence, and the best explanation of the existence of this convergence will require the actual truth of x.[44]

---

43. See D. Wiggins, "Truth as predicated of moral judgements", in his *Needs, values, truth* (Oxford: Basil Blackwell, 1987), p. 157, for a related point.
44. Ibid., p. 147.

Glossing this, he writes:

> If the convergence in the belief that item t is F is to be relevant to truth – if this is to be a case of the interesting, significant convergence that truth commands – then what puts that belief there and holds it there has to be nothing more and nothing less than the fact that the item t really *is* F. . . . We have the kind of convergence in belief that truth commands where *the best explanation of agreement in belief that p is inconsistent with any denial on the explainer's own part that* p.[45]

It is perhaps important to warn against an incautious understanding of what is said here: there is certainly no commitment to the claim that for *every* convergence in belief, the best explanation of that convergence will require that what is believed is true. Wiggins' second mark can happily allow the possibility that people can come *en masse* to believe falsehoods because they are gullible, say, or religious or defer to authority. The substantive point in the second mark comes in the first half: that if x is true, then it will command convergence (under favourable circumstances).[46] The second half is simply drawing out the consequence of this: if there is a convergence on the belief that p and *that* convergence comes about because p is true, then the explanation of that convergence will require the truth of p. If it can be shown that the best explanation for convergence on the moral belief that p requires citing the fact that p, then this will, in the terms of the present discussion, give the moral realist the explanatory purchase he needs.

The idea that realism can be secured by the need to cite the relevant facts in the explanation of our beliefs has, however, recently been called into question by Crispin Wright in his 1991 Waynflete Lectures, and the book *Truth and objectivity*.[47] In these lectures, Wright considered the question of what has to be true of a predicate if it is to function as a truth-predicate, and argued, interestingly, that more than one predicate could in fact satisfy these constraints. With this claim in hand, he was able to reconstrue the various debates about realism in terms of what sort of truth-predicate would be appropriately satisfied

---

45. Ibid. p. 151. The italics are Wiggins' own.
46. This would be consistent, I think, with the claim that some sentences may be simply unverifiable, in which case there will be no circumstances favourable to commanding convergence.
47. See *n*. 22 above.

by different classes of sentence. Rather than worrying about whether moral sentences, say, or mathematical or modal sentences are capable of being true (and false), the disputants to the various realist/anti-realist disputes can simply accept the truth-capability of the relevant sentences and look to the question of whether the sort of truth of which sentences of a certain class are capable is the sort that goes with a realist construal of the relevant subject matter, be it morality, modality or whatever else.

A sentence, on Wright's view, will be truth-assessable just if it meets certain syntactic criteria – for instance, that it can take a negation operator and function as the antecedent of a conditional. All that is required of a truth-predicate is that it satisfy certain very basic requirements – Wright calls them platitudes – such as: "that to assert is to present as true; that any truth-apt content has a significant negation that is likewise truth-apt; that to be true is to correspond to the facts; that a statement may be justified without being true, and vice versa."[48] In accepting the force of these platitudes, the minimalist allows that truth is a "genuine property", and one that "warranted assertions are not guaranteed to possess."[49] Any sentence that meets the syntactic criteria will be such as to satisfy a truth-predicate that satisfies these platitudes, that is, it will be capable of what Wright calls "minimal truth." The question then is whether it will be such as to satisfy a truth-predicate that meets more than these minimal requirements – and, according to Wright, when the sentences of a discourse do not, that discourse is not realistically construable.

In explicating minimal truth, Wright makes much use of an analogy with the account of reference that he had provided in his earlier book on Frege's philosophy of mathematics.[50] There the notion of an object was taken to be a formal rather than a substantive one; that is, instead of defining singular terms as those that refer to (individual) objects, singular terms are defined syntactically and then objects are taken to be what singular terms refer to. On this conception of an object, and given that there are true sentences that have numerical singular terms as constituents, it will not make sense to ask whether there are numbers; that there are numbers is simply given by the linguistic facts. It is here that Wright finds the parallel between the

---

48. *Truth and objectivity*, p. 34.
49. Ibid., p. 35.
50. C. Wright, *Frege's conception of numbers as objects* (Aberdeen: Aberdeen University Press, 1983).

referents of abstract singular terms and the "states of affairs purportedly depicted by merely minimally true sentences" – the latter do not "do anything except answer to the demands of our minimally true thoughts."[51]

If it can be made good, the comparison between abstract singular terms and minimal truth-conditions focuses the force of the challenge presented by Wright's account to the moral realist. For it makes it more obvious why the realist cannot rest content with demonstrating that there are moral truths and, hence, moral facts. If the moral facts he establishes are merely the inevitable consequence of there being true moral sentences – sentences, that is, which meet whatever are the assertoric norms of moral discourse – and no more can be said about their role in things than this, then they will have no more substance, as it were, than facts of algebra or set theory. Rather than seeing our discursive practice as regulated by the attempt to secure a set of truths that are either antecedent to, or at least independent of, that practice, the dependence will be the other way around. What truths there are will be dependent merely on the norms of that practice.

The point can be seen if we consider an instance of the explanation of convergence offered by Wiggins in the paper cited earlier. "How", he asks, "can there be values and obligations 'out there' that will account for such agreement as we achieve in our moral and aesthetic beliefs?"

> Well, [he answers], there is at least one general way in which we might try to conceive of the prospects for moral judgements' commanding the sort of convergence that truth requires. This is by analogy with the way in which arithmetical judgements command it. There is an impressive consensus that $7 + 5 = 12$; and, when we rise above the individual level and look for the explanation of the whole consensus, only one explanation will measure up to the task. There is nothing else *to* think that seven and five add up to.[52]

But, in the light of Wright's discussion, this now seems too weak – at least if the fact that a set of beliefs meet the convergence condition now needs to show that those beliefs can satisfy a truth-predicate that is more substantial than the minimal one. For even if one could not explain the convergence on the belief that $7 + 5 = 12$ other than by cit-

---

51. *Truth and objectivity*, p. 181.
52. "Truth as predicated of moral judgements", p. 153.

ing (possibly amongst other things) the fact that $7 + 5 = 12$, this itself could be explained merely by the fact that the norms of mathematical discourse are such that they (conclusively) determine the warranted assertibility of "$7 + 5 = 12$."[53]

In his explication and justification of the second mark of truth, Wiggins makes reference to the fact that "a subject or interpreter has to try to see other subjects as constantly adjusting their beliefs to something – as responding constantly to some reality or other (and, wherever this applies, as responding to changes in those ins and outs)."[54] The effect of Wright's discussion is to block any straightforward move from the existence of some convergence in belief, even where that convergence is to be best explained by citing the truth of what is believed, to the acceptance that, in so converging, those who hold the shared belief are responding to any reality at all – if, that is, the reality in question is taken to be something explanatorily prior to our practices of describing it. If mathematical sentences can satisfy only the minimal truth-predicate, then we might say that Wiggins' explanation of mathematical convergence gets things the wrong way around: it is not that we explain the fact that there is nothing else to think than that $7 + 5 = 12$ by reference to the fact that "$7 + 5 = 12$" is true, but rather that the truth of "$7 + 5 = 12$" is to be explained by the fact that, given that one is operating within the norms of mathematical discourse, there is nothing else to think.

6. Wright's own criterion for determining whether the sentences distinctive of a particular discourse are capable of being more than merely minimally true is what he calls the "width of their cosmological role":

> Let the *width of cosmological role* of the subject matter of a discourse be measured by the extent to which citing the kinds of states of affairs with which it deals is potentially contributive to

---

53. Some may (reasonably) object that talk of "the norms of (some) discourse" is unpleasantly vague as it stands. All that is required for the moment, however, is the acknowledgement that in possessing a concept, or range of concepts, the subject will be governed by some determinate criteria in his application of the concept or concepts to particular cases. What criteria are relevant to the question of whether something falls within the extension of the concept will be (at least partially) constitutive of the concept itself. See C. Peacocke, *A study of concepts* (Cambridge: Mass.: MIT Press, 1992), Ch. 1. I shall continue, for the moment, to follow Wright in talking of "norms" and "discourses."
54. "Truth as predicated of moral judgements", p. 150.

the explanation of things *other than*, or *other than via*, our being in attitudinal states which take such states of affairs as object . . . The crucial question is not whether a class of states of affairs feature in the *best* explanation of our beliefs about them, but of *what else* there is, other than our beliefs, of which the citation of affairs can feature in *good enough* explanations.[55]

The point is clear enough. Let it be the case that people, suitably situated, converge on a particular belief and that we seek to explain that convergence by reference to the fact that what they believe is true. As we have seen, there are two possible explanatory relations here. The convergence may be explained as the result of the world's impinging on suitably sensitive subjects in the same way. Alternatively, the truth of the belief may be explained rather as the result of the acceptance of a set of norms warranting assertion and belief, where those norms can be characterized somehow other than as what are required for the project of discovering facts that are explanatorily independent of the norms themselves. We can find in Wright's criterion of cosmological width a way of determining the direction of any particular explanatory relation. For if the facts cited in an explanation of a convergence in belief can *also* be cited in the explanation of other, non-cognitive, states, then they will be susceptible to characterization *other than* as the objects of the beliefs and assertions distinctive of a particular discourse. If a fact enters into such explanations, then this will provide it with the sort of independence that realism requires. This meets the challenge posed by Charles' modern realist head-on. There is no suggestion that what distinguishes realistic discourse is that we can somehow capture its subject matter without using the concepts which are distinctively employed in that discourse. The point is that there is nevertheless a significant distinction between claims whose only explanatory role is in respect of that discourse itself and those that enter into explanations more widely. Wright's contention in *Truth and objectivity* is that moral facts will not satisfy this criterion for realism. The *only* explanatory role of such facts will be in respect of peoples' moral beliefs and the human activities that arise from their having the moral beliefs they do.

Even if the realist accepts this last point, however, his position is not lost – for it is open to him to challenge Wright's criterion of "cos-

---

55. *Truth and objectivity*, pp. 196–7.

mological width." It is here that Aristotle's emphasis on the fact that the principal evaluative concepts are acquired through experience will prove important. For what is of interest to the debate is not how the truth of a belief is determined by the norms of some discourse but also how those norms themselves can be acquired. On Harman's model of moral education, for instance, perceptual concepts play no intrinsic role in the formation of moral beliefs; what are required are rather general beliefs of the form "Xing is wrong", where the action term is a non-evaluative one. All that would be required in the particular case would be the ability to identify an action as an act of Xing and this would be sufficient to produce the belief that it is wrong. When we turn, with Aristotle, to consider more determinate evaluations such as "That's courageous" or "That's brutal", we will be hard-pressed to find any prior general descriptions such that by identifying an action as something that satisfies them, one can conclude that it is courageous or brutal. One acquires the concept through exposure to a series of actions, and an explanation *is* required of what it is about *those* actions that makes them such that exposure to them, rather than others, is such as to bring about the relevant conceptual ability. In the absence of any reductive account of courage or brutality or elegance or whatever, the only available explanation is that which makes reference to these properties.

It is this that makes Wright's criterion of cosmological width misguided as it stands. Let us accept (without argument here[56]) two claims that are controversial (but which I take both to be true and to be Aristotelian). The first is that mental events are not identical with physical events and the second is that there is mental–physical causal interaction.[57] If this is right, then one could not have a full understanding of the causal history of the world without making use of a propositional attitude vocabulary. A scientist who ignored the fact that some of the organisms that have effects on the world, and are affected by it, enjoy a propositional attitude psychology would not be able to understand why many of the events that occur do occur.[58] Once it has been accepted that explanations of our cognitive states can

---

56. But see the final section of J. McDowell's paper, "Functionalism and anomalous monism", in *Actions and events*, E. LePore & B. McLaughlin (eds) (Oxford: Basil Blackwell, 1985), pp. 387–98.
57. For Aristotle's acceptance of these propositions, see my discussion, "Psychology", in *The Cambridge companion to Aristotle*, J. Barnes (ed.) (Cambridge: Cambridge University Press, 1995), pp. 168–94.

be wider than the merely rationalizing and that those states are to be brought within the realm of causal explanation, then we will need to provide particular causal explanations for particular beliefs. If we cannot provide a causal explanation of a set of beliefs, or of people's convergence on particular beliefs, without making reference to a set of facts (say, moral facts), then this will give us the reason we need to take the corresponding sentences to satisfy a truth-predicate that is more than minimal. It will serve no proper metaphysical or explanatory goal if, in our unwillingness to cite states of affairs that have a narrow cosmological role, we leave ourselves simply unable to explain our ability to acquire certain concepts and to make certain judgements.

On Aristotle's account of the acquisition of moral concepts, the subject has to be exposed to a range of actions – as a result of which he will come to recognize what they have in common. He is not taught a set of rules for the application of moral terms that he can understand antecedently to such exposure. The norm for asserting that a particular action is kind or courageous is just that it should be kind or courageous, i.e. like those he has already encountered. What needs to be explained is what it is about *those* actions, exposure to which has enabled him to proceed cognitively in a determinate and predictable way. This last point is important. The fact is that the attribution of the relevant conceptual abilities to people makes available a psychological theory with quite some *predictive* power. We can predict with complete certainty that anyone who possesses the concept of cruelty, when confronted by Harman's hoodlums engaged in their inflammatory act, will judge that what they are doing is cruel (provided that they believe, of course, *contra* Descartes, that cats can feel pain). This emphasizes the nature of the challenge posed to an irrealist such as Harman: he has to say what it is about that act that makes it such as to be brought, quite determinately, within the concept, and must, in doing this, be able to specify what it has in common with those other acts that also fall determinately within it. Here we can note a demand made by Wiggins against those who see convergence in belief too readily: that the convergence in question should be "not

---

58. It is important to note here that to abandon propositional attitude psychology would be to lose the ability to talk of *actions* rather than just of bodily movements. See Jennifer Hornsby's article, "Physical thinking and conceptions of behaviour", in *Subject, thought and context*, P. Pettit & J. McDowell (eds) (Oxford: Oxford University Press, 1986), pp. 95–116.

a *mere intersubjectivity* or a chorus of agreement in which each new voice that is added sings the note it joins in upon just for the sake of unison, reinforcing thereby the voices that are already singing that note."[59] It is not that, when one learns an evaluative concept through ostension, one learns to apply a word to those particular objects to which others are already applying that word: someone could certainly mimic the ability of those who do have the concept of, say, elegance merely by using the predicate of those objects one has heard them apply it to. This would be mere mimicry, however, and would not constitute agreement in judgement with them. The latter requires that one be able to apply it, broadly as they would, to objects as yet unencountered. The ability to predict what others will judge to be elegant runs in tandem with the ability to judge what is elegant.

The reason why it is important to focus on the explanation of concept acquisition, rather than just the formation of beliefs, is that although what is to be explained is the ability to hold those beliefs, what is changed in the acquisition of the concepts is a subject who does not *start out* with that ability. The actions and objects to which the subject is perceptually exposed thus have an effect on him even at the stage when he cannot recognize them for what they are. The reason why it is important to emphasize the role of ostension in the acquisition of the concepts is that one cannot get a grip on the norms governing the application of the concepts without standing in a direct cognitive relation to instances of the kind of thing that falls under that concept.

The realist has a ready explanation for the acquisition of evaluative concepts, of course. He can say that what one acquires in acquiring such a concept is precisely a sensitivity to the way things are. What secures the relevant conceptual ability is that one comes to spot that the set of things in question are relevantly similar – and will claim that the relevant similarity can only be captured by using the concept itself. The best explanation, he will claim, both of suitable subjects' convergence in evaluative beliefs and of their ability to become suitable by acquiring the relevant concepts will require that things are, generally speaking, as they are believed to be. Indeed, if he is bold, he will claim that the only plausible candidate for an explanation of these things will make essential use of the claim that objects and actions have the properties that they are believed to have. *Any* expla-

---

59. "Truth as predicated of moral judgements", p. 150.

nation of people's ability to acquire and determinately to use the relevant concepts will need to show what the things that fall determinately within the concepts have in common, what their relevant similarity is. The Aristotelian realist, emphasizing the observational nature of the concepts in question, will maintain that moral facts will play a necessary role in this sort of explanation and this is sufficient to give them the response-independence needed for realism.[60]

---

60. As they stand, these claims are too crude, since they are taken to apply to evaluative concepts *en masse*. It is important to recognize, however, that there is no reason to think that all evaluative concepts are acquired in the same way. While many evaluative concepts are acquired ostensively, some – perhaps that of chastity, for instance – may not be. Of course, those that are acquired in other ways will be vulnerable to challenge in a way that ostensively acquired concepts are not.

The later part of this paper draws on a longer discussion "Realism and the explanation of moral belief" presented to a graduate class given by myself and Joseph Raz in Oxford in 1993. I am grateful to him and to David Charles for discussion of these issues.

Eudaimonism and realism in Aristotle's ethics

JOHN MCDOWELL

1. Aristotle evidently holds that all, or nearly all, mature human beings (at least those who are proper subjects for ethical assessment) organize their lives in the light of a conception of eudaimonia (*Nicomachean ethics* 1102a2–3).[1] A conception of eudaimonia is a conception of *eu prattein*, doing well (1095a18–20). The relevant idea of acting with a view to eudaimonia is the idea of acting in a certain way because that is what doing well comes to.[2] That occurrence of "well" signals a distinctive sort of point, or worthwhileness, that one takes oneself to see in acting like that; I think Aristotle aims to explain what this distinctive sort of perceived worthwhileness is when he in effect glosses the "well" in "doing well" as "in accordance with virtue" (1098a16–18).

Now it is clear that Aristotle thinks some such perceptions are correct and others not. That is, his attitude towards the question whether

---

1. *Eudemian ethics* 1214b6–12 may leave room for some who do not ("a mark of much folly", Aristotle says); that is why I put "or nearly all." (Unattributed citations henceforth will be from the *NE*.) My parenthesis is meant to register Aristotle's well known views about women, slaves, and so forth. Having mentioned the point once, I shall ignore it from here onwards; this embarrassing feature of Aristotle's thinking is irrelevant to the philosophical issues that I want to consider.
2. No doubt one can act for the sake of doing well without conceiving what one does as itself constituting doing well. One's purpose in acting for the sake of doing well may be instrumental: to get oneself into a position in which one can act in the sort of way one sees as doing well. But this sort of action is not revelatory of character in the same direct way as action undertaken, because it is seen as exemplifying doing well, as opposed to conducive to it. I think it is the latter that is Aristotle's concern.

some action has that kind of worthwhileness is realistic in some sense. (At least to begin with we can leave it open whether the sense is one that implies anything seriously metaphysical). Aristotle's thought is that there is a right answer, and wrong answers, to the question of what doing well consists in. And his usual remark about rightness on this kind of question is that the right view is the view of the person of excellence (the *spoudaios*), or the person of practical wisdom (the *phronimos*).[3]

It is often thought that this Aristotelian realism points to an extra-ethical basis for reflection about what eudaimonia consists in. The idea is that, in Aristotle's view, it is possible to certify that a virtuous person's conception of eudaimonia is genuinely correct – that the actions it singles out are really worth undertaking in the way it represents them as being – by showing that a life organized in the light of that conception would be recognizably worth living anyway; that is, worth living by standards that are prior to the distinctive values acquired in what Aristotle conceives as a proper upbringing. These prior standards would be standards for worthwhileness or choice-worthiness that any human being, just as such, could accept, independently of any acquired values and the motivational dispositions that are associated with them. So the idea is this: Aristotle thinks he can authenticate the distinctive values that are imparted by what he conceives as a proper upbringing, and establish that that is indeed how people ought to be brought up, on the basis of the thought that a life that puts those values into practice is one that is worth going in for anyway, for a human being just as such.[4] On this view, when Aristotle says that it is the excellent person who gets things right, the ethical assessment expressed by "excellent" is not a stopping point for his thinking about getting things right. That the relevant kind of person is really excellent, and that he is really right about what is worth going in for, are together grounded on an extra-ethical basis.

I do not believe there is any sign of this supposed external validation in Aristotle's text. On the contrary, trying to read it into him

---

3. See for instance, in a different context, 1176a15–16. Continent and incontinent people also have (in some sense) the correct conception of eudaimonia. But this just reflects the fact that they are, so to speak, imperfect instances of what excellent people are perfect instances of; we do not need to consider them separately, or as a counter-example to the thesis that Aristotle comes at rightness in the conception through the character of its possessor.
4. This talk of values is no doubt anachronistic, but I think harmlessly.

disrupts our understanding of things he actually says. The external validation is an invention on the part of modern readers. I shall spend some time trying to make this plausible, and then offer some reflections on what underlies the invention: on what makes modern readers tend to suppose that Aristotle needs external validation to sustain his realism. I hope this will suggest some general conclusions about the prospects for ethical realism, independently of issues in the exegesis of Aristotle.

2. The supposed external validation involves a particular interpretation of the claim that the good life is the life that is really worth living for human beings: the assessment expressed in "really worth living" has to be prior to anything specifically ethical. People who take Aristotle to think like this credit him with an idea of the choiceworthy life that is related in some suitable way to the idea of an optimal combination of component goods. I shall distinguish some options for interpreting "related in some suitable way" in a moment, but first I want to put into place the appropriate idea of an optimal combination of component goods.

For the purposes of readings of this sort, the goodness of the component goods has to be established without presupposing the distinctive conception of worthwhileness in action that is supposed to be validated, the conception of worthwhileness in action that is inculcated when someone is brought up into the virtues. Only so could an external validation be forthcoming. In readings of this sort, the requirement is supposed to be met like this: the goodness of the component goods is revealed by the fact that they appeal to motivational forces – needs or aspirations – that are built into the human organism as such. The goodness implicit in the idea of optimality, in the combination of component goods, has to be handled similarly. We need not go into detail about what the component goods, or the specific values involved in assessing combinations of them, might be in a specific view of this kind; the point I want to make is about the shape of the position.

The simplest version of the kind of reading I am considering takes it that, for Aristotle, the good life, the life of eudaimonia, *consists in* such an optimal combination of component goods, independently certified as such. (This can be encouraged if we translate "eudaimonia" by "happiness", as we almost have to if we translate it at all; alternatives such as "flourishing" make no difference on this point.)

But in this form, it is very hard to make the reading cohere with a central Aristotelian claim about eudaimonia: that what it consists in is activity in accordance with virtue. (See 1098a16–18, a passage I have already cited. The explicit claim there is that the good for man is activity in accordance with virtue, but the claim is offered in the course of spelling out further an equation between the good for man and eudaimonia, 1097b22–24.)

Of course it is not impossible to make sense of a conception of the good life as made up of component goods, shown to be good by the fact that they appeal to motivations built into the human organism as such. But the idea of components has to work rather differently if we conceive the good life in the way the central claim indicates, as made up of actions. It might be natural to suppose that an optimal combination of goods is, if all goes well, *brought about by* the actions that, in this different sense, make up the life. But then if we say that the optimal combination of component goods is what eudaimonia is, we cannot also respect the central claim, and say that eudaimonia *is* the actions that, if all goes well, bring about the optimal combination of goods.

Consider also a remark that Aristotle makes in the course of a discussion of how the intellect is involved in choice (*proairesis*) (1139b2–4):

> what is made is not an end without qualification (but only in relation to something and of something), but what is done (*to prakton*) is; for doing well (*eupraxia*) is an end, and the desire [sc. the desire that is *proairesis*] is for this.

When one acts with a view to doing well (here *eupraxia*: the abstract noun is obviously equivalent to the verbal phrase *"eu prattein"*, which we are told is equivalent to *"eudaimonein"* by common agreement, 1095a18–20), what one does (*to prakton*) is itself the end with a view to which one acts. Doing well does not figure here as something brought about by the actions undertaken for the sake of it; it figures simply as what those actions are.[5]

This recommends a more sophisticated version of the reading. In this version, we are to respect Aristotle's equation of *eudaimonein* with *eu prattein*, doing well (1095a18–20); we are to take "doing" there to mean *doing*, and we are to respect the central claim's interpretation of the "well" in "doing well" as "in accordance with virtue". So eudaimonia *consists in* virtuous actions undertaken for their own sake; it is not something brought about by such actions if all goes well. An optimal combination of independent goods cannot now be what eudaimonia is. But on this reading, the notion of an optimal combination of independent goods still figures in an extra-ethical certification of the correctness of one rather than another conception of eudaimonia; that is, in this context, of one rather than another conception of which states of character are virtues. The thought is this: by appealing to the idea of an optimal combination of independent goods, we can show that the states of character that Aristotle identifies as virtues, and thus alludes to when he says that eudaimonia is activity in accordance with them, are worth cultivating anyway, independently of the distinctive habits of valuation of modes of conduct that one acquires when one has the virtues instilled into one. Virtuous activity for its own sake is what eudaimonia is, not some supposed optimal result of filling one's life with such activity. But it is worth becoming the sort of person who lives like that because such a life is likeliest to be satisfactory by independent standards – likeliest to secure an optimal combination of component goods whose goodness is independently established.[6]

This version of the reading does not flatly ignore the central claim. But it still has difficulty in giving full weight to what Aristotle says there, together with his claim that the action that manifests virtue is undertaken for its own sake (1105a31–32). Aristotle evidently wants the point of a bit of virtuous behaviour to be intrinsic to it, and it is hard to make this cohere with the idea that the worthwhileness that a virtuous agent sees in such behaviour is to be authenticated in this external way: by arguing that it is a good plan to cultivate the states of character that such behaviour would manifest, on the ground that acting out those states of character is likely to secure a life that would come out best by standards that are independent of a specific ethical outlook.

---

5. Compare T. H. Irwin, "Some rational aspects of incontinence", *Southern Journal of Philosophy* **27** (supplement), 1988, pp. 49–88. At p. 65 Irwin represents "decision" (his rendering of *proairesis*) as involving thought about what *promotes* the agent's "happiness" (eudaimonia). That fits this first version of the kind of reading I am considering. If we take doing well to figure in a *proairesis* as what is *promoted* by the action it fixes on, we lose our grip on how doing well can be what the action is.
6. For this version of the reading, see John M. Cooper, *Reason and human good in Aristotle* (Cambridge, Mass.: Harvard University Press, 1975), pp. 124–5.

We can make the difficulty vivid by considering cases of virtuous behaviour that seriously threaten the agent's prospects of achieving an optimal combination of independent goods, on any plausible interpretation of that idea. Take a case of courageous behaviour as Aristotle conceives it, for instance standing one's ground in the face of the dangers of battle. Suppose the result is, as is surely not unlikely, that one is maimed, or cut off before one's life has had a chance to exemplify to the full the combination of independent goods, whatever they are, that this reading takes to underlie the choiceworthiness of a life of virtuous activity. Surely that should not even seem to reveal that the point a courageous person thought he saw in the action was illusory. But how can we prevent it from seeming to have that effect, if we conceive the point of cultivating virtue as derivative from the attractiveness of a life conceived in terms of its procuring those independent goods? That is a kind of life that any courageous action is likely to deprive one of the chance to live, and that this particular courageous action *ex hypothesi* makes unattainable. This would be a case where acting out a virtue undermines the supposed point of having it in the first place. How can that not have the effect of making the action's value at least open to question?

On this reading Aristotle surely ought to have a problem about the value of this kind of action. But he shows no sign of disquiet anywhere in the vicinity of this issue. The closest he comes is when he says that if things go badly enough, in respect of "external goods", that can spoil blessedness (1099b2–6). But what he is getting at there need be no more than the sensible concession that in such cases the distinctive point of doing well, that is, of acting in accordance with virtue, can intelligibly lose its motivational pull. There is no suggestion that the distinctive point of doing well is rationally derivative from the motivational pull of goods that are independently recognizable as such.

3. If Aristotle thought he could establish, from first principles, that a possessor of the virtues as he conceives them is thereby equipped to get things right on the question of which actions really have the distinctive kind of choiceworthiness signalled by the concept of eudaimonia, we would surely expect him to make much of it. But any such argument is surely conspicuous by its absence from the ethical texts.

Early in the *Nicomachean ethics* he notes that he is addressing only people who have been properly brought up (1095b4–6). I believe this implicitly excludes from discussion issues, raised from outside, about whether their perceptions of choiceworthiness in action are correct. Substantive ethical questions are not under discussion in the *Nicomachean ethics*. This is borne out by a feature of Aristotle's practice that I have already had occasion to mention. Where the topic of right and wrong views about this or that comes up, one might expect an allusion to an external validation of the right view if he thought he had one at his disposal, but he always disappoints any such expectation. As I remarked at the beginning, his standard move is simply to say that the correct view is that of the virtuous person or the practically wise person. (See, for instance, 1107a1–2, 1139a29–31, 1144a34.)

When Aristotle makes his identification of the good life for human beings with a life of activity in accordance with virtue (1098a16–18), he bases it on a train of thought that connects what doing well is, for a thing of a given kind, with the *ergon* or "function" of things of that kind (1097b24–1098a15). It is sometimes thought that in thus invoking the idea that human beings have an *ergon*, Aristotle is pointing to a special view of human nature, as something that would enable us to locate human beings in a teleologically organized account of nature at large. Then the details of this teleological view of human nature would be available for validating Aristotle's specific conception of the good life without presupposing the habits of evaluation and motivation that he assumes his audience shares with him. The idea would be that acquiring just these dispositions of conduct and feeling, the ones that correspond to the virtues as Aristotle conceives them, sets a human being on a pattern of life that would conform to some "inner nisus" built into human nature; so that it comes naturally to a human being to live a life of activity in accordance with just these dispositions of character, in something analogous to the sense in which falling comes naturally to a heavy body.[7]

---

7. I take the phrase "inner nisus" from Bernard Williams, *Ethics and the limits of philosophy* (London: Fontana/Collins, 1985), p. 44: ". . . in Aristotle's teleological universe, every human being (or at least every non-defective male who is not a natural slave) has a kind of inner nisus towards a life of at least civic virtue." The suggestion is only that there is an analogy. There is room for a disanalogy as well: that in this case it takes habituation to get an individual on a path of behaviour on which – according to this interpretation of Aristotle's thinking – it follows its natural bent. So this reading cannot be quickly dismissed on the ground of the distinction Aristotle draws between human beings and stones at *NE* 1103a18–23.

However, even if we believe that Aristotle's talk of the *ergon* of a human being points in this sort of direction, the passage does very little towards bringing the supposed external validation back into the ethical texts. The most we could suppose is that the passage directs us elsewhere, for a validation for the conception of the good life that Aristotle assumes to be correct. (Elsewhere: where exactly?) If we take Aristotle to believe he can justify the specifics of his picture of the good life from first principles, it should still seem surprising that he should be so unforthcoming about the details of the justification in the ethical works themselves. (And is he less unforthcoming anywhere else?)

In any case, there is no warrant for taking talk of the *ergon* of a human being as an allusion to a general teleology. The notion of the *ergon* of an X is just the notion of what it befits an X to do. Exploiting the thought that X's have a place in a grand teleological scheme might be one way to cash out the notion of what it befits an X to do. But the mere word "*ergon*" is no indication that that is what Aristotle has in mind here. If he were asked to tell us what it is that it befits a human being to do, there is no reason to suppose he would offer anything except the sort of thing he offers on similar questions elsewhere, always disappointing those who think he promises to validate his ethical outlook from first principles: he would say that these things are the way a virtuous person, or a possessor of practical wisdom, takes them to be.[8]

What Aristotle achieves by invoking the *ergon* of a human being is only this: he enables himself to represent his thesis that the good *for man* is activity in accordance with human virtue as a specific case of a general connection between good and virtue, or excellence. What he exploits is a conceptual link between an X's being such as to act as it befits an X to act and its having the excellence that is proper to an X. The conceptual link is truistic, and it leaves entirely open what sort of evaluative or normative background fixes a substance for applications of the notions of *ergon* and excellence, in any particular exemplification of the general connection.

4. I am objecting to the view that Aristotle thinks he has an external validation for a conception of worthwhileness in action that he takes

---

8. On the appeal to the *ergon* of a human being, see John McDowell, "The role of *eudaimonia* in Aristotle's ethics", in *Essays on Aristotle's ethics*, A. Rorty (ed.) (Berkeley: University of California Press, 1980), pp. 89–102.

for granted in his audience, the conception characteristic of someone who possesses the virtues. The view I am objecting to belongs with a reading of "eudaimonism" that casts it as a general theory of reasons for action. In such a context, the thesis that eudaimonia consists in acting in accordance with a certain specific set of character dispositions would have to be read as saying that the conception of reasons for acting, of choiceworthiness in action, that is characteristic of a possessor of those character dispositions is correct because it matches up to the deliverances of a correct general account of which actions are choiceworthy. Just because it was general, this envisaged account would give no special position to distinctively ethical reasons for acting. Indeed, eudaimonism on this understanding would hold out a prospect that often tempts ethical theorists: that distinctively ethical reasons for acting might be authenticated by representing them as derivative from perhaps less contentious rational considerations. The envisaged external validation that I have been considering would be an instance of this kind of thing.

I think this is a misconception of eudaimonism as a context for ethical reflection. The idea of eudaimonism is indeed the idea that a life of virtuous activity is a life worth living, a choiceworthy life. But the relevant application of the notion of choiceworthiness need not be given its substance independently of the distinctive values that are instilled into someone who acquires the virtues.

From Aristotle's detailed discussion of the virtues, it emerges that we can summarily capture those values under the concept of the noble (see, for instance, 1120a23–24). In acquiring the virtues of character, a person is taught to admire and delight in actions as exemplifying the value of nobility. Coming to value the noble integrally includes an alteration in one's motivational make-up, in what one finds attractive: it shapes one's conception of what is worth going in for. It is true that eudaimonism attributes choiceworthiness to a life of virtuous activity. But the relevant choiceworthiness can be a choiceworthiness that such a life is rightly seen as having when, and because, it is seen as made up of actions that exemplify the value of nobility. It is not that "It would be noble to act thus and so" is certified as giving a genuine reason for acting on the ground that a life of such actions would meet independent standards for being worth going in for. The choiceworthiness of a noble action is simply a reflection of the action's being rightly seen to exemplify the value of nobility. It is because the value is authentic that the choiceworthiness is genuine, not the other way around.

The concept of eudaimonia is indeed the concept of a kind of choiceworthiness, but it is not choiceworthiness in general, something present wherever there is a reason for acting of whatever sort. There are many dimensions on which we can assess choiceworthiness in general. The concept of eudaimonia, as Aristotle uses it, marks out just one of the dimensions: one that he tries to delineate for us, in a general way, when he connects the idea of eudaimonia with the idea of how it befits a human being to act and the idea of human excellence (in I.7). It is obvious that not just any reason for acting can be sensibly glossed in those terms.

This may seem hard to reconcile with the passage (1097b6–20) in which Aristotle says that eudaimonia is self-sufficient. He explains the self-sufficient (1097b14–15) as "that which on its own makes life pursuit-worthy and lacking in nothing." And he goes on to say (1097b16–17) that eudaimonia is "most pursuit-worthy if not counted in with other things; if it were so counted, clearly it would be more pursuit-worthy with the addition of the smallest of goods." This can seem to support the idea that eudaimonism is a general theory of reasons for acting, since it is easy to suppose that, according to this passage, eudaimonia embraces anything whose presence would in any way make a life more desirable.

But I do not believe Aristotle means the scope of eudaimonia to include just any contribution to the desirability of a life. There are places where he seems to be trying to insist that eudaimonia is an agent's own achievement rather than a gift of chance.[9] Not that mere effort (or good willing on some roughly Kantian construal) is by itself enough to ensure eudaimonia. Factors outside an agent's control can make it impossible to live the life of a virtuous person (even if they leave isolated bits of virtuous behaviour still feasible), as perhaps in cases like that of Priam (1100a5–9).[10] But chance goods can surely make a life more desirable, in some obvious sense, otherwise than through their effect on what it is possible for the agent to achieve by

---

9. See Cooper, *Reason and human good*, pp. 123–4; he cites *Politics* 1323b24–29, *EE* 1215a12–19, *NE* 1099b18–25.
10. There are difficult issues in this area about what it is for something to be a person's achievement. But Aristotle resists or is immune to the temptation, familiar in modern philosophy, to discount anything for which there are conditions that are not themselves within the person's control, with the result that one's achievement is restricted to something like the disposition of one's will (everything else being at the disposal of stepmotherly nature).

his own efforts, and the ranking of lives as more or less desirable that is operative here ought not to be relevant to their assessment in terms of eudaimonia. On these lines we are required to discount at least some sorts of desirability when we try to understand what Aristotle means by saying that eudaimonia is self-sufficient. On a suitably restricted reading, what the passage says is that eudaimonia is self-sufficient precisely on the dimension of desirability that is connected with the idea of human excellence and how it befits a human being to live. Eudaimonia is self-sufficient with respect to the kind of desirability that Aristotle thinks is correctly captured by rightly applying the concept of the noble.

The point of saying that eudaimonia is revealed as "most pursuit-worthy if not counted in with other things" is, I think, the same as the point of its being *the* good with which eudaimonia is equated. This latter claim does not say that eudaimonia embraces all possible reasons for acting (all goods, in one obvious sense; see 1094a1–3). The point is that the relevant dimension of desirability is not just one dimension among others. Choiceworthiness along the relevant dimension – the choiceworthiness that actions are rightly seen as having when they are seen as noble, in the trained perception of a virtuous person – is choiceworthiness *par excellence*. If a consideration of the relevant type bears on an agent's practical predicament, someone who has learned to appreciate such considerations will rightly take it that nothing else matters for the question what shape his life should take here and now, even if the result of choosing the noble is, as it surely may be, a life that is less desirable along other dimensions than it might have been. If the result is a life that is more desirable along other dimensions, that is in the nature of a bonus. It is irrelevant to the point Aristotle is making when he says that eudaimonia is self-sufficient.

At one point (1102a2–3) Aristotle says "it is for the sake of this [eudaimonia] that we all do everything else that we do." Taken at face value, this may seem to make eudaimonia embrace all reasons for action, of whatever kind. But we know anyway that Aristotle does not think all human behaviour is aimed at eudaimonia; for instance, incontinent behaviour is precisely not aimed at eudaimonia. We could discount this remark as merely casual. Alternatively, we can read it so as to be consistent with what Aristotle says elsewhere, by taking it to employ a special, quasi-technical concept of "doing" (*prattein* in the remark; also *praxis*), to be understood precisely so that doings, in the relevant sense, are bits of behaviour undertaken as falling under a conception of eudaimonia, of doing well.[11] This way, the passage does not undermine my thesis that the concept of eudaimonia marks out a special category of reasons for acting.

5. Aristotle's habit of citing the judgement of the virtuous person as the standard of correctness, together with his insistence that only people who have been properly brought up are a suitable audience for his ethical lectures, may make it seem that on the substantive questions of ethics his stance is one of smugly accepting the outlook of a particular social group. Presumably he would say that what determines whether someone has been properly brought up is the judgement of the virtuous person. It is easy to want to complain that his thinking moves in a tight circle.

No doubt there is something right about this accusation of dogmatism. But we should not forget that when he puts his restriction on his audience, Aristotle says (1095b4–9):

> those who are going to be adequate listeners about what is noble and just, and in general about political matters, must have been nobly brought up in respect of their habits. For the starting point is the *that*, and if that is sufficiently clear, there will be no need in addition for the *because*.

In the immediate context, the point is that there is no need to have the *because* if one is to be a suitable member of Aristotle's audience. But it is also true, I think, that one does not need the *because* in order to shape one's life as one should; if one's grasp on the *that* is correct, and one acts on it, one will be living in accordance with virtue. However, Aristotle here registers at least the possibility of graduating from having only the *that* to having the *because* as well. He leaves room for a transition to a comprehending acceptance of a scheme of values, and thus connects himself to a tradition that stands precisely in opposition to dogmatism, a tradition that includes Socrates' commendation of the examined life.

What shape would the transition to having the *because* take? Obviously one possible answer takes us back to the style of interpretation I have been considering. The *that* is a piecemeal correctness, occasion by occasion, about what actions are worth undertaking in the distinc-

---

11. I elaborate such a reading in the article cited in *n.* 8.

tive way that the concept of eudaimonia signals, or perhaps about what features of situations require, in that way, what sorts of actions. The *because*, on this reading, is the story I have been considering, which could easily be cast as a story about *why* the actions that someone who possesses the *that* sees as choiceworthy are indeed choiceworthy: the idea is that acting in the light of such perceptions of choiceworthiness makes up a life that is desirable anyway, for a human being as such.

But that is not the only possible interpretation for the idea of a transition to the *because*. On a different reading, a comprehending acceptance of a scheme of values would not differ from an uncomprehending acceptance of it like that, with the comprehending view setting the accepted values on a foundation, so that the *because* would not only explain the *that* but also validate it from outside. Rather, in acquiring the *because* one would not be adding new material to what one acquired when one took possession of the *that*, but coming to comprehend the *that*, by appreciating how one's hitherto separate perceptions of what situations call for hang together, so that acting on them can be seen as putting into practice a coherent scheme for a life.[12]

We can picture the intellectual activity that would be involved in moving to the *because*, on this view, in terms of a version of Neurath's image of the sailor who has to keep his boat in good order while at sea. In this version of the image, the fact that the boat cannot be put ashore for overhaul stands for the fact that when one reflectively moves from mere possession of the *that* to possession of the *because* as well, one has no material to exploit except the initially unreflective perceptions of the *that* from which the reflection starts. One reflects on one's inherited scheme of values, or the perceptions of choiceworthiness in action in which that scheme of values expresses itself, from inside the ethical way of thinking that one finds oneself with, not by contemplating it from the external standpoint of a theory about motivations built into human beings as such.

Not everything in this Neurathian conception fits Aristotle's own approach. A feature of the Neurathian image that does not corre-

---

12. See M. F. Burnyeat, "Aristotle on learning to be good", in Rorty, *Essays*, pp. 69–92; see especially p. 81. (But I think it is quite implausible that Aristotle conceives the *Nicomachean ethics* itself as "setting out 'the because' of virtuous actions", as Burnyeat there suggests).

spond to anything in Aristotle is this: reflection on a collection of putative perceptions of the *that* from within, directed at seeing how they hang together, runs a risk of recommending the conclusion that they do not hang together at all, or at least that they do not hang together very well. If that happens, it should put the perceptions in question. Neurath's sailor may need to tinker with the boat. Reflection aimed at the *because* puts what has hitherto passed as the *that* at risk, and there is no sign that Aristotle recognizes this. It is partly for this reason that I did not simply dismiss the charge that he is dogmatic in his confidence about the particular ethical views he embraces.

In one way it makes an enormous difference to Aristotle's ethical outlook if we require it to open itself to the risk of revision, as a result of Neurathian reflection. But in another way the reform is quite easy. In particular, it does not disrupt Aristotle's realism. On the contrary, it suggests a shape for a defence of an Aristotelian realism, without either dogmatism or an appeal to an external validation. Reflection aimed at the *because* makes a collection of putative perceptions of the *that* vulnerable to being unmasked as illusory, on the ground that they do not hang together so as to be recognizable as expressing a coherent scheme for a life. In that case, if a collection of putative perceptions of the *that* has run that risk and passed muster, that is surely some reason to suppose that the perceptions are veridical. Indeed, wherever the Neurathian image is the right image for reflection (which might be argued to be everywhere), that is the only kind of reason there can be for supposing that some putative sense of how things are is correct.

So on this kind of reading as well as on the kind of reading that I have been opposing, reflection towards the *because* can after all be seen as yielding a validation of the conception of the *that* from which it starts. The difference is that on this reading the validation is not from outside. It belongs with that difference that in this case we cannot aspire to a validation that is better than provisional.

Possession of the *that* is what is imparted by the moulding of ethical character that Aristotle describes in Book II of the *Nicomachean ethics*. Full-blown possession of the *because* would presumably be the intellectual virtue, practical wisdom, that he discusses more particularly in Book VI. There is a tendency for commentators to overplay this distinction. The idea is that Book II is about the acquisition of motivational propensities that relate to reason only by way of obedience to its dictates (compare 1102b30–31); they prepare the agent to act in a way that conforms to prescriptions issued by the intellectual excellence, practical wisdom, which is going to come into view only later in Aristotle's text.[13] But Book II itself contains the claim that actions that manifest virtue of character must be chosen (1105a31–32). And Aristotle links the idea of choice to the idea of deliberation (1112a15–16, 1113a9–12), and thereby to the excellences of the intellect.[14] So it is already implicit in Book II that the virtue of character that is dealt with there, represented as the product of habituation, includes an intellectual excellence. A state of a person from which choices issue is itself a source of prescriptions, not just a motivational preparedness to obey prescriptions whose source is elsewhere.

In undergoing the moulding of character that is the topic of Book II, a person acquires a way of bringing behaviour under concepts, the conceptual scheme that we can summarily capture in terms of the idea of the noble and the disgraceful. A possessor of the *that* is already beyond uncomprehending habit; he is already some distance into the realm of the intellectual excellences. He has acquired apparatus for thinking and reasoning, and he is thereby equipped for reflection; he has the material for a transition to a full-fledged possession of the *because*. Aristotle's own presentation is defective in that it fails to register the possibility that reflection may undermine its starting points. But that is no reason to hold Aristotle to a clear-cut separation of having the *because* from having the *that*, which would be congenial to the idea that a transition to the *because* requires a shift of viewpoint. On the contrary, Book II indicates that a possessor of the *that* is already not devoid of the *because*. He can say "Because it is noble." Moving to

---

13. See John M. Cooper, "Some remarks on Aristotle's moral psychology", *Southern Journal of Philosophy* **27** (supplement), 1988, pp. 25–42.
14. Aristotle clearly envisages actions that manifest virtue of character but do not issue from deliberation (for instance at 1117a17–22). In conjunction with the link between choice and deliberation, this might seem to threaten the claim that all actions that manifest virtue of character are chosen. I think what has to give here is the connection between choice and (actual) deliberation. Note that 1117a21–22 is most naturally read as saying that an agent *chooses* spur-of-the-moment, and so not deliberated, courageous actions. This need not conflict with 1111b9–10, where the point need be no more than that actions whose occasions are sprung on one are not *in general* chosen. The point of the link between choice and deliberation is not that choice results from deliberation but that it reveals a shape to the way the agent is minded, a kind of shape that becomes explicit in actual courses of deliberation.

a more complete possession of the *because*, one sufficient to amount to full-blown possession of the relevant intellectual virtue, needs no more than internal reflection from the midst of what one already has.

6. I have been urging a Neurathian picture of reflection on an ethical outlook. One benefit of this is that it points to a way of understanding why it is so tempting for modern readers to credit Aristotle with a different picture of the sort of validation an ethical outlook needs: a picture in which, to modify the image, the boat is put ashore for a certification of its seaworthiness. Aristotle seems happy to assume that his outlook is simply correct. The tempting thought is that we cannot make sense of that in terms of no more than the prospect that his outlook would pass muster in Neurathian reflection, a prospect that, on the view I am suggesting, he assumes without even noticing that he is doing so. Neurathian reflection about an ethical outlook would be undertaken from within it. The tempting thought is that one could not achieve a justified conviction that a set of views about anything is objectively correct by reflecting from within something as historically contingent as an inherited way of thinking; except perhaps by sheer accident, objective correctness would require breaking out of a specific cultural inheritance into an undistorted contact with the real.

Intelligible though it is, I believe this line of thought is foreign to Aristotle. Here I do not mean merely to repeat what I have been urging, that he expresses his "realism" quite casually – he gives no sign that he thinks he needs to license it, even by anticipating a favourable outcome for Neurathian reflection on his ethical outlook, let alone by making a grand metaphysical gesture. I mean something more than that. Making historical contingency and cultural specificity into a metaphysical issue is distinctively modern. It is anachronistic to read into Aristotle, as an underpinning for his casual "realism", a line of thought that makes sense only as a response to a kind of anxiety to which he is immune.[15]

That might leave it looking as if we do Aristotle a favour if we equip him with a response to that kind of anxiety – even if he is too philosophically primitive to feel the anxiety himself. But that presupposes that susceptibility to this kind of anxiety marks an intellectual advance over Aristotle's immunity to it, and that is open to dispute. On the contrary, we might say: organizing our metaphysics around the idea of transcending historicity is profoundly suspect. Its true effect is to undermine the very idea of getting things right. We can conceal that from ourselves only if we think we can make sense of the idea of a mode of enquiry that transcends historicity. In our modern culture, natural science tends, quite intelligibly, to be cast in that role, but any such conception of science is an illusion.

Enquiry is an intellectual activity in which we aim to make our thinking, on whatever subject matter, responsive to reasons for thinking one thing rather than another. The anxiety I am considering is one possible reaction to a thought that we can put like this: we have only our own lights to go on in trying to ensure that the considerations that we are responsive to are really reasons for thinking one thing rather than another. But that thought is simply correct. It is no less correct about scientific enquiry than about any other kind of enquiry. That the concepts employed in laying out a scientific picture of the world are not anthropocentric – that they are in that sense "absolute", to use Bernard Williams' term – makes no difference to this point.[16] It is still true that how the concepts are taken to hang together rationally – what considerations are taken to be reasons for what conclusions of enquiry – is the product of the historical evolution of a particular human institution.

This is not to cast doubt on the idea that science is progressively revealing reality as it is. The moral is, rather, that we should learn not to see a threat in this thought: we have only our own lights to go on, and they are formed by our particular position in the history of enquiry. That should not seem to put in question our prospects for

---

15. What about the theme of *nomos* and *physis* in ancient thought? (Robert Heinaman raised this question). That is a large topic; obviously I cannot deal with it properly here. I think it is revealing that the theme surfaces in the NE only in connection with "justice" (V.7), and is there discussed in such a way that it is reasonable to connect *nomos* with the English "conventional". There is no sign of the general metaphysical anxiety that I am alluding to. More general ethical scepticism is of course a Greek phenomenon (even if not much in evidence in Aristotle). But, as represented for instance in Plato's *Gorgias*, it does not take this general metaphysical form. The Calliclean attack on ordinary ethical views does not scruple to exploit evaluative concepts, for instance the concept of the slavish, whose persuasive force ought itself to be open to question if the point were to express a metaphysical anxiety about what is culturally specific or historically contingent.
16. On "absolute", see Williams, *Ethics*, p. 139. For Williams' use of this notion in the reading of Aristotle, see p. 52: "Aristotle saw a certain kind of ethical, cultural, and indeed political life as a harmonious culmination of human potentialities, recoverable from an absolute understanding of nature."

getting things right. The prospects are live in scientific enquiry (indeed, we have more than just prospects there), not because scientific enquiry transcends historical determination of its lights, but because its lights stand up to reflective scrutiny. Our conception of how to conduct scientific enquiry, or, more exactly, the conception that is acted on by practitioners of scientific enquiry, is continually self-correcting. But if that is how we should neutralize the potentially disquieting effect of attending to our historicity in the case of science, our paradigm of enquiry directed at an "absolute" conception of how things are, the same thought can work directly for enquiries that do not aim at "absolute" results. A "realistic" attitude to such enquiries does not need a different kind of warrant, with any conviction that we are getting things right needing to be grounded in a relation to the result of an "absolute" enquiry.

We can express the role of habituation into virtue of character in Aristotle's thinking by saying that possession of the *that*, the propensity to admire and delight in actions as noble, is second nature to those who have been properly habituated. And I have suggested that someone who possesses the *that* is not devoid of the *because*; full-blown possession of the *because*, the intellectual virtue of practical wisdom, is no more than possession of the *that* in a reflectively adjusted form. Now something that we can appropriately conceive as second nature surely cannot be in all respects autonomous with respect to first nature, so to speak: the sort of thing that might be the topic of an investigation whose questions are framed in "absolute" or at any rate extra-ethical terms. If there are motivational tendencies that are built into human beings as such, they must put limits on what is possible in the way of habituation into an ethical outlook. So I am not ruling out explanatory connections between an ethical outlook and a pre-ethical account of human nature. But this is quite distinct from the idea that the perceptions that are characteristic of a specific second nature can count as correct only if they can be displayed as rationally derivative from truths about first nature.

I think that is exactly how *not* to be an ethical realist. Understanding the philosophical temptation to read such a position into Aristotle, and seeing through the post-Aristotelian philosophical ideas that underlie the temptation, is a good way of coming to appreciate the advantages of the different – less metaphysical – approach to ethical realism that Aristotle's thinking actually exemplifies.

Eudaimonism and realism in Aristotle's ethics: a reply to John McDowell

DAVID WIGGINS

John McDowell describes Aristotle's account of ethics like this.

(i) Mature human beings live their lives under a conception of eudaimonia, which is a conception of what doing well consists in – where doing well is doing well in the sense of acting well, or acting in accordance with virtue (cf. *Nicomachean ethics* 1098a16–18, 1139b2–4).[1] According to a conception of this sort, an action that manifests virtue is an action undertaken "for its own sake" (1105a31–32). The act is done *di' auto*. (It is a V act and done because it is a V act.) McDowell leaves the standard translation of this phrase, without jeopardizing his right to attend to the question of how the words are to be further interpreted or amplified.

(ii) A given conception of eudaimonia will be either correct or incorrect. In the latter case, it is a misconception. The correct conception is the one possessed by the excellent or practically wise person, the *spoudaios* or *phronimos* (the good or practically wise man). Conceptions of eudaimonia are not to be validated or corrected by standards external to the notions of the *spoudaios/phronimos*, or by reference to good things that can be seen as good from a vantage point outside the ethical conceptions of the *spoudaios/phronimos*. Nor can the correct conception be identified by reference to the biological or non-ethicized *phusis* (nature) of human creatures.

(iii) A conception of eudaimonia can however be described, explained and amplified for the benefit of Aristotle's listeners. Being well brought up, these listeners are well within the reach of the discourse, persuasion or advice of any *spoudaioi/phronimoi* who care to help them to enlarge a grasp of the *that* (*hoti*) into a grasp of the *because* (*dioti*).

---

1. All references to Aristotle's writings are to the *Nicomachean ethics* unless otherwise indicated.

(iv) Some philosophers may conclude, from the impossibility of any external validation of a conception of eudaimonia, that realism is unsustainable in ethics, or that irrealism or anti-realism are the only tenable positions. But McDowell himself arrives at a very different conclusion.

I shall come last to the last matter, namely (iv). See part (C) below. Among the points we ought to try to talk about before we arrive there, the most important all seem to me to fall, in one way or another, under two heads (A) and (B):

(A) What is to be the interpretation of "doing the act for its own sake"? And what interpretation is McDowell committed to give? We need here to distinguish the executive virtues such as courage, and the non-executive virtues.

(B) How content should we be with the extreme plainness or rigorism of McDowell's interpretation of eudaimonia? On behalf of this rigorism, McDowell adduces both methodological and ethical constraints. In what relation do these stand?

Under (A) I want to support McDowell's decision to content himself with the standard translation. But I also want to draw attention to the oddity or ethical distinctiveness of the doctrine that emerges. Contrary to the tenor of Bernard Williams' paper and most of the discussion that followed it, I shall claim that this oddity is not the product of a failure to see NE 1105a31–32 as a mere schema that Aristotle might himself have intended, but rather a consequence (one among several) of an utterly distinctive perfectionist strand in Aristotle's thinking. The passage means what it says.

Under (B), the question I shall raise is whether the rigorism cum ethical perfectionism of the position that emerges from McDowell's interpretation goes too far even for Aristotle.

(A) How to interpret *di' auto*

In the opening paper of the conference, Bernard Williams rehearsed a number of possible interpretations for *di' auto* (1105a31–32). He proposed that this condition of Aristotle's upon an act's taking place *kat' areten* (the act's taking place in accordance with such and such a virtue, or its being V of the agent to do the act) should be read schematically and filled out in different ways according to the nature of the virtue in question. If we are bent on aligning 1105a31–32 with what we ourselves think about the virtues and their exercise, that is surely right. But considering the question simply as one of interpretation, I am not sure whether McDowell – or Aristotle, as McDowell reads Aristotle – have quite so much freedom as Williams is proposing to exercise here.

The most prominent constraint upon interpretation is the sentence that McDowell quotes and makes so much of from Book VI of the *Nicomachean ethics* (1139b2–5):

> what is made (*to poieton*) is not an end without qualification . . . but what is done (*to prakton*) is [an end without qualification]; for doing well (*eupraxia*) is an end, and the desire [the desire that is in question, that is the *proairesis*] is the desire for this. Hence choice (*proairesis*) is either desiderative reason or ratiocinative desire, and such an origin of action is a man (*anthropos*).

A related constraint is Aristotle's perfectionism. Roughly speaking, Aristotle's perfectionism seems to come to this. We value our own existence and (by that same token) we must wish for the existent thing that is us to be as good a thing as possible. But the only way for that existent thing to be as good as possible is by our *eupraxia*. For what we are is what we are *in action*, and that is what we are by our acts. Our actions are part of ourselves in the same way in which our children are part of ourselves (1113b18–19) or (more aptly, I should say) they are part of us in the way in which a poet's poems are a part of himself, and precisely as such dear to him (1168a1–3).

> The good man wishes for himself what is good and what seems so and he brings this good into being in acting (*prattei*) – for it is characteristic of the good man to work out the good and try to implement it completely. He brings this good into being for his own sake (that is for the sake of his own rational nature, which is to be reckoned the same as the man himself). He wishes to be alive and be preserved – himself and the element by which he himself is conscious. For existence is good for the virtuous man and each man wishes for himself what is good. . . . Such a man wishes to live with himself, for he does so with pleasure, since the memories of his past acts are delightful and . . . he has, so to speak, nothing to repent of. (1166a13–28)

No doubt, one who propounds such an ethical view can mark *some* distinction corresponding to the one that Williams and Pears mark between the executive and the non-executive virtues. But, whether or not the perfectionist does mark such a distinction, it is unlikely to have the same ethical significance for him as it has for Williams or Pears. It will be extraordinarily natural for such a perfectionist to want to insist, just as we find Aristotle insisting, that the brave man will do the brave act because it is brave and in order to gain the noble for himself (bravery being one determination of the good/noble).

So I think McDowell's interpretation is beginning in the right place by concentrating upon the doing virtuously sense of "do well" and by engaging so with Aristotle's perfectionist outlook. I also think that we ourselves understand very well what it is that Aristotle wants to claim about such virtues as bravery. But this is not to say that there is no difficulty in these ideas. It will smooth the road to what I shall want to claim under (B) to mention now some of the difficulties that they create.

Suppose a brave patriot undertakes an act of heroism, but undertakes it in great anger at the necessity for the act. Suppose he rails at the incompetence or short-sightedness of those in command of the army in which he is serving. It is only their folly that has made the act necessary. Such a patriot may undertake the act in order to fend off certain disaster, and he may be *sustained* in his resolve to go through with the act, not by the fact that the situation puts him on his mettle (that is a part of what makes him so angry), but because at any point he can indignantly reflect that his future life would not be worth living if he refused at this point to do the act that is required of him. Is such a person less virtuous, I ask, or less brave or less practically wise than one who simply and cheerfully accepts this as his chance to act courageously? Is my patriot less virtuous or less brave even if, when the battle is joined, his resolution actually exceeds that of the person who rather likes to be put on his mettle? (Once the noble is offered in the way in which it is here, it cannot be refused. But why, *here*, he asks, did it have to be offered? The general in command is a blundering fool.)

I ask this question because I should like those who are prepared to speak on Aristotle's behalf to say whether the angry patriot ought or ought not to qualify by Aristotle's canon for courage. But I would add that there is a heavy price to pay if one will deny that this man is brave. If one denies it, then, instead of being strange to us, Aristotle's account of courage will move out of reach altogether.

Suppose for a moment that I am right to say that the angry patriot had better count as brave. Then let us go on to ask: does this patriot do the act for its own sake? Surely not. Does he do the act for the sake of *to kalon*, the noble? Aristotle says so, but that doesn't sound right either. One might do better to say that he is bent on avoiding the base. (cf. 1116a10. Moreover, avoiding the base is fairly simply related, I suppose, to acting for the sake of the noble).[2] But surely the thing that the man in our narrative is doing the act *for* is to fend off the disaster that will otherwise overwhelm the city. Admittedly, avoiding the base helps to define the space within which he deliberates and chooses. But that doesn't show that avoiding the base or preserving the noble is his *aim*. It doesn't show that he chooses the brave act *di' auto*.

Shall we say then that the patriot does the act "not for the wrong sort of reason"? Yes indeed. For us at least, preferring for all our own purposes to read 1103a31–32 only schematically and wanting not to say that bravery as we conceive it involves doing the act for the sake of its bravery, that suggestion of Williams' will do very well. But if this is all that McDowell's Aristotle says, then the connection between the agent's acting not for the wrong reason and his acting bravely for the sake of *eupraxia* itself becomes terribly tenuous. Saying the distinctive things he says about virtue and bravery and eudaimonia, McDowell's Aristotle surely needs a more direct connection between *di' auto* and *eupraxia*.

McDowell remarks that, on some readings of Aristotle's doctrine of happiness, Aristotle ought to have had a problem about the intrinsic value of acts of bravery, which are acts whose value consists in the act itself. "But [Aristotle] shows no disquiet anywhere in the vicinity of this issue", he says.[3] I agree that this is no accident,[4] but I shall pursue the matter a little further (without trying to speak for readings of "doing well" that connect this "doing well", in the manner that McDowell criticizes, with the motivational pull of goods that are pre-ethically recognizable as such). The point I want to make is this: that almost everyone now feels that there *is* a problem about human beings dying in battle or soldiers being mutilated in war and living

---

2. Well, fairly simply related – which is not to say that they are the same. Compare the audible difference between being glad you're not dead (after a near miss at a crossroads) and being glad that you are alive.
3. Above, p. 206.
4. I commend to you in this regard the remarks of A. Grant, *Aristotle's ethics* (London: Longmans Green, 1885), vol. II, p. 36.

on for scores of years in misery and futility. (Even if Greek warfare and Greek conceptions combined to make death in battle seem like something worthwhile, the second of these outcomes must have presented them with some of the same problems as it presents to us.) We see these *mutilés de guerre* sitting in the seats reserved for them on the Paris Metro perhaps, or wherever else, and we feel profoundly uneasy. The loss they have sustained unnerves us, however heroically and selflessly we may know them to have been fighting when they sustained injury. Of course, it would help to make what has happened to them more bearable if we could see their heroic acts as something somehow gained, as something actually achieved in the name of *eupraxia* itself. We are not strangers to that thought. But does it afford all the consolation that Aristotle wants to suggest? How can even Aristotle's listeners have felt *no* difficulty here?

If there are brave acts that are not done for the sake of *eupraxia* – or that we're uneasy to justify in that way, or that most of us *can't* consistently think of in this way – or if there are brave acts that an agent himself does not see in the Aristotelian way (if there were such acts and such agents even in Aristotle's time), does that show that we ought not to interpret *di' auto* as "chosen for themselves"? I don't think so. Is it not better to acknowledge that what Aristotle is offering is his distinctive ethical view of courage? Surely we ought to see the oddity of this and some of the other claims that he is committed to propound to us as all of a piece with the claim that all virtuous action is for the sake of *eupraxia*.

Among the several results that we ought to expect of this insistence of Aristotle's are these:
- the assimilation of the executive virtues such as courage, which scarcely need the *di' auto* condition at all, to the non-executive virtues, which require some version of some such condition, even where they do not require Aristotle's version (Williams spoke of this);
- Aristotle's assimilation of the virtues Hume would account natural to those Hume would account artificial (on the ordinary view, some sorts of reason for X's giving something to someone exclude its being generous of X to do so; yet generosity had better not be practised *di' auto*; whereas particular justice and the other artificial virtues *are* practised for their own sakes) – even as the doctrine of the mean represents (for other reasons) a third assimilation, namely

– the assimilation of the artificial virtues to the natural virtues (still in Hume's sense of "natural") with which Aristotle begins his exposition of the ethical virtues.[5]

What conclusion does this bring me to? The conclusion I reach is that nothing very accurate can be said about all the virtues in the space of a sentence such as the one we find at 1105a26–33; nor can anything very accurate be said in the space of a sentence such as 1139b2–5 about the relation of all the virtues to happiness. Understandably enough, Aristotle underestimates the difficulties. Nor then are the prospects very good for Aristotle to persuade us of the unqualified truth of doctrines like that which McDowell has quoted from 1139b2–5. Indeed it seems by no means obvious that Aristotle's own listeners ought to have found 1139b2–5 much easier to accept than we do, when it is read perfectly generally and fully literally.

A reprise. Someone may say that the points I have been rehearsing are a fuss about nothing, or that for all present purposes – contrast the purposes of a detailed study of the virtues – it will be better to see 1105a26–33 as a mere outline, in the way Williams urged, and not insist too much on that which "chosen for its own sake" specifically suggests. This objector may say that what is needed is to understand the phrase "for the sake of the noble" not as introducing direct or first-order aims or ends but as introducing *indirect* ends such as we ourselves commonly take safety or honour to be; and then the objec-

---

5. If Aristotle insists, as he seems to at 1107a10–11, that the reason why there is not a right amount of *klope* (theft) or of *moicheia* (adultery) is that these things are *already* excesses or deficiencies, then he must think that X's taking Y (here and now) represents, as *klope*, too much or too little of something or other (a way of feeling or acting) such that another amount of that would have represented (here and now) honesty and a third amount would have represented (here and now) some second vice. But what is unjust about X's taking Y at T under circumstance C has no constitutive connection of any sort (however weak) with too much or too little of *anything* the right amount of which would have had at T under C a constitutive connection with acting justly. It neither entails that nor suggests it. The same goes *mutatis mutandis* for *moicheia*. In so far as there is hope for the theory of the mean, the scope of the doctrine must be confined to the natural virtues. For the natural/artificial distinction as I mean it here and throughout (I never intend Aristotle's *phusikos* by "natural"), see Hume, *Treatise of human nature*, 3.2.1f. For Aristotle's difficulties with justice and the mean in Book V, see Bernard Williams, "Justice as a virtue", in *Essays on Aristotle's ethics*, A. Rorty (ed.) (Berkeley: University of California Press, 1980), pp. 189–99.

tor will say that the right thing to do is to gloss *di' auto* for the case of courage in *that* light. It is neither here nor there, it may be said, that the patriot I was describing does not have the noble as his direct aim or that his direct aim is only to fend off disaster. His indirect aim can still be *eupraxia* and *to kalon*. An aim can be both indirect and paramount.

There is much to admire, and yet more to develop, in this defence, but it could not completely succeed – not even, I think, with Aristotle's listeners – unless we were prepared to make certain changes to Aristotle's doctrines. Certainly we should need to abandon some of McDowell's interpretive emphases. Perhaps the whole issue can be reduced to this. The indirect aims of *eupraxia* and the noble would certainly play an important part in defining the space within which the patriot I was describing deliberates. But they cannot define it completely. Further determinants are needed, if the patriot is to have anything to complain of in the situation that he is confronted with, or if Aristotle is to connect courage satisfactorily with the aims and objectives that it is *worth* pursuing or defending. These must relate to the welfare – the doing well in the other sense – of the polis or of the citizens of the polis that the army is to defend. But in order to give these other determinants, which will make it harder than Aristotle supposes to see every truly brave act as done strictly *for its own sake*, we need ideas that are foreign to the pure philosophy of *eupraxia* and that exceed the range of ideas that are open to Aristotelian "virtue theory", not only ideas of character traits and their evaluation, nor only of the nobility of this or that practice, (cf. Hume's references to the "moral beauty of an observance"), but ideas of flourishing or happiness in senses of "happy" and "flourish" that go beyond the *eupraxia* of doing one's virtuous act (doing the act that the requirements of this or that virtue demand of one) in the name of *eupraxia* (as *eupraxia* occurs at 1139b2–5). We need a range of notions that the virtue theorists who take themselves to be following in Aristotle's footsteps ought not to regard as available to them at this point.

(B) Rigorism

The upshot of what I have said so far is to support the rigorism of McDowell's interpretation of Aristotle's idea of eudaimonia, as well as to stress that which is ethically so strange to us in some of Aristotle's notions. Not only is McDowell's gloss of *di' auto* at 1105a32 correct. The phrase scarcely needs any further gloss for its literal sense to be plain.

The next question is whether McDowell takes all this too far, even for Aristotle. Here I believe that it may be helpful to distinguish two claims (I am inclined to accept each, but I doubt that they are the same):
- the claim that the *phronimos'* concept of eudaimonia does not need to be validated from outside, or in non-ethical or pre-ethical terms;
- the claim that it is distinctive of the *spoudaios* that his motive to the virtuous act is not external to the ethical.

It is by putting these two points to work together that McDowell arrives at the extreme rigorism of his account of what a correct conception of eudaimonia has to be like. Such a conception must interpret the good for man narrowly, you will remember, and purely in terms of doing well rather than faring well – even though the "faring well" sense of *eu prattein* is open to view in *Nicomachean ethics*, Book I. What I want to suggest now is that considerations relating to faring well, however out of place they may be in a *spoudaios'* motivation to virtuous acts, do belong within the ethical evaluation of a kind of life. They need not import the sort of extra-ethical justification of the ethical that McDowell seeks to proscribe. For considerations relating to how one fares in a given kind of life can be perfectly at home in an account of the distinctive activities and particular ethical aims and objectives of someone who is living it.

Surely an account of eudaimonia that is not externally validating but stays well within the sphere of the ethical can begin in Aristotelian fashion by reviewing the different lives that seem to compete with one another to determine the good for man. In that context, faring well is not out of place. Considerations of faring well would be all of a piece with Aristotle's feeling (at 1098a20) that he needs to adjoin to his definition of the good, to the effect that eudaimonia is *activity in accordance with virtue*, the further words *eti d' en bioi teleioi* – "but we must add in a complete life." Indeed considerations of this sort are all of a piece with the charm (however philosophically troublesome) of the Aristotelian *ergon* analogy, namely, *seeing*: *eye*: *virtuous activity*: *man*. An eye that sees well not only does its work. It also flourishes and has all the distinctive satisfactions that an eye *can* have. The satisfactions that attach to the activities of a given kind of human life are part of that life, even if they may be lost or blighted. To take account of valued things that may be lost or blighted is not necessarily to stray outside the province of the ethical. If Aristotle had not been prepared to embrace such things in his account of the human good or in his review of the different lives that are open to us, it would have been exceedingly difficult for him even to have entered the claim that what he was attempting was to identify the human good. Nor would it have been so open as it appears in context to be for him to say that bad luck or misfortune can blight the happiness of a good man (1100a5–10, cf. 1153b19–21).

McDowell could concede all this (I think) without letting go of his claim that the correct conception of eudaimonia does not admit of validation from outside the realm of the ethical. For the truth is that that point of McDowell's underdetermines the extremity of the rigorism of his interpretation of eudaimonia, the human good and the value of acting thus or so. If McDowell relaxed his rigorism to the extent I am urging him to do, then I suggest he could arrive even more easily at the conclusion that the self-sufficiency of eudaimonia (1097b6–20) is simply equivalent to its comprising everything worthwhile that is recognized in the correct ethical conception.

Maybe there is something else that would trouble McDowell in this proposal. This is that the considerations mustered by the less rigoristic identification of the good for man might make an agent's eudaimonia seem more like a gift of chance than the agent's own achievement. The distinctive pleasures and consolations of a given life can be blighted or destroyed by bad luck or the malevolence of others. Can one be the author of one's own eudaimonia if one is not the master of one's own fate? In this connection, McDowell quotes *Politics* VII, where it is said that "God is *eudaimon* and blessed not on account of any external good but on account of himself and because he is by nature of a certain sort." My response to all this would be to say that there is a familiar tension here to which anyone will be subject who occupies a Platonic or Aristotelian position. One can move forwards, at whatever cost, to the Stoic conception of a man's inner citadel and place the human good there. Or one can stay where Aristotle is and make finer distinctions. An agent's happiness can be his distinctive achievement, and his *eupraxia* can be integral to that achievement of his happiness, without being essentially indestructible or essentially proof against bad luck – just as (according to Napoleon) a man can be great (and great of course by his own efforts), yet depend for the hazardous continuance of his greatness upon absolutely everything.

Here ends the plea for a less rigoristic interpretation of eudaimonia and the human good in Aristotle, an interpretation that reopens it at least somewhat to all the difficulties and instabilities that actually subsist within the human good as we pursue it.

(C) Moral realism

John McDowell says that there are philosophers who would draw an irrealist or anti-realist moral from his claim that the *phronimos'* conception of eudaimonia cannot be validated from a point outside itself. He says they must believe that one cannot achieve a justified conviction that a set of views is objectively correct by anything so straightforward as reflection upon it from within an inherited way of thinking. An inherited way of thinking is something historically contingent, but "objective correctness [as these philosophers conceive it] would require breaking out of a specific cultural inheritance into an undistorted contact with the real."[6] McDowell then goes on to point out that Aristotle himself is a stranger to all the philosophical perplexities that issue in the passion to find an undistorted contact with the real. Not only that. One is better off to be such a stranger. For it is highly questionable whether being open to such perplexities represents any intellectual advance at all. "Organizing our metaphysics around the idea of transcending historicity is profoundly suspect. Its true effect is to undermine the very idea of getting things right." It is sufficient, McDowell seems to say, to make the transition that any grown-up human being will make from the *that* to the *because*.

What conclusion shall we come to about all this? At one extreme, we have interpreters of Aristotle (some of them Aristotelians almost by conviction as well as by virtue of being interpreters of Aristotle) who see him as grounding a certain ethical conception in a non-ethical outer reality. (Perhaps they want to make the point that in Aristotle's world-view, *phusis* is already in some sense ethicized). Beside these, we have other interpreters who see him attempting the same thing but failing conspicuously and signally. That is the position of Bernard Williams as McDowell represents him. At the other extreme we have interpreters such as McDowell who would convict both parties just mentioned of a misinterpretation and would con-

---

6. Above, p. 216.

gratulate Aristotle upon his innocence of all the question of validation and vindication that trouble the philosophical mentality of nowadays. Are there any positions intermediate between these extremes? Well, someone might seek to ethicize the Aristotelian idea of nature or *phusis* (to do so in a manner that McDowell himself would recognize as ethicizing it – I note that he does not recognize Williams, for example, as doing so) and then redeploy the concept of *phusis* in a manner not so open to McDowell's strictures. There is more than one way of doing that. Some ways will be teleological and others will not. One non-teleological way would be to ethicize *phusis* rather in the manner in which human constitution comes to be ethicized in Hume's construction of morals. The Humean construction may seem at every point alien to Aristotle's – in its moral feeling, in its substance and in its attitude towards reason. But on some other occasion I think I might feel moved to try to show that the main differences between Hume and Aristotle are more attitudinal, more moral (first-order moral) and more rhetorical in character than philosophically or even methodologically structural. Attempting that, I should claim that an Aristotelian/Humean view of the sort I am conceiving might inherit from Aristotle a notion of the reasonable that is conditioned (as the *phronimos'* conception of practical logos is conditioned) by the actual sentiments, passions and propensities of human beings. It would do well to push Hume onwards from his youthful declaration (trivially true for Aristotelian theoretical reason, not otherwise trivially true) that it is not contrary to reason to prefer the destruction of the world to the scratching of his finger and urge him in the direction of the idea, which is no less Humean, that morality is the finest expression of the nature and second nature of man as a reasonable being – the idea that, by virtue of morality,

> The animal conveniences and pleasures sink gradually in their value, while every inward beauty and moral grace is studiously acquired, and the mind is accomplished in every perfection which can adorn or embellish a rational creature.[7]

One with such an outlook need not follow Hume in his claim (in the *Treatise*) that we are mistaken when we take moral feelings or sentiments to represent the deployment of ideas. Nor need he persist in the false contrast that is involved in Hume's claim (in the *Treatise*

---

7. *Enquiry concerning human understanding*, section IX.

again) that morality is more properly felt than judged of. (The falsity of the contrast is in a way evident by the time when Hume comes to think that his role is to *mediate*, as he promises at the beginning of the *Enquiry* to do, between reason and passion). Nor would one with such an outlook need to feel any enthusiasm for the project of finding a historically unconditioned contact with the real. Rather he would seek, in the face of multicultural demands that Aristotle himself never had to confront (still less see as a practical problem), to discover whether it is practically and constructively possible (or not) to do anything on the level of dialogue with the idea (itself a thoroughly Aristotelian idea) that different moral cultures represent different expressions of a unitary set of moral ideals that underlie the bewildering diversity of *ethos*. Surely the answer to that question will not be a simple *yes*. Nor yet need it be a simple *no*.

It is towards this question that we are turned by the question of realism in Aristotle, not towards any question generated by the lust for an unhistorical and unconditioned vantage point upon the ethical. Perhaps the insight and modesty of Aristotle's account of the way in which the *hoti* can become a *dioti*, supplemented by the humour and Neurathian trenchancy of the Humean condemnation (which is internal to morality) of the monkish virtues (his objection to them being at once structural and moral, namely that they harden the heart), may yet serve us as a model or ideal – in theory, in practice and in the application of theory to practice. Here I suppose – in the question whether such a project could or could not succeed – is a substantial content that we could give to the question of ethical realism.

Index of persons named

Aeschylus 89, 94
Aquinas, St Thomas 45n
Aubenque, P. 2, 5–6

Benhabib, S. 108n, 118n
Blackburn, S. 130
Bolton, R. 168n, 170n
Brink, D. 4n
Broadie, S. 15, 16, 20, 63n
Burnyeat, M. F. 101n, 213n

Campbell, J. 151n
Charles, D. 3, 8–10
Cooper, J. 174n, 205n, 210n, 215n
Cussins, A. 151n

Davidson, D. 138
Descartes, R. 197
Dickens, C. 166

Engberg-Pedersen, T. 115n
Euripides 89, 94
Evans, G. 100n, 151n

Foot, P. 30, 31, 32, 112n
Foster, M. B. 106n
Freud, S. 68, 72–6, 82, 83, 91, 112n

Gadamer, H. G. 44n, 57n
Geras, N. 109n
Gorgias 92n
Gottlieb, P. 157n
Gould, T. 86n, 87n
Grant, A. 223n

Halliwell, S. 76n
Hare, R. M. 59, 115n, 117n
Harman, G. 187–90, 196, 197
Hegel, G. W. F. 7, 104, 105, 106, 117n, 121, 122, 126, 128, 131
Heinaman, R. 217n
Homer 90, 94
Hornsby, J. 197n

Hume, D. 15, 24, 25, 224, 225, 226, 230–31
Hursthouse, R. 3

Irwin, T. 4, 174n, 205n

Jesus 41

Kant, I. 59, 61, 62, 66, 114–15, 117, 121, 129, 154, 210
Kendell, R. E. 163n

Lawrence, G. 159n
Lear, J. 4, 6–7
Loewald, H. 69n
Louden, R. B. 115n
Lovibond, S. 2, 4, 7–8,
Lyotard, J-F. 108n

MacIntyre, A. 106n, 108n
Mackie, J. L. 104
McDowell, J. 2, 3, 4, 10–11, 110–11, 127, 128, 141, 145n, 147n, 151n, 165n, 175–6, 180, 182n, 194n, 196n
Michael 57n
Moore, A. W. 115n
Moore, G. E. 136

Nagel, T. 105n
Napoleon 228
Neurath, O. 4, 11, 213, 214, 216
Nietzsche, F. 93
Nussbaum, M. 31–2, 37n, 109n, 121

O'Neill, O. 115n

Peacocke, C. 151n, 194n
Pears, D. 221, 222
Plato 6, 16, 37, 39, 47n, 68–72, 74, 77, 82, 83, 85–8, 90, 91, 92 and n, 93, 94, 121, 136, 137, 156, 171, 217n, 228
Plotinus 37
Prichard, H. A. 165n

233

Protagoras   47*n*, 136*n*, 137, 156

Rawls, J.   43, 54
Rorty, R.   105*n*, 108

Sayre-McCord, G.   182*n*
Schopenhauer, A.   93*n*
Sharples, B.   57*n*, 58*n*
Socrates   16, 88, 154, 156
Sophocles   77, 78, 88, 89
Sorabji, R.   151*n*

Tricot, J.   45

Vernant, J-P.   77, 81*n*
Vidal-Naquet, P.   77*n*

Walzer, M.   108*n*
Wiggins, D.   30, 141*n*, 161*n*, 190–91,
   193–4, 196–7
Williams, B.   2, 4–5, 8, 48–9, 60, 82*n*,
   104, 109*n*, 113, 114, 117, 121, 129, 130,
   132, 207*n*, 217*n*, 220, 221, 222, 223, 224,
   225, 229, 230
Winnicott, D. W.   78*n*
Wittgenstein, L.   112*n*
Wright, C.   99*n*, 111, 183, 191–97

Index of passages cited

Aristotle
  De anima
    418a12   180*n*
    427b9–11   151*n*
    428a3–4   151*n*
    428a12–13   151*n*
    428b3–6   151*n*
    428b19   180*n*
    429a5–8   151*n*
    III.5   171*n*
    431b10–13   155
    432a9–14   151*n*
    432a12–15   151*n*
  Eudemian ethics
    1214b6–12   201*n*
    1215a12–19   210*n*
    I.8   2
    1216a37–b2   186
    1221b33   101
    1228b4–8   144, 145*n*
  Magna moralia
    1194b30f.   56
  Metaphysics
    980b25–27   150
    981a10–12   149
    981a28f.   162
    981b2–5   150
    1036a28–29   112*n*
    X.1   157
    1053a31–b4   156
    1072b3   107
    1075a11–23   107
  Nicomachean ethics
    I   227
    1094a1–3   211
    1094a26–27   76*n*
    1094b14–19   49*n*
    1094b15–16   49*n*
    1094b19–22   49*n*
    1095a8   102
    1095a17–20   44*n*
    1095a18–20   201, 204
    1095b1   168

1095b4–5   169
1095b4–6   206
1095b4–9   212
1095b31–34   165
I.6   2
I.7   165, 186, 187*n*, 210
1097a26–30   167
1097b1–5   147, 169
1097b2   174*n*
1097b2–3 186
1097b2–5   169, 187
1097b5–6   169
1097b6–20   210
1097b10–14   168
1097b14–15   210
1097b16–17   210
1097b22–24   204
1097b24–1098a15   207
1098a5–7   167
1098a15–18   165*n*
1098a16–18   137, 147*n*, 165, 201, 204, 207, 219
1098a20   227
1098b9–12   103
1099a16–17   154
1099a31   36
1099b1–2   167
1099b2–6   206
1099b3   167
1099b3–4   165
1099b4   168*n*
1099b4–8   168
1099b18–25   210*n*
1100a5–9   210
1100a5–10   228
1101a6–21   165
1102a2–3   201, 211
1102b30–31   215
II   214–16
1103a18–23   207*n*
1103a31–32   149, 223
1103b6–8   149
1104b2–9   180*n*

235

1104b5–6 166
1104b5–8 144
1104b11–13 101
1104b31 101
1105a1 102
1105a5–6 150
1105a14–16 150
II.4 13, 24
1105a26–33 225
1105a31–32 15–19, 24–30, 205, 215, 219, 220–27
1105b1f. 14
1106b35–1107a1 166
1106b36–1107a1 157
1106b36–1107a2 112
1106b36f. 137
1107a1–2 207
1107a10–11 225n
1109b20–23 102, 112
III.1 179
1110a23–26 179
1110a28–31 146
1111b9–10 215n
1112a15–16 215
1113a9–12 215
III.4 157n
1113a25–33 135
1113a33 102
1113b11–14 58n
1113b18–19 221
1115a32–33 143, 144
1115b2 19n
1115b7–8 179
1115b10–11 179
1115b10–13 143
1115b12 16n, 144
1115b12–14 166
1115b26–28 147
1116a2–4 166
1116a10 223
1116b20 146
1117a9–16 166
1117a17–19 143
1117a17–22 215n
1117a17f. 144
1117a19 179n
1117a21–22 215n
III.9 177

1117a35–b5 177
1117b1–6 166
1117b3–5 146
1117b5 180n
1117b7–9 177
1117b7–11 143, 145n
1117b7–15 144
1117b9 144
1117b9–13 177
1117b9–15 166
1117b11 146
1117b11–13 146
1117b12–13 146
1117b13 146
1117b14 146
1117b15 180n
1117b15–17 166
1117b17–20 145
III.12 147
1120a23 16n
1120a23–24 209
1122b6 16n
1123b20–21 174n, 186
1128b15f. 18
1128b16–21 116
1128b21–29 58n
V 35–60
1129a7 50
1129a17f. 51
1129a27 36n
1129a31–33 51
1129a32 36
1129a32–b1 50
1129a33 35
1129a33–b1 37
1129b2–3 36
1129b7 36
1129b10–11 50
1129b31 36
1129b32 36
1130a2 36
1130a13 36
1130a14 36
1130a16–32 51n
1130a33 36n
1130b2 36
1130b5 35
1130b20 36

INDEX OF PASSAGES CITED

1130b31–32   36
1130b32   38
1130b32–1131a1   38
1130b33   38, 44
1131a1   38, 45
1131a13–14   50
1131a16   39
1131a22–23   40, 52
1131a24   39
1131a25–26   43, 50
1131a27–29   55
1131b25   45n
1131b28–29   45
1131b31   45
1132a1–6   46
1132a2   45
1132a2–6   58
1132a4–5   58n
1132a24   46
1132a24–29
1132b14   58
1132b19–20   58
1132b28–30   46n
V.7   217n
1134b18f.   55
1134b21–24   56
1134b32   56
1134b35–1135a5   55, 56
1135a2–3   57n
1135a2–5   44
1135a5   44n, 55
V.8   57
1135a27–29   44
1137b19–24   112
VI   214
1139a9–12   215
1139a29–31   154, 158, 207
1139b2–4   204, 219
1139b2–5   221, 225, 226
1140a10   158
1140a25–28   116, 137, 169
1140a26–28   167
1140a30   102
1140b4–6   116
1140b5–6   166
1140b17–19   151
1140b20–21   102
1141a22–25   156

1141a22–26   155
1142a15f.   162
1142b33   102
1143b1–5   159, 161
1143b12–15   140n
1143b13–14   102
1144a29   20
1144a34   207
VI.13   101
1144b5f.   149
1144b8–12   167
1144b9–12   140n
1144b14–18   164n
1144b19–21   167
1144b32–1145a2   101
1144b35f. 164
1145a21–23   147
1146a9f.   178
1146a11–12   178
1146a12–13   148
1146b23–24   20n
1148b19–24   91n
1148b19–34   163
1149a7–8   144
1149a10–14   163
1150a1–8   91n
1151a7   20n
1151a16–19   149
VII.9   178
1151b34–36   178
1152a1–2   152
1152a1–3   148
1152a2–3   178–79
1153b19–21   228
1153b25–32   101
1166a13–28   221
1166b16f.   169
1168a1–3   221
1169a18–22   166
1169a21f.   146
1169a23–26   166
1169a24–25   145
1169b9–10   174n
1170a31–b10   167
1172b36–1173a1   102, 130
1173b28–31   102
1174b14–24   167
1174b20–21   167

237

1174b26–31   167
1175a11–23   107
1175a18–19   101
1175a31–36   151
1175a32–34   167
1176a15–16   202n
1176a15–19   135
1176a17–19   102
1177a2–6   167
1177a21f.   167
1177a22–27   167
1178a9–11   165
1178a15–21   155
1179a16–18   168n
1179a18–24   168n
1179b7–16   102

On the generation of animals
775a15   104

Physics
246b5f.   162
246b6–8   162
247a1–3   164
247a1f.   164

Poetics   76–83, 88–95
1451a3–4   76n
1451a37–38   76n
1452a17–21   76n
1452a20–21   76n
13   68n, 91
1452b30–1453a8   76n, 78n
1453a5–6   91
1453a8–30   76n
14   89
1453b10–22   67n, 78n
1453b14   92n
15   68n
1454a17–20   77n
1454a33–36   76n
1454b8–13   77n
1455a16–19   76n
1461b11–12   76n

Politics
1252a26–34   63n
1252b27–1253a5   63n
1253a1–18   61n
1253a2   38n
1253a7–8   62n
1253a10   38n
1253a14–15   38n
1253a15–18   63n
1253a17   38n
1253a29–30   63n
1253a33   91n
1260a7–31   104
1263a11f.   41n
1263a11–15   53
1275a22–23   61n
1277b11–16   61n
1283a37   168n
1294a21   168n
VII   228
1323b24–29   210n
1329a2–17   61n
1332b3–7   61n
1332b25–29   61n
1332b41–1333a3   61n
1333a11–16   61n

Posterior analytics   159
II.2   161
II.8   161
96b15–25   162
II.19   160, 161
100a5   149

Rhetoric
1355a15–17   49, 130
II   92
1378a30f.   152n
1380a1   152n
II.5   91
1382a21–22   152n
1382a22–30   79n
1382a26–30   144, 146
1382b28–1383a12   79n
1382b31   79n
1383a10   92n
1386a19–23   80n
1386a21–23   92n
1386a24   92n
1386a24–25   79n, 95n
1386a24–27   79n

Plato
  Apology
    22b–c   76n
  Ion
    535b–e   92n

INDEX OF PASSAGES CITED

Gorgias 217*n*
  508a 39*n*
Phaedo 70*n*, 88
Protagoras 47*n*
Republic 37
  II-III 90*n*
  379a–383c 90*n*
  423e 39*n*
  430e–432b 70*n*
  441d–444a 70*n*
  443–444 171
  457a–466d 39*n*
  540d–541b 70*n*
  546a–547a 70*n*
  546a–547c 72*n*
  547a–c 71*n*
  567b–c 71*n*
  567c 71*n*
  568b 71*n*, 87*n*
  569b 71*n*
  571b–c 69*n*
  571c–d 69*n*
  571d 91*n*
  573c–579e 70*n*
  IX 86, 87, 91
  577d–e 70*n*
  X 87
  604b–e 90*n*
  604e–605d 71*n*
  605b 87*n*
  605c 87*n*
  605c–d 69*n*
  605d 87*n*
  606a 87*n*
  607c–d 76*n*

GENERAL THEOLOGICAL SEMINARY
NEW YORK